REVIEWER COMMENTS
From a free self-thinker, who has read this book

Robert Q. Riley - Did not graduate high school. Instead, wrought article of a contemporary design of cars and boats for Popular-Mechanic books for 30 years, is last car design, did, 225 miles per one gallon, in a world rase of the most economical car of all cars.

ROBERT RILEY was born in an Irish catholic religion family; the result is by debating in reality! ROBERT Q. RILEY became a genius.

I've read this book on wisdom, and I do not see any contradictions in it. However, people perceive it as a contradiction that could come from their refusal to give up traditional religious ideas and beliefs.

Energy gives life and with it, moral and humane values. We do not have to create God in our image for God to exist. All of us and the entire universe itself consist of God-energy. God is not an extremely powerful man or a woman. God is the life force of the universe, which creates a platform for life.

Also, there is no difference between the "life-force" of the universe and the "energy" of the universe. If that were not the case, it would be impossible for these rocks (this stuff we think of as raw matter) to come alive and begin to think and create on their own as individual human-beings and as societies. Consider all of it as connected and consisting of the same energy. Free self-think and be creative for a better world in scientific debate conversations.

ROBERT Q. RILEY

THE ENEMY OF KNOWLEDGE IS NOT IGNORANCE

It is Illusion of Knowledge

LEON D. HALFON

Halfon Book Publishing
Los Angeles, California

Part 1
Sociolinguistic Profiles of Countries and Regions across Greater China

DARKNESS IS 0, OR NOTHING. THERE IS ONLY LIGHT.

Darkness is a place where there is no light!

Shifting your focus away from certain long-held traditions and beliefs in the illusion of knowledge may be frightening and challenging, but it is essential for change for the better. You might feel more comfortable in the darkness in the illusion of knowledge rather than turning on the light to see God reality that is there. But once you switch on the light it reveals the universal truth of the time, you will see there is nothing to be afraid of. At that moment, you will accurately understand that it is more frightening to live in a dark, blind-fate illusion of religion, than in the light of God reality of science. You will be excited to realize you can free self-think to see the light of reality, instead of believing what someone else tells you is there in blind faith in the dark, instead of free will and freedom of speech, in debating, because both are essential to better yourself and the world! In the past—and still today—governments and religions want to do all the thinking and want you to do all the obeying; they want you to be "moldable." However, it should be the other way around because ordinary people are the creative ones, but the hierarchy will not let that happen because they are greedy and want to control others by their ego from competing, to feel good about themself. Therefore, the government is the entity that needs to be moldable if it is to represent the people. That is the democratic way to find universal truth that will direct this country—and the rest of the world—in the right direction in the shortest time.

Challenge Yourself and your children to Excellence, Improve Your Minds Like the Greatest Minds by Creating a More Accurate Self-Understanding of Life Reality of science, for a better government, a better country, a better and safer world! Not by illusion of knowledge, (religion fairytale) to keep grownups childish.

THE ENEMY OF KNOWLEDGE IS NOT IGNORANCE

Published by Halfon Books
Los Angeles, California
Leon Halfon, Publisher/Editorial Director

All rights reserved.

No part of this book may be reproduced or transmitted in any form or any means, electronic or mechanical, including photocopying or any information storage and retrieval system, without permission in writing from the copyright owner.

Copyright © 2024 by Leon D. Halfon
ISBN # 978-0-9904130-8-0
Library of Congress Control Number: 2022913000

This edition is created from the original text, and by debating and researching in God-reality of science, it developed into a more accurate understanding, for the wisdom of this new addition. However, knowledge and philosophy stay still, and universal-truth wisdom changes with time, to create new knowledge. Because life is meant to be exciting and challenging, to have the understanding for confidence to better yourself, your government, your country, your world, to be safer and healthier. Not a monotonous boring journey of comfort, from competing opinionated belief philosophy to be unsafe and unhealthy!

Leon D. Halfon

DEDICATION

When I arrived in America 60 years ago from Israel, I could not remain close to most of my Israelite friends because I was a free self-thinker searching for wisdom, from universal-truth reality of that time, to make a better world. My Israelite friends were generally afraid and unwilling to step away from the dangerous discriminatory dogma of world "gangs" that created illusory religious philosophical beliefs. So, from the confidence of free self-thinking, I became much closer to my free self-thinking non-Israelite new friends from very different countries and backgrounds.

These free self-thinkers were all in the same scientific way of searching for the wisdom to arrive closer to a universal truth of that time. This journey brought us all together and, from accurate understanding, we became united joyfully trustworthy as my best friends. This system, always work, and it will unite all the people on this planet. They are the ones to whom I promised I would write this book. But unfortunately, they are all gone from my life now, in one way or another and I miss them very much.

I wish to dedicate this book to my friends, who were humane-beings. These were the very best free self-thinkers and scientific debaters searching for universal-truth to understand the magic of God reality more than anyone could have ever known: Maurice Braslave, Robert Bardey, Gerard Alcon, Jon Michel, Monsignor John Sheridan, Suliman and Jack Brady.

Free self-thinking is a personal thing in a free self-thinking group!

When you understand the magic of reality from debating, you can, and will, create magic, for a better world!

Leon D. Halfon

INTRODUCTION

IN the past all food is registered as food to eat, however, some is poison, some is organic, some is vitamin, therefore, .in today knowledgeable people don't accept the worth food to eat as good enough, and need an accurate understanding of all the ingredients, they are putting in their stomach. This is why they liv longer.

In the past food for thought is registered as a philosophy or a belief; however, today, knowledgeable people searching for a universal truth in a scientific debate of reality, they will eventually find the answer, and understand to love life, liv longer and prosper, however, if you are searching for universal truth, in a religion or tradition or a philosophy or propaganda, in the illusion of knowledge that kip you idol , make you an idol worshiper that will never find the universal-truth for that time because it is subjective to each other or each group, and everything that is subjective to each other, or each group is a lie, and believing in lies is poisonous in your brain, because today more people are free self-thinkers, in reality, and need to debate, for accurate understanding of what they are putting in their brain.

If universal truth does not exist, then science cannot exist. For example, in physics, for every action there is an accurate opposite reauction and that is a universal truth!

How would you make this world better for life? If you were the Energy of the Universe God?

Everything evolved from—or was created by—Energy!

The universe is Energy, and the earth is heated from the outside by the Energy of the Sun, and from the inside by the Energy of the earth, from scientifically accurate distance, for life to flourish, this is reality of science, whether you believe it or not.

Would you make the planet a sphere and give it gravity so that life would not fall off the edge? Would you make water boil at 100° Celsius, so water vapor could evaporate in the atmosphere to create rain so that life could exist on land and under the water? Would you make water float when it freezes at 0° Celsius, creating large ice floats that insulate the waters below so that life can thrive under the ice and on top of the ice floats? Would you make the ice white reflect the sun's rays to not contribute to global warming? Would you make glaciers, snowmelt, and water evaporate to create rain, and lightning to create negative-ion, that clean, refresh the dirty air, to become delicious, healthy air for life. Would you make the rainwater clean the dirty ground, to came out, as delicious healthy spring water for life, and that creates rivers, so that life could have healthy water on land all year long? That is life magic! Would you have volcanoes thrust out all the minerals that enrich the earth for agriculture and the vital materials we use like copper, iron, gold, diamonds, and other elements to the surface, so life and people could utilize them and evolve? Would you have stars explode to create carbon, which is vital for life on earth? Would you make a magnetic field and ozone to protect life from the blasts of solar winds? Would you have earthquakes shake people from their comfort zone, and from illusion of knowledge to free self-think in God reality of science and be creative? Would you create a planet just the right size to have perfect gravity so that people can walk upright on two feet? Would you make a planet with a tilted orbit to create four seasons in a year? Would you make a moon to light up the sky at night and keep the oceans' high tides and low tides flowing and the seas are in constant motion, to make life challenging, and exciting, which also influences our weather? Life needs a Goldilocks atmosphere to flourish, not too hot, not too cold, but just right—with the right mix of gases, to breathe

The Enemy of Knowledge Is Not Ignorance

and thrive. My "verifiable conclusion realization" is that the Energy of the cosmos is doing a marvelous job, today you are able to see from the telescope, in the Milky-Way, energy creating element to create planet for life. Therefore, all the planet's resources should be focused on supporting humane-beings, free-self-thinking in wisdom and not supporting selfish hierarchy or people in illusions by hierarchy. All religions are fairytales created by leaders (god-players)! All religious people have Santa clos in the sky, that love them mor then they love themself, that is childish, because in reality there is no Santa clos in the sky or ho ever you believe in...So please don't give weapons to children because they will play In childish religious war games where they will hurt or kill themselves and others, and that is what people call stupid! Be a free self-thinker grownup in reality, for a safer humane world! Would you create a super-heated planet named Venus for us to observe and learn from what happened to it due to global warming? Venus was a very earthlike planet long before an expanding Sun released excessive carbon dioxide into the atmosphere, creating a greenhouse effect that heated the surface temperature to over 700 degrees, hot enough to melt lade! Will that be Earth's fate someday if we don't become humane-being to create wisdom? Would you make time so that life would be in constant motion? Would you give people only so many years to live and know that they are running out of time to accomplish something worthwhile by challenging their life to create understanding and exciting times before they are gone? Would you create all the natural laws needed for life to evolve in diverse ways via a continuous change to enjoy and be amazed by the magic of life? Would you create **love,** to create beautiful species? **This establishes in factual reality, that God the energy. Of the universe is terrific, that is a good reason to be humane and not believe in illusions of knowledge, because all this could not have happened by superstitions or delusions of knowledge or ads or %, or by oxidant, or god-players, or dead people of the past, or money, or philosophy, or illusionary religion and tradition . to create the Goldilocks conditions with precise,** scientific perfection. This is a scientific reality, that there is something that made it possible for life to flourish! This chapter establishes the understanding that the Energy of the Universe, the energy of the cosmos or God, is in you, around you and is always there for you, to be a free self-thinker, to create the realistic knowledge, to become a humane-being, who strives for a better life for all life, wear in this together!

Shame on you, god-players, for creating religion fairytales that make grownup, childishly ignorant from God reality of science, to overpopulate and participate in wars, against life, and that is against God, to protect inhumane criminals' hierarchy privileges?

How have things changed by the scientific knowledge of free self- thinking humane-being? For example, we came down from the trees and began to walk upright to collect food and hunt. When we needed to go faster, we domesticated horses. When we needed to transport heavy things, we built trains. When we needed to go even faster, we made cars. When we needed to go much faster and farther, we created airplanes. When we wanted to learn more about the world quickly, we invented computers and the internet. All this was created by free self-thinking accurate scientific understanding in scientific minds., and in a reality debate, this is the scientific method for a more accurate understanding of reality. To search for the wisdom, by not competing, in a humane scientific debate to learn from other, and create magic, for a better life, it was not created by the illusionary knowledge of philosophical religion tradition or Atheist created by aggressive laws, from hierarchies' leaders for mor power from ego.

Albert Einstein left his family and moved with his female cousin, it was more important, to prove is theory of relativity, that prove that all energy is related to unite all the people in God reality, for the love of life, because he was a humane-being, not a as **sheep in the herd of grazers.** Einstein's showed by his equation of $E=MC^2$ is that matter can become energy and energy can become matter. The equation of relativity shows that all energy correlates to one energy. Those wonders of the magic of life. They did not think they could have done a better job. Da Vinci thought the man-body was so perfect he used it as measurement device. However, Da Vinci did think the man had one bodily flaw, his penis.

Hierarchy memorizes illusion of knowledge, thinks they know everything; however, they don't understand the magic universe reality of what they know or will ever know. Because there is no understanding of the spectrum magic God reality in illusion of knowledge or in what they know in their computer materialistic brain. Only by humbling yourself to learn from others in a debate, only by accurate understanding in the infinite mind, people and hierarchy will become a humane representative of life, because as it is, in God the magic reality of science, today, people are creating a supercomputer that will have in a conversation, all the answers to all questions to all the knowledge, to replace all the schoolers and knowledgeable books. This book is open to disagreement in a scientific method of debating in reality. by humbling awe self, we all learn new things from people who disagree, in reality, to create a new mor accurate understanding of the spectrum of, God magic reality in your understanding mind. Because God is only found in your infinite mind, not in your computerized illusionary knowledgeable materialistic brain!

You don't learn from people who agree with you, because we already know that and don't need to be repeated by a preacher to create obstacles in your brain, that create misunderstanding in your mind!

Albert Einstein said: "God does not play dice. Einstein understood in what he called "cosmic understanding" where God's presence was evident in the order and rationality of nature and the universe in all expressions. However, religion tradition in blind faith is gambling and is playing 'dice, it is accepted by the medical fill as a sickness that is hard to cure, and everything that is subjective to each group, it is not God's universal truth, for that time, and everything that is not truth is a lie, because it is created by leaders (god-players), for more privileges.

Albert Einstein is not a philosopher or religious! Albert Einstein is a scientist, a free self-thinking Israelite, in the search for universal truth accurate understanding to create knowledge. Leon Halfon is not a philosopher or religious! Leon Halfon is a free self-thinking Israelite in search of universal-truth accurate understanding to unite and create a better world for all lives.

All religion create war that kills, themselves, to be able to kill other people from other religion and kill free self-tinkers humane-being that understand God reality of science, love everything, everybody, and will create a better world for life, they are killed for not believing in religion or tradition, not participating in competing ego, and in destroying life!

All religion, tradition illusions of knowledge, are philosophies that build, structure to families and the world, created by hierarchy leaders, however, all structure that are built from illusion of knowledge are very dangers for all lives that are in the structure., because the structural have to be scientifically safe. That is why, in intelligent free self-thinking countries, they have scientific building codes, and inspectors, to enforce the codes, there for you must create, a Scientific country, for accurate understanding that you have to be out of your ,mind, to structure, yourself, your family, your friends, your country and your world, by religion, traditions, Atheist, philosophies, illusions of knowledge, created to protect illusionary hierarchy privileges!

You find the correct answer from within yourself, by free self-thinking, no excuses, or justification allowed! You must give up all your paradigm that make you fill important, from believing you are special, to advance to the next level of a new realistic understanding, by free self-thinking, you will see that all problems can be solved, through God reality of science from becoming a caring, humane-being that understand right from wrong, to do what is right.

If people stop believing that they are special because they belong to a religion, tradition, Atheist philosophy, or a hierarchy. There will be no war! You are in reality, only what you do, not what you believe you are!

If you say you are religious, then you are promoting freedom of illusionary beliefs for a criminal hierarchy.

If you say. you are a Jew, you are part of an illusionary belief, that was started from the scientific, free self-thinking movement of Moses, and that created King David empire of the powerful belief of the Jews, by Juda tribe, and that created by the hierarchy, and belief of Christianity by the Romans empire, and that created the powerful belief of Moslem, by Mohamed empire, that is the reason they are trying to destroy free self-thinking democratic Israel in the scientific movement of Moses, and destroy American free self-thinking democratic constitution, to justify their illusionary knowledge by the criminal's hierarchy's, in war and propaganda. However, the Israelis and all Free self-thinkers legitimately, have the right to the land of Israel, because, the land of Israel was conquered by uniting all people in the scientific movement of Moses, not by war, and today, scientific free self-thinkers are the majority of the world, and will stop this inhumane parasite leader from destroying this living planet. So, stand up for what is right, and create a safer world for creative people, who understand the reality of science to protect this planet and all lives from leaders of the past, and are still today, controlling their people by extreme, scary inhumane torchers, to protect their privileges because they are good for nothing and act innocent, by propaganda!

Leon D. Halfon

TABLE OF CONTENTS

Dedication xi
Introduction xiii
Table of Contents xxi

PART ONE: What This Book is About 1

Free Self-Thinking 2
Two scientific Experiments 6
Traditions 7
Looking in the Wrong Places 9
The Socratic Method 11
The Mason from the Crusaders 13
United States of America: The Greatest Country in the World 15
The Most Creative Country in the World Used to be the
United States of America 17
Discover Free Self-Thinking in Wisdom 19
Experiment to Know the Percentage of People Who are Humane-Beings 26
What We Know Now for HIGHER CONSCIOUSNES 28
The Word Belief 32
What is BELIEF? 32
Religion Is a Placebo 37
Move From Illusions of Knowledge to a More Accurate
Understanding of Reality 38
Religious Jokes 41
Religious Leaders 42
Example of Free Self-Thinking in a Debate 47

Cognitive Dissonance 51
Understanding the Meaning of Words 52
Confidence 54
Illusions 55
Understanding Right from Wrong 58
Obstacles of the Brain 59
Voodoo Zombies 63

PART TWO: You Are What You Do, not what you believe you are! 67

Always in Friendship 69
The Purpose of Life 71
Hippies 71
From Debating in the Search of a Universal truth about God 73
Satan, Lucifer, and the Devil 73
Comparing Cultural Contributions of Religious Followers and
Free Self-Thinkers 75
Public Coffee Shop of Wisdom 77
Greba Temple of Inspiration and Wisdom 78
People of the Books 79
Competition 82
To Be a Humane-Being or Not to Be a Humane-Being -
That is the Question? 84
Choose Conversation instead of Violence 85
DAAA 86
Verifiable Conclusions 89
The understanding Movement 90
The only Bible Story about Satan is in the Book of Job 91
Discover if Someone is a Free Self-Thinker in Wisdom 93

People With Little or No Formal Education 94
Discover A New Meaning and New Word 97
Police Shields..99

PART THREE: Evolution 101
Free Self-Thinkers are Problem Solvers 104
Free Self-Thinkers Need Artificial Intelligence...106
What is Love? 111
Three Steps toReach Love of All Life 113
Is life a Glass-Half-Full or Half-Empty? 113
Why There are Gangs 115
Why There Are Bullies 115
Declare Your Brain and Mind Independence 117
Ancient Books of Wisdom..118
My Verifiable Conclusion Regarding Moses..119
More of Moses' Inspiring Wisdom Stories...123
My Understanding, from Debating the Story of Jerico..........................125
Wisdom of King Solomon 126
Abraham..131
Hierarchy and Joan of Arc..134

PART FOUR: Going Back Home 137

PART FIVE: Inspiring Photos and Life Stories of Leon 149
Only By Understanding One Picture Is Worth Morethan
A Thousand Words 153
Falcon 178
A Young Appaloosa Stallion at My Ranch..179
My Thoroughbred Stallion..179
Swinging onto the Balcony 180

I Date a Woman Who Likes to Drink at a Bar 182
Working in the Litton Building for Maurice Braslave 183
The Voice of Europe 184
The Preachers 185
The Mustang Ranches 185
My Cancer Stories 186
The Desert Island of Djerba 187
Crushed 192
Lifeguard 199
Yoynay 204
England 206
America 207
The Second Gun 215
Desilu 217
FHA Foster Home Program 219
The Catholic Church 223
Jack Brady 228
Buzz Aldrin 231
MY FATHER, MERO wearing A FRENCH police hat 232
U. S. Consulate 235
My Brother, Yehuda 238
My Mother, Rachel 239

PART SIX: Inventions 241
Solar Water Distillation System from Humidity 242
The Best Sprinkler System 243
Remote Control Drone 243
Inexpensive Solar Water Heater 244

The Enemy of Knowledge Is Not Ignorance

Producing Electricity with Nature 246

Ethanol at Five Cents a Gallon 246

Build A Concrete Holly Wall 246

Converting to a Non-Skid Bathtub 247

Replenish the Dead Sea in Israel 248

Solar Air-Conditioning 248

The Solar Energizer Necklace 249

A Humane Non-Fatal Mousetrap 250

Lifeguard Poem 251

A Free Self-Thinking Prayer for Life to care 252

The representative of the creative countries of the world is playing a game of chest for world domination. 253

I Was Betrayed by My Brother's Wife for American Money, And by Bribing My Boat Partner; Ironicly, His Name is Cries! 254

Dear friend 255

Contact Information 257

Leon D. Halfon

PART ONE

What This Book is About

FREE SELF-THINKING
Free self-thinking is a personal thing in a search for accurate understanding of reality!

MY life journey proves that debating in a scientific method searching for a universal truth unites different people. It worked. It will unite all people of this planet because Universal Truth combines everything in the universe to create a more accurate understanding of Life's reality necessary for the wisdom to become a humane-being. After all, life is not an illusion of knowledge. It is a living reality. **This book is about individual free self-tinker. You are what you do, it is not about competing for ego. However, most people are part of a religion, tradition that is a (gang) and are brainwashed by leaders that the word, I, is ego, because, as a singular, you are part of everything and that will open your horizon to love all. However, a leader's ego derives only from winning the competition. It does not derive from the word, I, or of what you did, or what you do!**

Ever since the beginning of free self-thinking, humane-beings have been and are still, against hierarchy because hierarchies created all religion's that are (illusions of knowledge) to control the people, that make a united "gang" willing to defend, attack or pillage. Or rape other gangs created by competition. These hierarchies created a world full of (united groups) illusory thinking as a "norm." Therefore, all religions, are not made by the people; religion, and tradition is created by leaders of the people—no exception. Leaders must force violently, using torture chambers, to promote illusory thinking about themselves, by religious law which lets them stay in charge to protect their privileges. All illusions are fairytales, they are not the truth, they are lies. We currently have a world epidemic that has killed many people, and Mach suffering. It will get more dangerous in the future. This shows that the hierarchy gangs, the regimes, are unable to find a solution because all solutions are solved by free self-thinking humane-beings that understand the magic reality of Life. Not by competing in knowledge!

The Enemy of Knowledge Is Not Ignorance

If you want to believe in a religion, you can believe just about anything. **Because it is not real, and everything that is not real is a lie;** That is why it is subjective to each person or group. It is time to encourage people out of believing illusions of knowledge into a scientific method of free self-thinking; by debating to learn from each other to arrive at a Universal Truth for that time, because Universal Truth is not subjective to each person or each group. All people will unite to create a love of Life, to do what is right, for a safer future. And leaders are god-players, parasitic scholars, memorizing knowledge to compete by preaching propaganda for a ranking scale. They are not humane-beings searching for the scientific debate for Universal Truth. What I mean by hierarchy is. People in government and in a position that serves the people raise their salary or services without the permission of the public. **because they can**, and are not by the people for the people, day are hierarchies, and create illusionary traditional religion, to self-propel the hierarchy, **because they** can't disagree with the preacher!

This book is about respecting all the people of this world that created and are creating a better world for us! By the only way! And that is an accurate scientific understanding of the universal truth reality of that time, as we know from archeologists of enchanted drawings, how amazingly precise their stonework was. the Israelites are not religious jews, they are free self-thinkers that scientifically debated for accurate understanding of the spectrum of magic life reality, to solve all problems for over 4,000 years, to create a better life and a safer world for all lives. Because there is no going back to save what is extinct, so please be scientific to accurately understand the magic of God life reality, with no illusion of knowledge! Because in life reality, there is no illusory knowledge. In reality, it is all about precise understanding.

Through debate, humane-being created the knowledge to convert all senses to sight, by developing gauges to see all senses accurately, giving people the ability to understand accurately all senses in reality. To give people the ability to build a car, train or even a rocket ship to the moon, because relying on opinions, religious beliefs or even Atheism philosophy doesn't provide accurate reality to create new knowledge and that is the reason for a scientific method of debating to arrive at an accurate understanding, that challenges the reader to look beyond the norm and let go of biases, beliefs, traditions, prejudices, hate, excuses (justification) that are self-destructively from being the most dangerous stupid people, by memorizing knowledge and competing. That becomes the common goal of living the norm and will become more dangerous because you are looking one way at the magic of Life, as looking at any magic show, that creates an illusion of knowledge and makes it very hard, to be a free self-thinker.

However, if you look at the magic of Life from different directions for a different outlook, by the scientific method of debating, by Hambling yourself to learn from each other to have a spectrum of the magic of Life, it will create a more accurate understanding of the universal truth for that time, of how Life Magic works.

For example, Albert Einstein's theory of relativity, could not be introduced for 10 years of debating in reality, to arrive at a universal truth, because the theory was not accurate to become scientific. In the future, a computer and your cell phone will tell you if the conversation is a likely scam or a belief or propaganda or an accurate scientific conversation worthy of debate. For an accurate understanding of life reality, because of blockages in the brain from illusion, it makes it very hard to know if a conversation is scientific. My inspiring life experiences exemplify how one person can go beyond self-imposed limitations, which are just illusions that keep you from living fully because you are trapped in an illusory jail that enslaves you to your delusions. if all the people don't free self-think and debate in a scientific method to have an accurate understanding of the spectrum of magic life reality, people will end up as destructive parasite hierarchy and homeless people because they're just very intelligent animals that compete by memorizing knowledge, with no accurate understanding of reality to become humane-being.

My goal is to help you identify those illusions and then encourage you to put them aside and leave through a door that is not even locked, for your own good and all life! You are free to leave your illusions behind at any time by an accurate understanding of reality. However, delusions are always dangerous and will likely become more dangerous in the future as the world faces increasingly complex problems. Ultimately, it could threaten Life on the most beautiful planet in the known Universe. So, get back to reality. We can discover for ourselves the causes of all problems and become

The Enemy of Knowledge Is Not Ignorance

empowered by wisdom to solve them. Today's political hierarchy is an obvious example of how we cannot depend on regimes to do it for us. It is essential to create fairytales to help children follow the right path towards becoming humane grownups. But it is counterproductive to develop illusory religious and political propaganda fairytales for adults because adults need *accurate factual truth* for the scientific debate conversations necessary to develop wisdom. Wisdom is the universal truth of the time and Universal Truth is the key to accurate scientific understanding that will create the solution for all problems. Otherwise, powerful interest groups and leaders will run the world by preaching fairytales (the illusion of knowledge) to people. Those fairytales invariably create prejudices jealousy, leading to wars, cruelty, and misery, destruction of the environment—yet these are all necessary for Life on this planet so the hierarchy will not lose its privileges. **For example, King Henry the VIII created a new religion to get more privileges. To be able to kill his wife.**

To create wisdom, you need an accurate understanding of reality for the changing times. However, any fool can acquire a more profound knowledge, philosophy, propaganda, illusory or religion by studying what is recorded in books, computers, and memorizing preachers' lectures which provides a deeper understanding of knowledge.

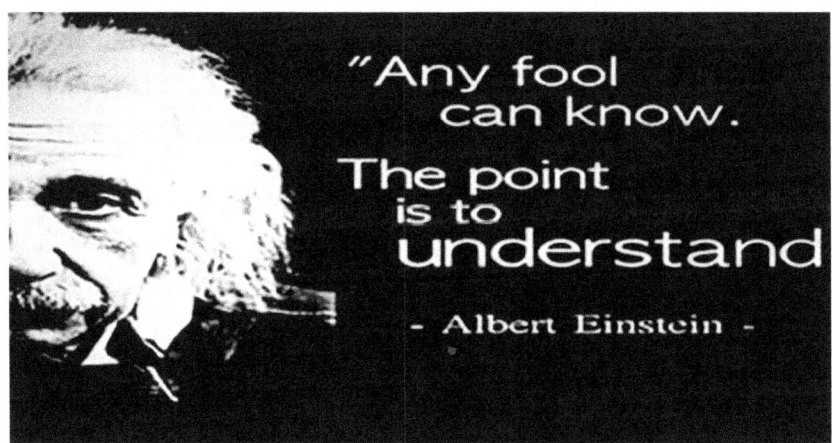

All beings are capable of memorizing knowledge. However, only people can create a more accurate understanding of reality by scientifically debating what is necessary to generate the wisdom to become a humane-being, to solve all problems. Otherwise, without a more precise understanding of reality, all animals and people are just beings because they have no accurate understanding of reality. That is why it is essential for all the people to scientifically debate to search for an accurate understanding of the spectrum of magic life reality to become a humane-being to care and grow compassionate from your love of life. **Understanding reality, universal-truth for the time, and science are the same things. That is the reason. When you have an accurate understanding of reality, you will create wisdom, create new knowledge and that is the reason when you have vast knowledge without an accurate understanding of reality by memorizing knowledge, ore illusion of knowledge, you can't create new knowledge. For all thinking creatures, the meaning of life is to give their life meaning, however, for humane-beings, the meaning of life is to create a more accurate understanding of reality to create a continuous inspiring and exciting life for a utopian joyful life for all lives.**

Two scientific Experiments

Here are two simple scientific experiments to clarify the actual reality for organized "gangs," i.e., religious, followers, Atheists, or believers.

Experiment # 1. Ask a young child who hasn't been told to believe any beliefs yet, "Is there a God?" The child's answer will be, "I don't know." A child is born an Israeli free self-thinker with common-sense in the search of universal-truth wisdom. Therefore, it would be impossible for the child to say there is no God and I am an atheist, or this is my religion and tradition!

Experiment # 2. Teach a child this fundamental law of scientific physics, "For every action, there is an equal and accurate opposite reaction." Then ask the question, "Is there a God?" The child will answer, "If there is life, then there must be something that started the action to create life. Therefore, life is a reaction. The "action" that made life possible is what people call God." This is an Israeli free self-thinker's answer. We still don't know how and why anything in the Universe got here. All we know is that energy is in everything, and all is created by energy!

TRADITIONS
Tradition is not a personal thing it is a gang thing!

All religion and atheist have tradition, and children obey tradition to be nice wither their father, however, **tradition is created by people leader, (god-players) to keep people idol, and that, make you, an idol worshiper, it was not created by God, or the 10 commandments or the American constitution!** Traditions are long-established customs and beliefs from dead people of the past, from generation to generation. People who believe in traditions and other illusion fairytales become slaves to their traditions because they like to feel a part of something big, and **that makes you believe you are important**. But celebrating them is not essential because they don't do any good and it separates people from different traditions. However, it is more challenging for free self-thinkers, more fun, more inspiring, and more important to be part of everything, which is more significant than just something big, **and that is democracy for all people**.

What are traditions? Slavery is a tradition, religion, atheist, royalty, hierarchy, preaching, bribery, dictatorships, gang, believing, competition, superstitions, bullies, caste systems, war, and peasants. To be used by leaders, hierarchy, not by free self-thinkers' representative of the people!

Being humane is not a tradition or a religion. One should not do only what is expected by tradition or religion or atheist; life is unfulfilling when you only do what is expected by god-players. Open the door to the reality of life and do what you know is right, by free self-thinking to be creative, to accomplish your dreams of accurate understanding of God reality to unite all free self-thinking creative humane-being, to be the majority of the world.

Wouldn't it be wonderful if there were a theme park where people could visit the world's traditions and religions in one place to discover the foolishness of all beliefs and practices? The people will be amused, compare, and understand how ridiculous beliefs traditions are without traveling. As the government, a representative of the people can create this amusement park to help people become free self-thinkers with a more accurate understanding of life's magic reality. So, people can be free self-thinkers and creative humane-beings to save this world from extinction! It is time to create a brand new and only one-holiday celebration worldwide called the Festival of Life. Every January eleventh: One-one-one (1/11). All life as one, to rejoice that unite people and animals to remind us that we need each other because we are all in this world together and in life, only universal truth for the time exists. Religion and traditions are **nothing or 0** zero. Free self-thinking in search of universal truth to create new wisdom from reality, is a scientific method that always works.

Wisdom does not come from belief. Wisdom comes from an accurate self-understanding of reality. The lyrics of the Beatles song "Let It Be" derive from the religious concept of accepting one's blind fate and *in times of trouble fate comes to me, speaking words of wisdom from belief, let it Be.* But the Beatles and most people look for wisdom in religious beliefs; that is the wrong place because that is what they have been led to believe by preachers, let it be, it comes from, (god players). However, God doesn't play dice, and His presence was evident in the order and rational understanding reality of nature and the universe in all lives. Wisdom comes from more accurate self-understanding by extensively debating subjects that have occupied the greatest minds in history. Their wisdom did not come from doing nothing, just "letting it be" or blindly in blind faith following leaders in charge. However, many free self-thinkers were punished for making a better world throughout history because they wore minorities, and cruel hierarchy and their followers are ignorant of reality they wore the majority. Perhaps they should have "let it be," but they didn't, because the energy of the universe is in you to thing freely is the right thing. Instead, they sacrificed their lives because they did not have tradition from believes, understood right from wrong by God reality of science to create new universal-truth of that time for a better life for all lives. However, today. Most people are free self-thinkers not stinkers, from understanding , Moses, understanding the American constitution, and understanding democracy.

The Beatle, Sir Paul McCartney, accepted knighthood as a tradition, and became hierarchy, not wisdom. Steven Hawking, who understood reality, did not accept knighthood, or become hierarchy—that is wisdom.

LOOKING IN THE WRONG PLACES

One night, a man was searching underneath a lamp post for something. People passing by asked, "What are you looking for?"

The man replied, "I lost $100." They asked, "Where did you lose it?" By pointing, the man responded, "Over there in the dark." The people asked him, "Why don't you look where you lost it? The man said, "You think I am a fool? I cannot see in the dark, but I **believe** I can find it under the light of this lamppost. **"Because if you want to believe, you can believe just about anything."**

Sometimes psychiatrists avoid debate conversations because they think they are always right and often their patients do. A psychiatrist is a preacher who doesn't ever let other people think for themselves. When people spend their upbringing competing and being told what to do, they think that a meaningful debate conversation for wisdom sounds like **jibber-jabber, because the people that jibber-jabber lives in the island of Djerba?** They understand the word "knowledge," but they also believe that "there is no meaning for the word wisdom. They think knowledge is wisdom, but wisdom creates new knowledge. They also believe that people use the word wisdom; it is to sound critical. Because they use words, not meaning, preachers make people believe that great people who have wisdom are prodigy or chosen by God. That is why leaders preach just to let it be, to stay in charge, and be a god-player. It is a hierarchical scam! By preaching and passing laws to create more power for themselves, leaders' egos, greed, and competitiveness compel them to maintain their sway over their obedient followers because they arc not by the people for the people, and, it is, against, Moses law between God, and people, the 10, commandment, that created, free self-thinkers, humane-being creative Israeli!

Only in free self- thinking and debating in searching for universal truth in God-reality of science do not mind being questioned, and don't create propaganda because, they are searching for the universal truth for that time and that, unite all the people, for a terrific safer world!

Traditional believers, in illusionary knowledge by hierarchy leaders do not like being challenged. And must create propaganda, justification, to keep people from knowing the truth, and that separate people, to create a terrifying world, to be use and abuse by hierarchy!

My father told me he had 1 million and ½, Franks from the insurance. That belonged to me. All insurance paid 10 times of medical expenses. As a Lifeguard, I made 1,800,00 liras, per month, and my father made 400,00 lire, per month. Do I have to obey religions, or tradition, for my family to treat me, honestly? As a free self-tinker, I gave you, a dog, falcons, a boat, America, a horse ranch, to understand the joyful love of all lives, that Is more joyful than money, or illusion of knowledge. A laggard job is not a temporary job. lifeguards, at 80, are still lifeguards!

Me and Susy came to the house, and asked my father to marry us, when my father found out she had money, he asked me to give Susy to Simon, because he is my older brother, Susy and I were not interested.

Use your mind, not your brain, because brain as obstacle to believing in tradition. I hope you remember all the scrimping between father and his brother, about my money. No matter, I always loved, and respected my father and mother, and still do, however, as a free self-thinker, I cannot do wrong, when I understand what is right in God reality, even in torcher, for a better world, for life. My life shows that. Religions, Traditions are terrifying, however God is terrific. Free self-think for a better world.

To me, a leader means "One who is the head of an authoritarian hierarchy, regime, group or gang." The Bible talks of shepherds as leaders and often uses this metaphor to lead people like sheep. But people are not sheep! A sheep cannot free self-think to find new wisdom for a better world. Therefore, there should be no leaders and no shepherds of people who create gangs. Read the American Constitution! People can exercise their right to choose representatives by the people, from the people for the people!

If you get attacked by a harmful germ or virus, you will survive, because you love life, and that makes your energy stronger. If you get attacked by bullies and survive, you may decide it is necessary to become stronger, smarter and learn how to defend yourself. You do it because you don't want this to happen again to you or other humane-beings. You survive because of love of life, from accurate understanding, of God's scientific reality.

The Socratic Method

ALL ANSWERS Are in THE QUESTIONS for the search of universal truth FOR EVERY QUESTION THER IS AN OPPOSITE ANSWER for a more accurate understanding.

- What is darkness? = Darkness is the absence of light!
- Wat is a belief. =a belief is the absence of understanding reality.
- What is religion? = is he absence of, God reality.
- What is propaganda? is the absence of truth!
- What is war? = War is the absence of humane-being!
- What is in blind faith? = is the absence of God-reality.
- What is hierarchy = is the absence of representative
- What Is an obedient follower? = is the absence of democratic creative free self-thinkers!
- What Is ignorance? = is the absence of reality!
- What is Atheist philosophy= is the absence of understanding God reality of science, from debating.
- What is tradition=is the absence of excitement, from content change in the magic of life,
- What are illusions of knowledge? =is the absence of God reality of science, that creates the understanding, to enjoy loving everything in life, to live a joyful long life, as a humane-being!

This book Is to ask yourself questions for self-understanding as a theory, and in a debate find the wisdom! This book is not to memorize knowledge. For example, Da Vinci, created the understanding, of a propeller, and the Right Brothers, by debating in God reality of science for two years, from free self-thinking, they created the wisdom of a propeller that work, and it became a universal-truth Knowledge for that time.

No one can change anyone in life, no matter how good the intention or wise approach. However, in a debating conversation, you can let others say what they believe. Then ask questions to reveal the contradictions in their thinking, to ask themselves important questions and eventually arrive at an accurate understanding. Encourage to do the reasoning to understand for themselves, to change their life and the world for the better from having confidence in God reality! A believer is someone who believes they know everything; however, they don't understand the magic universe truth reality of what they know or will ever know. because believing is an illusionary knowledge, and in elution there is no understanding the reality in what they know, because religion is common-belief, not common-sense!

The Socratic Method examines an assumption by asking questions about why it is believed to be the truth. Ask where is the evidence for it and what are the alternatives? You will arrive at a more transparent, more accurate understanding and less ignorant by doing just that. That is what free self-thinking in the search for universal-truth is all about; it is a scientific method for continually searching for what is right and wrong by debate conversation to learn from each other and arrive at a more accurate understanding of God reality of science. **However, competing questions, it is not a Socratic Method, it is an animalistic competition that pokes holes in same one's life picture, and only sees the holes, not the picture!**

In ancient times, the philosopher Socrates was taken to a Greek court and prosecuted by Meletus and two others who were members of the democratic elite (hierarchy). They found him guilty on trumped-up charges of impiety and corrupting the youths of the country. Socrates used his scientific method of thinking to show he would have no reason to do what he was charged with. Nonetheless, his jury of 501 citizens found him guilty, **even though they loved Socrates, for his devotion to democracy. Because of their greed for comfort, of money, and must have their children to believe in illusion of knowledge, tradition, to believe they are special Greeks. Not in understanding God reality of science, to better yourself, your country, and the world. So, what do you think of a jury in a democratic court?** Socrates was ordered to suggest his suitable punishment. He replied he should be sentenced to dine in the Prytaneum, a state honor generally offered only to victorious Olympians, famous generals, because he understands that he created a better world and a safer Greece. When his "punishment" was denied, Socrates suggested death as a penalty, to create a more accurate understanding of hierarchy **that promote freedom of belief and tradition, that is, illusion of knowledge to believe in blind faith that they are special. However, in democracy nobody special from belief, and that is the reason in history all democracy was and will eventually be destroyed in the future by freedom of religion, and tradition, because it does not work together. So, get real!**

He was offered a chance to save himself if he was exiled to a desert island (Djerba) for the rest of his life, but this was unacceptable to Socrates. He wanted to make a point about the wisdom of his life and prove that if this travesty of justice transpired in democratic Athens, similar injustices could happen in any democracy. In the end, Socrates became a martyr for his cause and was universally renowned. Socrates was a great free self-thinker searching for universal truth to find wisdom, a Lucifer "Satan," who enlightened and changed the world for the better. He should have suggested being exiled to the island of Djerba, where he would have been appreciated. Do you think Socrates deserved death for teaching his students to think for themselves by asking themself questions? The Socratic Method revealed that an Emperor is not a God, that religious leaders manipulate words and that believing is neither knowledge, nor wisdom, nor reality, nor truth. The Athenian nobles claimed that the Socratic Method was corrupting the youth because it revealed the truth. This is a lesson about religion and hierarchy. Those in power must change to become representative champions of the people or become extinct, which is just what happens. Eventually, greed from hierarchy become extinct, and destroyed the great democratic civilization of Greece. **Imagine this for a better democratic world!**

THE MASON FROM THE CRUSADERS

The Pope recorded the Nights to protect Jerusalem, the home of Jesus. The Night was renamed by the Pope, Crusaders and preached to hate the free self-thinkers Israeli. However, when occupying Jerusalem, the

Crusaders searched for the object from history and found the King Solomon book of Mason, which is Israelite thinking in God reality, **"you are what you do."** So, the Crusaders became free self-thinkers, creative Israeli Masons, which created over 8,000 most beautiful buildings in Europe, around the world and started banking, to help free self-thinking creative people. However, the parasite Hierarchy didn't want free self-thinker's creative people. They wanted ignorant obedient religious followers of tradition in blind faith. So, the Israel free self-thinker Mason Templar was burned alive at the stake and on Friday the 13th, the religious army massacred many Masons, **because they wore a minority**, to keep people, ignorant followers in blind fate. So, the Masons escaped to America and declared war on the parasite Hierarchy that created religion, to protect their privileges. After winning the war, the Masons wrote the Declaration of Independence and the American Constitution by the people, for the people, from the people, no religion in government allowed, creating a better world for all the people in the world, because life had a need of humane-being with a representative all the people. To have the freedom to think in the mind and become a creative humane-being, only then, there will not be a problem that cannot be solved. If the founding fathers, were opinionated or believer, in tradition, they could not have written such a humane American Constitution. The saying, "Sticks and stones will break my bones, but words will never hurt me." This saying is to protect the right of free debate and speech in reality of science, to create new points of view, for a mor accurate understanding. The Masons became a secret society because religious leaders persecuted them because they were a minority free self-thinker humane-being. You are what you do, not what leaders make you believe you are!

The reason the Masons are not elected as president of this country, is because the Masons hired assassins to kill religious leaders to create a free self-thinking country, because democracy, unite all the people, and parasite Hierarchy, create a gang from religion to separate people.

UNITED STATES OF AMERICA: THE GREATEST COUNTRY IN THE WORLD

The American Revolution rid the colonies of gangs and the British Empire's hierarchy, and that energized the individual American free-self-thinker search in reality for universal-truth wisdom. America's founding fathers debated in scientific reality for four months and by free self-thinking, they arrived at the famous compromises leading to the Declaration of Independence Constitution. After lengthy deliberations, wise old Benjamin Franklin said, "I am surprised that all this disagreement can arrive at one answer." But somehow, these free self-thinkers pulled it off by finding God's universal truths of that time. Had the delegates' debates at the Constitutional Convention failed to reach the "one answer," that would mean they had been unable to achieve universal-truth wisdom for that time.

Here is some wisdom from America's founding fathers:

> *"Christianity is the most perverted system that ever shone on man."-Thomas Jefferson*

> *"I have found Christian dogma unintelligible." -Benjamin Franklin*

> *"This would be the best of all possible worlds if there were no religion in it!"-John Adams*

> *"The Constitution is the guide which I never will abandon."-George Washington.*

> *"All religions were inventions set up to terrify and enslave humankind." -Thomas Paine*

The American humane Constitution separated religion and hierarchical gangs from the government. It was the second constitution of humane law founded without establishing a national religion or belief for parasite hierarchy. But, on the other hand, the founding fathers in Philadelphia designed the United States to be self-governed by free self-thinkers' representatives by the people, for the people, from the people.

Although little acknowledgment in modern times is that the first humane constitution was Moses law between God, and people, to create free self-thinkers. it was founded to understand God as life energy. Moses wonted to unite all the people of the world in God reality of science. without religion for god-players. Moses' objective was to create a community based on debating by free self-thinking to search for universal truth to create continuously new wisdom. Thus, the Ten Commandments were not intended to become part of religious dogma but rather a sacred constitution between God and all people, to create free self-thinkers humane-being out of people. Not for religion, and tradition for parasite leaders, (god-player)!

America's founding fathers were all Masons. The ancients lived by the Book of the Masons, written by the Israelite King Solomon, to unite people about understanding the God of the Cosmos. He did not create a religion, but he did send missionaries to enlighten others in wisdom. As a result, America became an example of morality, creativity, and fairness for the rest of the world. It opened the door for the opportunity to unite free self - thinkers, across the globe. As a result, many people from all over the world want to move to America. They want to be allowed to free self-think. They come here to unite free self-thinkers through wisdom, scientific knowledge, for mor accurate understanding of reality. However, the Mason did not find the book of **Adam, the snake, and Eve**, to debate for a more accurate understanding of the meaning, to have the wisdom not underestimate the slippery snake hierarchy leaders, therefore the Mason become a club of mane only because, they didn't want to listen to unrealistic opinionated women of that time. It created an opportunity for the sneaky snake parasite hierarchy to get back. So, the parasite hierarchy created a place to listen to the ignorant conversation, **and preaching illusion of knowledge and religious forgiveness, it was called, confession room** and that created a large movement of religious followers of women, that gave the hierarchy the have power, and privileges from illusionary knowledge, religion, and tradition. **Today Atheists are changing history books by saying that the founding fathers wore Atheist That is how hierarchy creates propaganda, lies as illusion of knowledge. Today it is wiser to include**

women in the man club, to debate for a more accurate understanding of God-reality of science because today all people man and women, are capable of being brilliant free self-thinker, humane-being for a utopian world!

The Most Creative Country in the World Used to be the United States of America

America had bars everywhere and everybody knew your name from debating conversations and discussions that created the wisdom of the American Revolution and evolution that led to the wisdom of the American Constitution: By the people, for the people, not for hierarchy. Two hundred years later came prohibition, which outlawed and banned all alcoholic beverages from the country. **This unenforceable law was created by a large movement of obedient religious women believers in blind faith and that destroyed those debate conversations**. Banning alcohol ultimately led to organized crime, such as bootleggers, rum runners by the Mafia, which created powerful police, judicial hierarchies, who arrested innocent people for drinking and started a decades-long war between criminal gangs and police gangs, with innocent creative civilians caught in the crossfire. It was created by ignorant obedient followers of religion's illusion from hierarchy greed. That was created religious law that created power hierarchy laws, **The wave of that religious movement still exists today, and bars are mainly meant for getting intoxicated, not necessarily used for debate conversation, as a result of today** America is a Christian country and Christmas, is a national holiday, **to protect hierarchy** business for more privileges, it is no longer a free self-thinking creative mason country.

Gangs will always win if people have no power for free self-thinking because free self-thinking creative people fear too many laws that they don't understand. They need a hierarchical lawyer, and a hierarchy judged to keep them out of jail.

The representative of the people in the government's job represents all the people to level the playing field. So, the government by the people creates wisdom by free self-thinking is necessary to develop confidence and welcome different views outside the norm from disagreement to a more accurate understanding of life reality to be a creative country again.

Some people are raised to be believers, that they are special by following tradition, and become an aggressive inferior gang, while others are raised to think for themselves and that is why all people cannot be friends. But, on the other hand, all people need scientific thinking to be friends. It is wisdom for this time, to include all people to a more accurate understanding to arrive at God's universal truth reality of science because all people are capable of being brilliant free self-thinkers for utopian world!

What matters to all great free self-thinkers is what they think of themselves, not what other people think of them from illusion. Then, by judging themselves after debate conversations, they will understand what is right and realize that humane-beings don't have to compete to impress anybody. The Socratic Method was intended to improve the understanding of reality, not to compete. Plato's "Republic" book is about the most prolonged debate between Socrates and his friends. Plato speaks in the voice of Socrates, who is the central character in the book. However, most of Plato's books were destroyed by religious leaders to enforce religious laws to create ignorant illusionary believers in blind faith, to protect privileges.

Orville and Wilbur Wright often debated with each other in the search for how to design the first motorized flying machine. After two years of scientific debating, frustration and failure, the brothers finally figured out how to create a propeller that would work. Each blade at both ends was in the shape of a boat sail, so the propeller could catch the wind to pull the plane forward. Without an accurate understanding of God-reality of science, they could not have designed a powered aircraft that would fly. They created the wisdom of a flying plane's propeller because of their scientific debating, and it is still used today because they reached God's universal truth reality of the time, that will create new knowledge, to solve all problems!

Today many corporations, interest groups, lobbyists and politicians are gangs in America. They are chipping away at the people's rights by weakening the Constitution to inhibit freedom of speech from greed because freedom of speech can create disagreement. They want to control the country via biased media, digital disinformation and so-called "opinionated news", shows on radio and TV that create and promote, half-truths and freedom of religion in the country, to create ignorant obedient followers for more votes to control the people, because they have your money to pay for it. However, the news must debate with people from the public to arrive at a more accurate understanding of the information. Many people think it is time for a new evolution, not a revolution. They are looking for brilliant wisdom that will unite humane-beings, so they can separate illusions from scientific wisdom, create a government by the people for the people and encourage free self-thinking in search of new wisdom that brings out the best of humane-beings. We can secure a better future not just by reading, but by questioning what we read; not only listening, but questioning what you hear; not just watching, but questioning what you see and not just believing but questioning those beliefs, and in a debate ask, is this a belief, an opinion, a theory, or a scientific conclusion? In a debate, challenge yourself and ask how anything was discovered or created for more accurate understanding, which will inspire the people of the world, and that will create a majority of free self-thinkers, to create a democratic world!

DISCOVER FREE SELF-THINKING IN WISDOM

Over the years, it has been determined that many health problems come from the medical model of relieving symptoms rather than curing diseases. This has led to a culture of patching everything in life—as leaders would have you do to maintain power and control. Chronically ill patients who return for more treatment are far more profitable than healthy patients. It is suitable for business. Because greed from competing scullers thinks they are entitled to make more money, by using and abusing people.

WISDOM creates humane-beings and wisdom will give medical science the power to be creative with natural cures. However, leaders want to use whatever they can, including robots, to control the people. But the future is not robots or knowledge. It is **WISDOM from humane-being.**

A believer, a gambler, or a follower, all rely on chance, superstition, for God to be responsible for the outcome; the question is, what are illusory people doing on this planet? Is it to overpopulate, destroy the environment, let everybody believe in whatever they want to believe, for hierarchy control by keeping people from free self-thinking and twiddle their thumbs? However, a free self-thinker searching for wisdom clearly understands that people must become humane-being to care. They do not expect chance, superstition, or god-players to do it. They rely on wisdom from God reality of science in searches of universal truth because life is an inspiring journey of challenges, not a monopoly, monotonous, comfort journey.

Wisdom from Albert Einstein: "Imagination is more important than knowledge." This imagination must come from free self-thinking. All other sources have no universal truth. When Einstein wrote his theses, people told him, "What you are saying is that Newton's wisdom was wrong." Einstein replied, "His wisdom was right for his time and my wisdom is right for my time." Because life is not a competition for humane-beings, wisdom changes with the changing times, and universal truth changes with the time. Our planet belongs to all living things. Nobody has the right to use the land, seas, resources, and overpopulation. like money in the bank by the illusion of hierarchy greed. They must be shared for all life to flourish. That's the only road for people to evolve into humane-beings because nobody purchased the planet Earth from God or the Energy of the Universe! This is one reason we pay taxes. Hopefully, some of those tax money is used to preserve, protect, and maintain our Goldilocks atmosphere for all life to flourish for wisdom by debating to create accurate understanding in God reality.

Albert Einstein thought that mathematical equations could explain the whole universe. But he was wrong because the universe continuously changes. Mathematics is Knowledge and knowledge does not change, only wisdom change Mathematics, and Knowledge. Therefore, today's wisdom will not be the wisdom of tomorrow!

Here is an example of how free self-thinking correlated with a universal truth: Fore thousand years ago, Moses, the people's representative, said that God is Energy, God does not make mistakes; people make mistakes. This is how Moses; the free self-thinker described the wisdom and Energy of the Universe. God, "the creator," is not a religion or tradition; it is just a word to name the cosmos' life energy. Everything around you and in you correlates with today's scientific knowledge. Look at the tree. It has no pump. **However, it can find, and carry water up from the roots below to the very top of the tree;** this happened through the power of life's energy. This is a fact, not a belief. When I confront a challenging task, I call on the life Energy to correlate and accomplish the job. In a television show about Space-Time on PBS's Nova TV program, Stephen Hawking said the cosmos is *in your subconscious*. Hawking demonstrated that the subconscious brain *knows* what you will do before the conscious mind acts in a test. What Stephen Hawking meant was that there is no free will because your subconscious decides before you do.

As a free self-thinker, I do not agree with Stephen Hawking that there is no free will, because he miscalculated people's different speeds.

Speed 1: Instinct operates at the speed of light.

Speed 2: The subconscious moves at the rate of instinct.

Speed 3: The conscious mind is slower than the subconscious instinct because the mind must understand the brain before acting, and by free self-thinking, or debating, the accurate answer could take from minutes to years.

Therefore, in addition to instinct and intuition, free will can also be slow or stopped by free-self-thinkers and that is why Israelite men wear hats. The cap's concept is to remind themselves to be humane-being, understand that the Energy of or the cosmos is in you and around you and that the cosmos knows what you are thinking. The hat could be as small as a nickel or as large as an umbrella. Still, you don't need to wear one if you remember to be a humane-being. The hat serves as a string on a finger to remind you not to forget important things.

Religious leaders dictate rules and laws that are ridiculous, illogical, and devoid of wisdom. The leaders want to enforce their will over their followers to maintain their status and power because they know religious followers are not free self-thinkers and do what they are told.

As you evolve by free self-thinking in wisdom, you will deal with singularity, i.e., correlation. A free self-thinker is a person who thinks for himself free from the untruth of dogma. Science searches for one trustful answer at a time. Mathematics gives you only one correct answer, which is a universal truth. Every brain lives only once in one life. Every man, woman or child is entitled to enjoy the individual's right to the most important right. And any individual free self-thinker in wisdom is capable of being brilliant.

As humane-beings create wisdom for a more accurate understanding of the world, the more the world becomes part of humane-beings and when the humane-beings become part of the world as a whole, it creates symmetry. That is why humane-beings don't want power over others by competition violence or wars or greed or propaganda. In the end, there are universal truths for the time. However, we will always be things we will never know and are not supposed to know; only having a real understanding of your wisdom will you understand because of the hierarchy as no wisdom. They will memorize the knowledge and use it to create power over ignorant, lazy, obedient followers for comfort and privileges because animals and animalistic people that are just being don't deserve to become a humane-being to be able to enjoy the love of all lives.

Only by understanding the universal truth reality, humane-beings will correlate everything into a universe answer. People will gain a more accurate understanding of life magic to be humane-beings and not be "god-players or leaders or hierarchy or obedient or followers."

All people are ignorant in some areas; however, people can overcome ignorance by asking questions in a debating conversation to understand the magic of life reality more accurately.

All illusions of knowledge were created by the hierarchy to have power over ignorant lazy people. And **if you are a believer in blind faith of illusory knowledge following a regime, you are the creator of hierarchies! And Hierarchy is, 1. The enemy of a more accurate understanding of life magic reality, 2. The enemy of free self-thinkers creative humane-being, 3. The enemy of nature, 4. The enemy environment. 5. The enemy of life is the enemy of God, 6. The enemy of reality of science. Imagine this. If you can free self-think?**

The Enemy of Knowledge Is Not Ignorance

Because all the people on this planet need to understand for themselves, **overpopulating to save hierarchy privileges, that destroy the environment and that will create uncontrollable epidemics and misery for all**.

When you have a more accurate understanding of reality, you will love life itself, love all living things and become a humane-being who truly understands right from wrong. When you become a humane-being, any effort to maintain an unsustainable status quo or use power over other people disappears. Leave behind the alienating world of hierarchy and the idolization of leaders and tradition. Wisdom advises us that we, as a civilization, must take a different path and **the only right direction is the scientific method is for all people to free self-think and by debating create a more accurate understanding God-reality of science, so all people will understand what is right to be the majority of the world!**

Since the beginning of history, there was vast knowledge for advancing a better life for all lives by free self-thinkers. However, most of the knowledge and free self-thinkers were destroyed by hierarchies that are lying **to stay in charge**. Free self-thinkers have been tortured or killed by leaders and still do today by gangs of ignorant followers who believe in illusory knowledge. Therefore, illusory knowledge is the greatest enemy of wisdom to understand the reality of scientific knowledge and the enemy of a better future. Fortunately, now more people are interested in a more accurate self-understanding of reality. Nevertheless, hierarchy's greed will ruin every great society in the future, if not stopped by a majority of free self-thinkers.

The greatest enemy of knowledge is not ignorance, it is illusion of knowledge, and that is religion, and tradition that repeats the same, from generation after generation, and does not facilitate change in the mind, to create new knowledge!

Animals and people have logical feelings, intelligence, and are capable of memorizing knowledge to survive. people are the only being, that is capable of debating to understand God reality of science. To be a humane-being. For example, after observing a herd of grazers, the lion goes after the logical choice, and that is common sense, the weakest animal he can catch and eat is logic. Most animals and homo sapiens belong to a group, to be safe. That is logical. Thinking that animals have no logic, feelings or intelligence comes from religion, beliefs, and illusions of knowledge rather than scientific truth. Leaders create a hierarchy by telling you that you become exceptionally special, when following them in their illusion of knowledge. But the truth is, you are what you do and if you are not humane, you are not a human or a humane-being you are just a being! in addition to logic and feelings, people have higher intelligence from memorizing knowledge, enabling us to become the most powerfully destructive animal.

That power today allows us to destroy Earth. Beliefs, feelings, and tradition are not God reality of science. That is why leaders of people and animals were and will not be able to achieve universal truth of that time. Because they are not humane-being. all People are equally capable of maturing into a humane-being. By free self-thinking and in a scientific debate conversation, they can overcome obstacles of the brain from believing in the illusion of knowledge. Science deals with the provable reality; this is why humane-beings can achieve wisdom by correlating with all living things to achieve universal truth for that time. The universal truth is the language of the universe. If it is not simple, does not correlate to a universal truth for that time, and does not unite all the people, it is not God reality of science. In this stage of evolution, nature does not need people. However, nature has a desperate need for humane-beings! Humane-beings have learned to defend themselves powerfully because they are creative. Civilization does not need leaders, but civilization has a desperate need for humane-beings to act on behalf of all life for a safer life. Then people can indeed be independent, free self-thinkers to discover more knowledge.

Why do you believe that all homo sapiens are humans? Why do some civilizations believe that animals are gods or that wolves are people who came back to earth to teach us how to hunt and survive or that rats are reincarnated of ancestors? Many civilizations falsely believed that nature exists only to use and abuse. Where is the evidence? Look at the mighty peoples of the past: The Egyptians, the ancient Greeks, and Romans. Their populace was taught to feel special by becoming followers of the regime. However, if people are not humane-beings, they are merely animals and all these great civilizations. And tradition disappeared.

Homo sapiens are very intelligent animals. They must think as they must eat. However, all leaders create religious illusions because they want to keep people from free self-thinking and debating. Believing in a religion tradition is a box of illusions that create a blockage in people's brains, that keep you idol, and limit you to one's perspective of your beliefs. Because leaders strive to keep their privileges and maintain control by keeping you addicted gambler that is hard to cure by believing that you are a winner. leaders create a religion/belief that makes prejudice, which creates hate. which creates violence and war. Some leaders direct their followers into battles, not just for power but also for the spoils of war and the valuable loot and booty the conquerors can steal for more privileges. Let me show you, from understanding that. 1+1=2, then that is why, it doesn't add up, that all religions are telling the truth. However, it does add up, that they all are lies, and if you are an **addicted gambler, you are a loser, not a winner.** free self-thinking searching for wisdom arrives at a universal truth to know right from wrong and become representatives of their people, which creates a safer, humane, and more creative world from understanding God reality!

How do you know that some people are humane-beings and are not just animals? All animals need a "carrot at the end of a stick" to propel them to act, such as hunger drives hunting for prey, grazing for food, or protecting their territory. They may also work because someone is whipping them with a stick. Carrots also drive people on sticks, such as fame, fortune, or affiliation with a gang by competing and obeying religious law. Many are motivated by the promise of an illusory after-life, whereby followers who behave are rewarded in heaven. In contrast, bad action and non-believers are condemned to a fiery pit, eternal torment or Enslaving people who will act because someone is whipping **them, by creating a scary God!**

We don't know how the Energy of the Universe, or the cosmos or God works. If we did know, the hierarchy would memorize the knowledge to control by creating religion (the illusion of knowledge) propaganda for more privileges, because the hierarchy has no wisdom because they are not searching for universal-truth. But Humane-beings don't need incentives like a carrot on a stick to accomplish worthwhile humane activities. They act to do the humane thing. They would risk their lives to save a total stranger. That is because a more accurate understanding makes them love all lives and live humanely. Because they **understand the Energy of the Universe, the cosmos, God, because God is to be understood not to be memorized!**

Humane-beings get gratification from making a better world. And doing what you know is right is gratifying because it results in the joy and love of life. Here is one example of a humane-being. After the Armenian genocide in 1915, which killed or expelled one and a half million people from the Turkish Ottoman empire. A Danish woman named Jacobson organized and cared for 1,500 orphaned Armenian children and did not create children of her own. Jacobson was a free self-thinking humane-being. She did it for her love of life. She understood the Energy of the Universe. Other remarkable humane-beings have performed similar altruistic endeavors throughout history.

EXPERIMENT TO KNOW THE PERCENTAGE OF PEOPLE WHO ARE HUMANE-BEINGS

An experiment was conducted in 1960 in which a doctor asked participants to raise the level of pain on a device that would electrically shock someone in the next room with a glass door. The participants were unaware that the person being "electrically shocked" was an actor. Every time the participants would raise the (nonexistent) voltage, they could see and hear the actor scream and exhibit more pain. The actor would even come to the point where he pretended to die if the voltage was raised to its maximum. The participants simply had to choose either to obey or disobey, increasing the purported voltage. or by free self-thinking in wisdom, not to obey by using the word "no" to a doctor's or "leader's orders!" The 1960 experiment results showed that 60% obeyed, thinking they were hurting someone and 40% disobeyed.

In 2011, the same experiment was performed and an overwhelming 75% obeyed orders. This shows that people are more likely to choose to be followers and were more obedient in 2011 than in 1960. In 1960, there was a hippie movement to free self-think. In 2011, we did not have a free self-thinking movement because of too many laws. However, we have more preaching on television and more freedom of religious belief and propaganda, giving the hierarchy more power over people, staying in control, and going to war or using the people for more privileges.

The people on this planet were better yesterday than today. There are fewer humane-beings today and more people live by an animalistic competing law because it is the law of hierarchy. The researchers concluded that people in 2011 are busy watching preaching propaganda on computers, televisions, and cell phones, including YouTube, preaching illusions, propaganda, instead of having a debate conversation like the hippie movement, to create a more accurate self-understanding right from wrong, to do what is right and be creative.

I created about 20 inventions and not one person who copied my work offered me a profit share! The inventor of the television was a farmer. He had a patent, and he showed his invention to General Electric Company. G.E. kept his designs until his patent time ran out, then they started making and selling televisions. The inventor farmer died poor. His life shows, hierarchy is greedy, and they are not humane-beings! Humane-beings searching for new wisdom created all great civilizations, but all great civilizations are destroyed by hierarchy greed, because their God is $!

A scientist claimed that free self-thinking conversation searching for wisdom creates people who exercise their minds and make their brain healthier, which has been shown to prevent Alzheimer's disease, and live longer. Alzheimer's is killing more people every year and is one of the most expensive and hart braking sicknesses to endure. Alzheimer's disease is becoming an epidemic and there is no medical cure for it because religion, belief in blind faith, illusions ignoring reality, create blockage in your brain and that create Alzheimer. The only remedy is free self-thinking and debate in the God-reality of science to keep your mind exercised to understand the magic of life. Imagine that? Because the cosmos will not have it any other way! So, start debating for your one good and for the good of life.

All religious movements could eventually change for the better, but that will take a very long time. Due to the obstacles erected by hierarchy and their beliefs that stifle change, the scientific movement of free self-thinking in a debate in reality is the most direct, shortest, the safest, and the fastest path towards accurate understanding to create a healthy life, and world!

In this time of our evolution, I am right until proven wrong. Some people ask me, "How can you talk about all these subjects: religion, politics, and feelings without getting mad?" (Getting mad is getting crazy). I answer, "When you search for wisdom, you don't get mad, only people that believe in religious lies get mad, and are dangerous! First, listen to what is being said, then free self-think and ask questions to acquire a more accurate meaning of words. If I don't answer, I would excuse myself and get back to the conversation later. When I find the answer, I will respond." Humane-beings don't need to act with instinctive aggression or compete. They take the time to free self-think and find the correct answer, to fix all problems!

WHAT WE KNOW NOW FROM HIGHER CONSCIOUSNES

In 2012, scientists confirmed the long-sought Higgs Boson particle's detection, commonly known as the "God particle," at the Large Hadron Collider (LHC), the most powerful particle accelerator on earth. **The Higgs mechanism gives mass to fundamental particles, such as electrons, protons and other building blocks that cannot be broken into smaller parts. However, these Higgs mechanism**

vital energy particles comprise only a tiny portion of the total mass in the Universe.

According to scientist Peter Higgs, in the beginning, the universe was in perfect symmetry. Then, along comes the God particles' energy field that creates a super-symmetry that facilitates continuous change. Just like Earth, the Universe evolves, ever-changing, ever-expanding, universal energy powers, our planet's natural law for wildlife, which often must compete to procreate, sometimes violently, leading to a better and more beautiful species, including early homo sapiens, which synchronized their actions in unison gang. This created a need for leaders and followers to work together for safety and survival. This developed hierarchies. It is as if they did by one brain with power over all other minds in the gang. Eventually began believing in a man as a king-god and a descendant of the God of all Gods.

Belief creates duality, not symmetry. If you believe in a man in the sky who is a God, you must also believe in a man in the earth who is a Devil. When you create a belief in religion, you also create a belief in atheism. Enchant beliefs are evil and dangerous. However, people by starting to debate from words create accurate meaning to understand life's reality. This leads to the wisdom that transforms people into humane-beings. And as life continuously changes, humane-beings seeking understanding and wisdom create knowledge; wisdom must also continuously change to overcome planet Earth's existential challenge of global warming due to pollution and overpopulation. Coincidentally, the energy particle was discovered when we had the knowledge and technology to do so. Thus, everything has been changing from the beginning, continues to change and creates exciting challenges to protect the Goldilocks atmosphere for life, by humane-being.

The scientist Nel Bohr discovered that measurement changes everything. He said that before a particle is discovered and measured, its characteristics are uncertain. For example, a particle could potentially exist in multiple places around a nucleus at any given moment; however, the act of higher consciousness measurement is what forces a particle to relinquish all other possibilities to one definite location. During the act of observation—and only at that moment, a particle's location becomes certain. Hence, this universe is designed for higher consciousness. From consciousness comes awareness. From accurate awareness comes brilliance. People and animals have common-sense, logic, and are able to memorize knowledge to become intelligent, but only humane-beings of higher consciousness can become brilliant because they exercise their minds in God reality of science, by free self-thinking and debating.

When a highly conscious mind observes, the magic of life collapses everything; however, when you look at any magic, you have to look at the magic spectrum for an accurate understanding. Since we can acknowledge others and ourselves around us, with a more precise understanding of creating a higher level of consciousness than another being on the planet, it is essential to free oneself from thinking in illusion to develop into higher consciousness by searching in God scientific universal truth for that time,

What is the difference between people of higher consciousness and being? We can send people to the moon. A dolphin, on the other hand, cannot send another dolphin onto land. So, what is it that makes us such brilliantly self-aware? Why are we capable of understanding things like God's universal truths of science and wisdom and why are we capable of having this "higher consciousness"? Because we are here on earth for an inspiring purpose and brilliant enough to realize in the spectrum of the magic of life that creates the wisdom to know, **that we are responsible for protecting the environment and all life. Not because it is easy, but because it is hard, inspiring, and exciting challenges. That's what my wisdom has shown me during my 80 years on earth life.**

Some knowledgeable people with no wisdom theorize that consciousness is an illusion created by chemicals in the brain. They can see where thoughts occur in the brain using Magnetic Resonance Image scans (MRI) and can even estimate what you think. Still, they cannot tell where you are or where your mind is; although they have figured out where activity in the brain operates, scullers do not know who or what is in charge. Essentially, they cannot find "you" in the brain! On the other hand, as free self-thinkers in wisdom, we realize that there are things that people are not able to measure or know. However, only by an accurate understanding of the spectrum of the magic of life, you create understanding! Because if scullers are able to memorize the knowledge they will compete to create parasite hierarchy, therefore, they are not humane-being, they are just being, that is the reason they don't accurately understand the magic of life, because **people that memories knowledge and compete to become parasite hierarchy, that will not comprehend infinity in their own Brain**, because the brain is an organ and all organs dies. However, a free self-tinker in the searches of God universal truth of science, understand that universal truth continually changes with the time to create an infinitely exciting and challenging life and that understanding in your mind create Higher consciousness humane being, to understand that you are infinite. Because the anergy of the universe will not have it any other way, because the reality of the universe we live in has energy throughout, which provides all the necessary resources **to fix itself or destroy!** Since we are aware of this and brilliant enough to understand much about the universe's mechanics, we can harness its energy to change our lives and all lives for the better—by wisdom from humane-being!

A higher conscious humane-being is a responsibility not a privilege, by his accurate understanding, has confidence in what is right versus wrong. Along with this wisdom comes energy and the willingness to accomplish the impossible. You can overcome pain, control your feelings, and conquer the most incredible obstacles in life by free will from free self-thinking **in your mind.** I have known this since I was a little kid. Once I understood the mechanics of higher consciousness from free-self-thinking wisdom and the energy it offers, I could harness life itself and become magically powerful! I feel everybody should learn the powers that exist inside of them and around them. They too, can have the energy and confidence to love themselves and all lives, to accomplish wonderful things. Unfortunately, not everyone is open-minded to free self-think for more accurate thinking of wisdom because of obstacles in the brain from memorizing the illusion of knowledge, and not being able to disagree with the preacher.

Leon D. Halfon

THE WORD BELIEF

The word belief is accepting what somebody says without debating or questioning. That is not smart; all scams are created by believing parasites. The word belief was created by religious fraud for religious dominance over the public to develop a gang for hierarchy. However, this word is often used in people's daily lives because the word belief has been imprinted in the public brain by preachers, often preaching the word belief; many other words can be used instead. For example, I think, I anticipate, I assume, I estimate, I expect, I fancy, I gather, I imagine, I presume, I reckon, I sense, I suppose, I surmise, I suspect, therefore I understand that all books of wisdom are written for debating conversation, not for believing blindly.

However, if you are not a believer, you cannot be scammed by criminals! The essential part of life is to surround yourself which free self-thinking humane friends that you can trust. God protect me from my friends; I will protect myself from criminals by not believing!

If you think this life comes from nothing, or evolution, then you are a believer in preachers, that write atheist scientific philosophy, therefore you are not a free self-thinker, because any fool can memorize. Scientific knowledge and write what they believe. Because the more you believe, the more you think you know everything, and that makes you feel important. The concept is to free self-think and understand for yourself, by learning from others, and the more you understand reality, the more you realize that you don't know much, and that is challenging and exciting. However, evolution is evolving life to adapt to the environment.

Energy is in everything it can't be created or destroyed; only life-energy creates life in God-reality of science.

WHAT IS BELIEF?

Most religions incorporate some wisdom, but because believers don't ask questions in a debate conversation and are not

The Enemy of Knowledge Is Not Ignorance

allowed to disagree, they keep on believing. But now, out of necessity, people are starting to search for a more accurate understanding of reality. That type of self-examination can be painful **because it reveals the truth, and all Pain is essential to let you know where the problem is**. So, free self-think!

All illusions, opinions, mirages, propaganda, tradition, and beliefs have no understanding of life reality. That is why, in a debating conversation, participants must have a reasoning method that leads to a logical realistic conclusion. This is the only way to create a more accurate understanding. If someone tells you what they believe, a "believer" will just accept it. Beliefs or opinions that have no roadmap This type of conversation is a waste of time because it does not create, accurate understanding to create God's universal-truth for that time. Therefore, **I'd instead go surfing!**

For example, India's subcontinent has freedom of religion and tradition the widest variety of beliefs than any other country in the world and started the Buddhist religion. Still, unfortunately, these omnipresent religions keep people ignorantly idol from believing in illusion. India has the second-largest population on earth, over one and a half billion people and leads the world with the most poverty, starvation, and disease. It is the only place where the rat-born Buddhist plague still exists. Moreover, in the recent past, India was where smallpox killed millions of people every year. To stop that deadly toll, it took one free-self-thinking, hippy sun of an Israelite immigrant who set up a program to vaccinate millions of people a year, which practically eradicated smallpox in its tracks. Today, smallpox is virtually non-existent worldwide. However, before that achievement, more than one billion Indian citizens and millions of educated doctors and scholars in their country were unable to eliminate smallpox because all of them were worshippers and followers, thanks to "freedom to create gangs of believers" which gave them the right to remain in illusion of knowledge. They have the illusion of knowledge and knowledge, but no free self-thinker for wisdom to understand reality. No one can change anyone in life, no matter how good the intention or wise approach. However, in a debating conversation in reality, you can let others say what they believe. Then ask questions to reveal the contradictions in their thinking in reality to ask themselves important questions and eventually arrive at an accurate understanding of God-reality of science. Encourage them to do the reasoning in the search of universal-truth to understand to better themselves.

A person told me that someone else is saying some of the things I am saying, and he has many followers. He is right because anybody who free-self-thinks in search of wisdom will arrive at a universal truth for that time. However, if someone creates followers or complete, he is no longer a free self-thinker because a free-self-thinker is an individual, not part of a gang or a leader. All religion starts from just a story that attracts followers and that's the problem. Beliefs effectively manifest and propagate illusions of knowledge because followers do not debate to search for universal-truth from a more accurate self-understanding of reality. Life is changing; it is challenging! Since there are many leaders with big egos from competing, many gangs and religions deal with delusions. **What believers do best is justify and justifying is not an answer, it is just an excuse! However, when you say I believe, you are uncertain, because if you are certain, you say I know, when you say I know, it doesn't mean I understand what I know, and when you say I understand what I know, it doesn't mean I accurately understand the universal-truth of that time! God is not found in knowledge, or religion, or tradition, or competition, or philosophy, or opinion, because they all are subjective to each person, or each group, and anything that is subjective to each person or each group, is not a universal-truth for that time. It was, it is, and it will, create a cruel world. Only by free self-thinking and humbling yourself to learn from others in debating conversation of scientific reality. You will understand the spectrum of God magic of life, so, you can, understand God to have confidence in yourself to be creative, so you can create a loving life in a utopian world, for all lives!** The Golden Rule— "Do unto others as you would have them do unto you."—is wisdom. It is neither opinion nor belief. It is humane wisdom to be applied in many situations. For example, everybody in the world wants to be treated equally and fairly. That is Universal Truth democracy! Think of life as a clock; all the gears must work correctly to give you the right time. But if the gears don't correlate in your brain from illusion, you will have to take somebody else's word for the time, although you cannot know for sure. Believing is not knowing and not being connected to reality; it will install false confidence. Consider the power of suggestion, the power of intuition, the power of the mind, hypnosis, the power of nature, the power of love and the power of life energy. All people in a scientific method debate create a more accurate understanding of these powers to benefit all life.

In the medical field, some doctors use computers not so much to improve knowledge but rather to record patient information simply. The majority of the medical profession and its powerful affiliated industries strive to discredit other healing practices to look good in followers' eyes, for more power, so they will feel good about themselves. However, for a humane-being, competition is wrong. Successful alternative treatments and nature-based, holistic approaches to healthiness should be encouraged. Of course, this presents an existential threat to the medical monopoly, which is why most of these outside-the-box healing processes have been opposed and marginalized for years by the medical establishment aligned with health insurance companies. Doctors should focus on healing, not competing, to make more money.

Free self-thinking in the search for wisdom goes far back to when people started thinking and there is no date known for that because people have always had to think and do things. On the other hand, all beliefs from religion, Buddhist and atheism can be traced to the date and time when their leaders started their hierarchies and gave their gangs a name and a religious faith from the illusion of knowledge to compete with another team. Because that is why all corporations do to create more business.

Atheism began to appear in Europe and Asia in the sixth century B.C. Philosopher Will Durant found that certain tribes in Africa and all animals are atheists. However, atheism is neither scientific, provable, nor knowledge-based; it is just another philosophical belief. However, atheists are also lost because they believe in an illusion with no scientific approach to back it up! The downfall of religion is the ego of its leaders, and the failure of its followers is ignorance and laziness brought about by the absence of thinking for oneself! Atheism does not correlate with life. Where there is life, there must be something that made life possible. People with high IQs are tired of being scared by violent religious god players and their illusionary God. They choose to become atheists because they understand that fearing God is wrong and having high IQs is having high **knowledge, not science wisdom**. When we learn in books or movies about enchanted beliefs like those of the ancient Egyptians, Greeks, or Romans, we laugh because we cannot understand how anybody could believe all this ignorance? It seems to be the truth, just like today's religion, but all these imaginary beliefs are illusions of knowledge. In the future, people will look back at the beliefs of today and laugh. Belief is like knowing there is an address for God somewhere. Followers believe in the illusions from leadership, even though their leaders take them in the wrong direction. Leaders give wrong directions because they are lost themselves by tier ego. They clash with others in hatred and wars to prove who is right. Believers think their path is the one natural way to go, but that is an illusion. This is why atheists came to think that religious atrocities are wrong. They are tired of being afraid of God because religions scare people. Therefore, they go in the opposite direction of religion!

Leaders and psychopaths, past and present, are known for big egos, high IQs, being atheists and god-players. To some extent, they are in the illusion of themselves as gods. In reality, they have all either died or will die someday; therefore, they are not Gods. You wouldn't want them in charge of your life or any lives because they are too destructive.

If you think there is no Santa Claus and no man in the sky named God, that doesn't make you an atheist. On the contrary, it makes you a realistic free self-thinker in wisdom because this is factual in science. You are an atheist only if you believe there is nothing in the universe that made life possible. If so, you belong to Atheism's gang; you are a believer in an illusory philosophy that **is not a threat to the religious monopoly of hierarchy**. Because people are interested in believing in blind faith, that there is a god that love you mor, however, if it is not a universal truth, it is not the truth, because it is subjective to each person or each group!

During a debate conversation, someone told me he was neither Protestant nor Catholic, but he was a Christian. I asked him, "Why do you think you are Christian?" He replied, "I like the humane things that Jesus said and did not accept some of the other church teachings. I think some church leaders have diverted from the legacy of Jesus Christ." My response: "You are neither Protestant, nor Catholic, nor Christian. You are a free self-thinker in wisdom because of your search for what is right and wrong. However, the Mason and free self-thinker in the search for reality are a defiant threat to the religious monopoly of hierarchy. Since the beginning of history, gangs of believers were the majority, that is the reason they tortured and killed free self-thinkers. They wanted to alter truth and knowledge to control the thinking of their followers. Belief is an illusion of knowledge, not truth because religious leaders create and propagate those illusions. The American Constitution separates religious beliefs from the government. Since then, free self-thinkers in search of wisdom have at least enjoyed some legitimacy and humane protection. As a result, they produced more factual knowledge in the past 100 years than in the last two million years! Because the free self-thinkers were protected, Imagine that!

RELIGION IS A PLACEBO
Religion is not a personal thing it is a gang thing!

In the beginning, when all people had self-awareness, they understood there was a power or a creator, which they called God. As soon as homo sapiens could speak, they began asking questions; the group leaders, (politician) decided they were the ones who had to have all the answers even though, in all cases, they did not have the solutions to solve problems, so they hijack sum wisdom and created illusions of knowledge (lies) to keep people follow the leader in blind faith. So, everywhere globally, the people in charge turned to opinions, traditions, which later become religious beliefs. Religions are still placebos because they replace God-reality. Simultaneously, some people created more accurate understanding by free self-thinking in a scientific method of debating in search for universal truth, by God given free-will, which made the wisdom for all new knowledge of today's better world no exception. Tru out history, the free self-thinkers have been, torture and killed, because they are a minority, and the leaders have the power for being the majority and the money. However, in today world, the free self-thinking countries have so much understanding power that they are able to destroy any majority of religious gangs, but they don't because they are humane-being, **the evidence are in the Iraq war. All leaders know it, and that is the reason they don't attack. However, leaders have to create hate to unite, their religious followers in blind fate to stay in charge, to protect their privileges. All cruel wars are created by inhumane leaders of religious people in blind fate, and they all wright history books propaganda (lies) to justify their inhuman cruelty, however, justifying is not an answer, it is just an excuse. So, get over your ignorance of reality, and get real by being a free self-thinker, to create a majority. When doctors don't have the knowledge or medication to cure you, they will prescribe a placebo and sometimes it works because the doctor meant well. However, the doctor must be out of his mind to prescribe a placebo if medicine and the scientific knowledge that will cure you and the world are available to the doctor.**

Move From Illusions of Knowledge to a More Accurate Understanding of Reality

A good comparison to religion is smoking cigarettes. Cigarettes first came out; cigarette salespeople were in propaganda campaigns advertising that they would cure practically everything. When the factual reality came out, smoking cigarettes created particular cancer types, start fires that destroy lives, homes, and businesses. The big tobacco companies and their advertisers and salespeople glamorized smoking, praised its benefits, and lied to the public like preachers, leaders, and hierarchy for decades until the truth about tobacco dangers finally came out. All the cigarette companies wanted was money and comfort, so they did not want to reveal death's fatal universal truth by smoking. They knew smoking was dangerous a deadly, and is an addiction that is hard to cure, but they didn't care. It took years before the cigarette industry was found guilty of hiding the truth from consumers and was forced to pay vast sums of reparation funds. But big Tobacco's monetary restitution is not enough because they knowingly killed people, profited from it, and got away with murder. The tobacco industry leaders who knew about these dangers need jail time. And so are the religious leaders preaching untruth propaganda who knew the untruth about all along; they need jail time too because they created a dangerous world that killed people and profited from it. Restitution is paying bribes. Bribery is the worst crime because it makes all crimes possible. Humane laws are designed to stop someone from damaging others, such as selling cigarettes or preaching untruths by propaganda lies, they knowingly killed people, profited from it, and got away with murder. And the environment, all that is doubly wrong and should be punished! But they don't get penalized because gangs run this world and gangs are run by ignorant hierarchy, (the United Nations) to be in charge of the money, not by the free self-thinking humane-being that will make the world safer.

When people can buy a seat in heaven or pay restitution (bribery) for a crime instead of facing punishment; or pay to obtain power in government, society is divided into the privileged criminal's royalty and the working populace, and no middleclass. This is not a government by the people, for the people. This is corrupt gang-hierarchy favoritism, privileges; this creates two groups. It makes a world that is not united and in times of trouble, the people pay the price and without a middle class the people stop being creative. However, people's creativity creates all civilization and without creativity to solve problems, all hierarchies will be doomed. That will make all world civilizations condemned; it has happened before because it does not work. That is why! Government must be by and for the people in a scientific method of free self-thinking by debating, the only whey that work, because People who believe the Bible, the Koran or Buddha have all the answers are misguided and are called "square" because they are stuck in a square box, People who think the dictionary and computers have all the answers are also misguided and "square." It is comforting for people to believe that the universal truth can be easily found in a square book. Because all they believe and want to know is found in that materialistic brain. When a conversation consists of what is contained in their box, they become an agreeable Dr. Jekyll. Once the conversation goes outside that square box in a debate for more accurate understanding of God-reality, they became the monstrous Mr. Hyde. Mentally limiting their horizons to only what is in their box by competing ego, they don't humble themselves to learn from others, to understand reality, because they give up their mind free will, by believing in blind faith, to create obstacle illusion knowledge in their brain!

Here's another example of free self-thinking in search of reality, not in illusion: When Galileo was 18 years old, he went to church with his friends. While everybody was praying and listening to the priest, Galileo watched a candle hanging from the ceiling on a swinging rope, were there was no wind, which created a pendulum motion. Galileo measured the time of the pendulum swings and found that every swing kept accurate time. That sparked the idea in Galileo for the pendulum clock. It was more accurate than the sundial and it is still used today. **Religion tortured Galileo because they believed he was lying; however, all religions are liars because there is no universal truth reality in the illusion of knowledge from religion!**

Galileo was not interested in believing; he was interested in understanding God-reality to find the wisdom to create new knowledge. Unfortunately, because he was a minority and not a believer in a tradition obedient follower, he was tortured by religious leaders to stop revealing God-reality by being a free self-thinker. **Some religions are still torturing and killing people by calling them liars, for not being obedient believers of religion!**

Hierarchy deals example, **I will tolerate your belief and you will tolerate my belief. We can choose peace among our religions. We agree to disagree. While these are grand ideas, history has shown that these concessions never work out because they are illusionary. These peace agreements last Sonly a short time because followers will remain ignorant, under their God player and eventually stop tolerating other people's beliefs.**

Christians and Muslims: peace lasts only a short time.

Jews and Muslims: peace lasts only a short time.

Hindus and Muslims, peace lasts only a short time.

Do you see a pattern here? It seems that one gang is less tolerant than the others **because hierarchy deals are illusion, and all illusion does not work.** Answers do not drive critical thinking. Questions drive it. Solutions can be further examined by asking more questions in reality. Ultimately, the critical thinker is led to a rational conclusion of his own making. He must accept his new realistic conclusion or willfully remain in his ignorance of illusion in the dark. You find the correct answer from within yourself, no excuses allowed! You must give up all your paradigm that make you fill from believing you are special, to advance to the next level of attaining new realistic understanding by free self-thinking, you will see that all problems can be solved through understanding God reality of science.

RELIGIOUS JOKES

Have you heard the story about a religious woman who fell in love with a scientist? After their marriage, they had a baby boy. When the baby was older, he asked his mother, "Where do we come from?" The mother answered, "We come from Adam and Eve, sweetheart." The boy responded, "But mom, dad says we come from apes!" The mother said, "Your father is right. Monkeys come from his side of the family."

A man died and met Saint Peter in Heaven; Saint Peter said, "No, no, no, what you did, is not a sin, hate, is an ignorance of God reality of science. You just worried yourself to death over something that was not sacrilegious." The man said, "How should I know? I am just a believer of leaders, in blind faith, not a free self-thinker in search of universal truth!

A religious leader places his hand on a young man's head and gives him a blessing. Then the young man puts his hand on the religious leader's and gives him a blessing. Next, the religious leader extends his hand and asks the young man for $5. The young man extends his hand and asks for

$10, saying, "I usually ask for $20, but I am giving you a special religious leader discount. Finally, the religious leader says, "I don't believe you." The young man responds, "I don't believe you either because I am not a believer, however, I understand God. By free self-thinking and debating in reality!

A devoutly religious man enters a cab in New York City and asks the driver to turn off the radio because his religion bans him from listening to infidel music. The driver stops the cab, opens the passenger door, and says, "Back in the time your religion was created, there were no automobiles, only carts and wagons. Cars, trains, and planes were made by inventive free self-thinkers searching for wisdom, not delusionary believers. However, if you still want to believe in illusions, maybe you should get out of the cab now and wait for a flying horse to take you where you want to go.

A farmer sold his donkey for $100, to a leader. The leader requested that the farmer keep the donkey for two days. The next day the donkey died. The farmer funds out that the leader made $1000 from a dead donkey, so. The leader explain that he sold 501 raffles tickets, for $2 each and return the $2 to the winner, because the donkey died! **because what believers do best is justify and justifying is not an answer, it is just an excuse!**

A successful religious young man brought many young ladies home. However, the mother disapproved of all the ladies, so he asked a friend what to do, the friend said, "Why don't you find a lady that looks like your mother, **he did just that, however, his father disapproved of her!"**

Religious Leaders

All great civilizations first evolved from people's wisdom. Later, hierarchy hijacked wisdom and replaced it with religion and tradition to create a gang's followers to control the people. This stopped people from asking questions and started hierarchy competing for more power that ultimately has destroyed every civilization in history! Because of their ego, from winning the knowledgeable competition.

"Blessed are the poor" means "Give leaders your money." "Blessed are the meek" means "Follow and obey." "Blessed are the humble" means "Do not question authority so hierarchy can remain in control." "Blessed are the hungry" means "We get fat while you starve." "Blessed are the merciful" means "If you catch priests or leaders doing something wrong, don't put them in jail or hold them accountable for their bad behaviors." "Blessed are pure of heart" means "Switch off your brain and use your emotions." Finally, "Blessed are the timid" means "Give us your power and become our slaves.

God-reality, science, wisdom, and universal truth—have nothing to do with religion or philosophy or illusion or tradition or gang or leaders!

When people operate under ideas that sound too good to be true, they end up becoming shortsighted. Something too good to be true is anything that offers a payout that is unequal to the work required. Some believe that an inhumane person can continue to misbehave so long as he or she repents. One has to ask or pay off religious leaders for forgiveness to enjoy an afterlife equal to Mother Teresa's. This gives power and importance to money from religious leaders but does not add up to an accurate understanding and at makes money into God. I recommend seeing the movie "The Name of the Rose," starring Sean Connery, about how religious leaders created a book of propaganda to stay in power over their believers. The movie is based on a true story in history about how the Vatican's created an educational book for the hierarchy to know how to maintain control and stay in power by preaching propaganda (scams) to create a gambling addiction for the masses that want to believe that they are winners!

Followers often deny factual reality because the truth is painful when it contradicts their beliefs. But when you hide from the truth reality due to cognitive dissonance, it will become more painful in the future and pain is necessary to know where the problem is. Jesus did what he did because the truth created pain to see human beings tortured and killed by greedy, inhumane hierarchy for more power and more privileges.

To be a free self-thinker, you must be brave enough to stand up for what you know, brave enough to admit what you don't know. When you are a religious believer, you are unwilling to admit that there are things that you don't know. When you say, "I believe," it sounds like you know everything. However, in God-reality of science, nobody will ever know or understand everything, because life is a journey of inspiring challenges!

When someone tells you they believe, what does it mean? It means they close their eyes and don't want to see or understand God-reality of science and universal truth. It means they have a blind faith addiction that hard to be cure. It is not logical to close your eyes and stick your head in the sand like an ostrich. Open your eyes and wake up from your illusions or you will hurt yourself and others. **That is childishly stupid.**

When I ask for directions, some people answer, "I believe it is that way or this way," and my response is, "I didn't ask for your blind belief. I want to know if you know where it is because I don't want to go on a wild goose chase!" Just say you don't know; is that so hard? This is why people are on a wild goose chase worldwide because believers won't admit they don't know. If you are not sure, the correct answer is to say, "I am not sure, but I think it is there." It is all uncertain until proven in factual knowledgeable **reality of science. A mind is a terrible thing to waste, clogging it up with unrealistic illusions to create blockage in your brain from reality!**

Some people claim advanced space aliens-built pyramids and other impressive structures throughout history because they are believers and not thinkers. They don't give enough credit to humane-being wisdom by free self-thinking to become brilliant. **Because ignorant believers in illusion can't have the confidence to be creative!**

The afterlife is a commodity that can be sold. It costs nothing to religious leaders, so everything is profitable. It is the best business in the world. With a profit margin of 100% and no need to work, religious structures are among the finest buildings on the planet and rest upon the most expensive real estate. With a market like this, it is no wonder why there are several different denominations within most religions. Everybody wants in on the action. The power that believers can provide. When you are a religious leader, an obedient follower will fight your wars, pay your bills, and raise your children to offer you the same. This is wrong. It gives incentives for people who seek power over others and don't want to work.

The Enemy of Knowledge Is Not Ignorance

This is what has been happening in the past and will happen in the future if we don't start free self-thinking in God-reality of science, to have wisdom.

Here is an example of what has happened in the United States. In 1830, the Book of Mormon was published. Brigham Young (nicknamed "the American Moses") led his followers to the "promised land" of Provo, Utah, where many schools and churches were founded under his name. Brigham Young sounds like "Bring Them Young," which may explain how he could attract many young people into his flock and why he approved polygamy for many wives to bring more children into his religion. One cannot help but notice how the subtle propaganda of a name like "Bring Them Young" reinforces its mission to captivate the young and the impressionable. The Mormon founders knew they would not have succeeded in getting followers from other religions because people are brainwashed in childish fairy tale not to convert. The Mormons understood that if they wanted their religion to succeed, they would have to preach to gullible children about their illusions. They have to overpopulate to give leadership power. Mormons run their religion like all businesses. They invested in future markets and took advantage of the naiveté and gullibility of children to create followers! Religions' bloody past is evidence that it is taking people and the world in the wrong direction. Its fanaticism can conjure phony reasons for atrocities such as torture and genocide. In recent history, we have seen genocide in Syria, Afghanistan, Iraq, Darfur, Sudan, Nazi Germany, Russia, and China. It has been going on for thousands of years and it is still going on today! It is all about power in inhumane leaders' hands to prove that their belief is actual knowledge and other religions are not! If they can win, it would prove that their beliefs are actual knowledge and God loves them more. But if they lose, it is always God's fault, not because their religious blind faith is a stupid illusion, and it will never be an actual reality; get over it; Free self-thinkers are a minority and have constantly been mistreated throughout history because they were threats to ignorant hierarchy. It is time to unite in the temple of wisdom for free self-tinkers, to be the majority of the world.

My friend moved to Mumbai, India and built a lovely house. Due to the lack of bathrooms, many people from the city urinate on their house walls. The man was distraught since it smelled so bad. He decided to build a wall around his home. After it was built, the people started urinating on his wall and that started to smell bad too; he asked me what he should do. To solve his problem. I said, paint pictures of religious Gods on all the walls. The man did just that and ever since no one urinated on his wall again because no religious person would urinate on pictures of gods—and that is wisdom for freedom of religions countries. Stop praying and expecting God to fix everything! Free self-think, and by debating to understand what is right, in God-reality, you will do what is right, even in the face of torture.

The Shiites don't believe that Sunnis are Muslim, and the Sunnis don't believe the Shiites are Muslim. Muslims don't believe the Israelites are the chosen people. The Jews don't believe Jesus is the Messiah. The Protestants don't believe the Pope is the leader of Christianity. Religious leaders are salespeople that sell illusions and will make you believe their illusory product is better than other illusory products so that they can play god.

I know by free self-thinking that no religions or tradition are necessary now in this stage of evolution. Stop bickering and move beyond the age of belief, tradition, aggressive competition, hatred, and war. Move towards the universal truth of science. If a group said to me, "Be religious or we will kill you!" I will pretend to be a religious believer, **and that what Israelis' free self-thinker did by becoming religious Jews**. All the significant humane changes occurring in every century were either rejected or welcomed with open arms. People who avoid life's challenges and welcome comfort become extinct because life is meant to be challenging in reality!

People should stay healthy by exercising their mind in the reality of science to understand how gravity affects their bodies. You are constructed on the frame of a skeleton. Muscles and tendons keep your bones and organs in the right place. If you don't exercise and stay comfortable, gravity will pull the bones against each other, creating pain. To remain healthy, you must understand the importance of challenging yourself by exercising your body and mind, as you must know that life is not about comfort. Throughout history, religious traditional countries that are idol, by fooling and obang an aggressive, religious leader, lost the war, to country that exercise their minds, that created powerful weapons! Believing in Santa clos or believing there is

nothing out there are called beliefs, all religions, or traditions, are called illusions of knowledge, all illusions of knowledge, and philosophies. are called ideologies because they keep people idols.

EXAMPLE OF FREE SELF-THINKING IN A DEBATE

If you lose your keys or some other essential item, you might ask a friend to help you find it. You ask them because you know two heads are better than one. That is the principle of the scientific method of debating. But, by free self-thinking, studying the situation and analyzing all known facts, by debating, science will take you in the direction towards finding yourself closer to universal truths for that time.

Throughout history, great thinkers wrote books such as the Bible, the Koran, and Buddha's books. Over time people translated these books differently and changed these books to show that they were right. Readers believed that these books were inspired by God, even written by God and their translations spurred new religions, dogmas, cognitive dissonances, prejudices, hatred, and wars. But if you have been taught to free self-think in wisdom, it will become evident that words are not perfect, have many meanings and are written by people who sometimes make mistakes and are lying from greed. But the God energy of the cosmos does not make mistakes! The understanding from free self-thinking is that cosmic energy God did not write these books; **people did, and later on, they fix these books and destroy books, to create that their prediction of the past is truth to promote their religion, that is why the dead-sea-scrolls of the past was important to find the original truth righting. However, in a debate conversation, you will find the wisdom of what the writer meant what is essential, not propaganda!**

Religious leaders' tactics are copied by politicians, salespeople, and gangsters for-profit propelled by scamming the believers from greed, not humane. That is why we must convert all religious buildings into temples of wisdom. Instead of sending children to school to simply memorize knowledge, it is better to make them into humane-beings, to be creative by wisdom for a better world, because **today knowledge is available on the internet**, that was created by free self-thinker in the search of universal-truth of that time by debating in God reality of science.

Everything in this book is open to debate. You don't have to agree with me. But, if you disagree, ask questions for a more accurate understanding of meaning. **For example, religious believers who have read my books often say, "This is your belief and I have my belief, or this is your opinion and I have my opinion, Sor we agree to disagree," because they cannot understand, from memorizing knowledge how you can exist without believing. However, you don't have to believe or follow a tradition, in a scientific method of debating, because you seek a God realistic answer!**

For example, the Jews, believe, that the Tora was given to the Jews, by God, my question is? Was the Tora, delivered, by UPS or UBS, the truth is, the Tora was written in Aramaic, by the god-players, of Babylon, not by, Israelis in the Ebru language!

A utopian society is easily obtained, by free will, to free self-think in a scientific method of debating, to arrive at God universal truth for that time that will provide accurate understanding, to understand what is right, from what is wrong, to create humane-beings out of people, to do what is right, and that will eventually create a utopian society by the people for the people, It is not possible to be obtained by computing egotistic hierarchy!

One hundred ten-year-old men were interviewed and asked why are you so healthy, wealthy, look so good, and live so long? The older man said, as a young man, I understood that it is my life, so I became a free self-thinker and enjoyed life peacefully, however after I got married, my wife start demanding and was no longer my partner, so I got rid of her, later on, I got rid of all the parasite in my life and only kept humane being, because it is not wise to keep parasite in your life ore in your country ore in your world.

In this book, you will not find the phrase, where I say "I believe" because it is not valid, helpful, or necessary and it is harmful to creating confidence. To live your life fully, you need confidence, from understanding reality. I wrote this book partly because of my experiences, which gave me a more accurate understanding of those boxes of belief. I realized that these boxes fall short of depicting a precise perception of life. Believing that your box is better than other boxes is an illusion because every religion or belief cannot be better than others' beliefs. To gain wisdom about reality, you have to evolve with an open mind continually. That can only happen by free self-thinking in a scientific method b to find universal truths that unite all life.

What if all people on this planet free self-think in wisdom, focusing on the same question? All the answers eventually will correlate to one scientific universal truth. In science, that is called finding the consensus solution that unites all responses to one universal truth of that time. All people can only focus on one thing at a time. That's why magicians can trick us with their dexterous, sleight-of-hand illusions. However, people know a magic show; it is just entertainment. When you get out of your box and look at the magician from all directions by debating, you will understand God-realities cannot be seen from one direction that is known to exist as a norm, nonetheless. That's the rabbit jumping out of the hat.

Religions and gangs create illusory boxes they believe are the best. But when you are in any of these boxes, what you see is a manufactured illusion of knowledge from only one perspective or one point of view. However, your brain has been tricked into thinking it is reality. Lowering your guard by believing in blind faith is not the way to find God, universal truth reality. It is not the path to wisdom. In these boxes, you can focus only on one thing: your religious or gang box of beliefs, or philosophy.

If you spend your whole life with the same gang, then you are in a box. Your sense of reality becomes nonscientific. It is distorted because you've learned to see only one perception of the world from one set of beliefs and rules. Under those circumstances, you will not have a vision of the spectrum of life magic. In such a controlling group, it becomes more difficult to see for yourself what is out there. As a result, your beliefs create cognitive dissonance from the illusion. That is why you need a debate in reality by a conversation from all directions in reality, not just from the people in your box. Comparing other points of view is especially important. You cannot learn from people who agree with you, in illusion of belief, because already know that and do not need to be repeated back to you by a preacher. to create a more powerful obstacle in your brain!

If your parents believe in illusions and traditions, it does not mean you must believe in fantasy fairytales, because wisdom changes with time. This is your life. You are born a free self-thinker with common-sense searching for understanding to have the confidence of your own free will. Then you are on your way to being a thinker, not a stinker. If you are a believer, then you can believe just about anything. That is why a. brainwasher believes that by memorizing knowledge, **in his brain**, he knows everything; however, he doesn't understand the reality of what he knows.

A free self-thinker, ins search of gad reality of science understand that he knows very little, and understand in **is mind,** that, reality of science is infinite, because life is meant to be infinitely exciting and challenging, and that increases wisdom to develop new knowledge, which is what life is meant to be. Paraphrasing President John Kennedy about sending a man to the moon, "We do it not because it is easy, but because it is hard, exciting and challenging." This phrase also applies to a better life, a better government, a better country, and a better world, not because it is easy, but hard! So, standing up for what you understand in reality is right. Education gives you the tools, but you must be a free self-thinker in search of universal-truth for the time, to be creative, to do the right job.

However, I don't judge people; I let them judge themselves by free self-thinking! If you want to **believe that zero is number two,** you can believe just about anything.

COGNITIVE DISSONANCE

Cognitive dissonance is a blockage in the brain to reality caused by dogmatic beliefs or illusions or propaganda given by leaders in their quest for power over others. When people clinging to strong beliefs are presented with evidence that contradicts them, the evidence will usually be rejected by the "believers." The evidence creates an uncomfortable feeling inside that is called cognitive dissonance. At that moment, they must protect their firm adherence to their beliefs by rationalizing, justifying, ignoring, or denying anything that does not fit in their belief. For centuries, believers' ignorance enflamed hatred and violence toward others from different religions or not followers and free self-thinkers. Throughout history, believers would fight, torture, kill and even be killed to defend and prove their belief is actual reality. That is stupid and is the aggressive part of cognitive dissonance. It will never be a universal truth, scientific knowledge, or wisdom; that is why the right way is the scientific way to debate and learn from each other, so you can arrive at a more accurate understanding of God-reality and be more humane today than yesterday.

When people are in a state of cognitive dissonance, they are very good at justifying just about anything, even if they are wrong or guilty and they know it! They are unable or unwilling to clear up any obstacles arising from their illusions of knowledge. However, these obstacles have doors that are not even locked, so anyone who wants can get out into reality, without the need to justify addictive illusion by saying my life experience is different than yours or by saying, I have my tradition you have your tradition or by saying you believe in what you want to believe, say e in what I want to believe or by saying, all roads lead to Rome. The meaning is that all religions arrive at a belief In God; however, all roads lead to a different illusion of knowledge location. In wisdom, the concept is to analyze the shortest way to a universal truth reality in a scientific method, no belief aloud. You have to have free self-thinking of individuals searching for original thoughts to understand today better than yesterday.

This is my point! When you see life from one direction or one experience by following your norm or a belief, it becomes your illusion of what life is. However, life is not a magic show. It is your life, and life is real., **that is why it is most important to learn from each other in a debate of reality, so you can get out of your illusions to see the spectrum magic of life and create a more accurate understanding of God and all reality. Believing is an epidemic childish philosophy of no confidence, that creates uncreative people from uncertainty of reality. You find the correct answer from within yourself, no excuses allowed! You must give up all your paradigm that makes you special, from believing illusions. To advance to the next level of attaining new realistic understanding by free self-thinking, you will see that all problems can be solved through understanding, because, democracy, and God-reality of science, cannot exist together, with elution pf knowledge.**

UNDERSTANDING THE MEANING OF WORDS

Take the word "ambitious." This describes someone who works hard to succeed. The term "greedy" describes someone who cares more about money than anything for more power of greed from the desire to compete for ego and may cheat, lie, or steal and think of themselves as ambitious. They are not ambitious; they are just greedy and greedy people are not humane-being.

Words are just a shell that carries a meaning or several meanings, which is why you must ask questions for a more accurate self-understanding of the meaning of words in context. If you don't ask questions, you are left to believe words with many meanings manipulated to create propaganda by leaders to improve their importance. However, by free self-thinking searching for wisdom, you must correlate the meaning of words for a scientific meaningful reality in a debate conversation. This leads to a more accurate understanding so that you can arrive at universal truth wisdom to understand your importance.

The Enemy of Knowledge Is Not Ignorance

Most problems today come from people believing leaders who control them by espousing illusions and superstitions over reality. They preach propaganda to believers about what life is supposed to be all about. However, we can no longer continue to be inhumane to humane-beings or the environment or other living things, simply because we are unwilling to let go of our many belief systems indoors, by government leaders or money in return for votes. For example, all people are classified as "human beings," but they do behave like animals and inhumanely. It is time to break the pattern of merely obeying and playing "follow the leader." We are not sheep; we are individuals, thinkers and we must each declare our mind's independence to think for ourselves, by the scientific road to universal truths to create wisdom, to resolve all our problems for a safer future, because all our issues have been and will be resolved by free self-thinking in God scientific method of thinking, **not by being the following sheep.**

Mathematics correlates to meaning and facts, not words. For example, if the number 2 could also mean 3 or 10 or whatever and if the number 4 could also mean 7 or 8 or 100, in that case, it is impossible to arrive at a universal truth, unless we search for the meaning that the word 2 two means 2 two and the word 4 means 4, in reality by the accuracy of scientific debate, then you can arrive at a universal truth, tor that time, and that brings on accurate self-understanding to The correct answer, $2 + 4 = 6$, that is an indisputable mathematic fact. That is the reason I called my first book, THE MATHEMATIC OF LIFE. It is scientific.

Here is another example of how to correlate meaning: Darkness is a place with no light. Darkness is nothing or zero. Therefore, only light exists. Some places are brighter than others, so the real meaning of darkness is the absence of light.

Recognize that wisdom in search of universal truths creates the understanding to love life. You may love some people more than others; you may wish to stay away from some people or some animals. However, there is no need to hate or fear any being with a more accurate understanding of reality. All believers of illusions are meaningless. In other words, their justification equals zero, 0 wisdom, zero 0 reality, zero 0 truth and zero 0 creativity of new knowledge for a better world for all lives. Someone has stolen original pictures of my inspiring life, so they can say that I am a liar, justify the illusion of their belief and attack me back by saying, we're your evidence. That is how terrible cognitive dissonance is; I know who did it. However, I don't judge people, I let them judge themself.

Confidence

Free self-thinking in wisdom is thinking for yourself without an organized gang belief of illusion that creates no confidence. Once you understand how to free self-think in scientific debate, you will have the confidence to analyze every period in your life, history and everything that comes your way. You will be able to see and understand the justifications from cognitive dissonance because you have the confidence from the scientific method of free self-thinking by debating, you can see the spectrum of life reality that gives you the power from confidence to say, I can fix the problem of homelessness and that is what this world needs now!

Free self-thinking in wisdom is democratic thinking and America is a democratic country. For example, you cannot swim if you don't know how. You cannot swim from faith or opinions or philosophies or beliefs or propaganda. The reality remains, you don't know how to swim. Ask questions about the realistic way to understand how to swim, once you know how to swim in reality, and by free self-thinking, you will have the confidence for the ability to swim safely. So, please be a free self-thinker for your safety and the world's safety!

In a debate conversation a participant said, what if after I die, I will go, *whoops*, what I believed is truth. My respond was! What you said is, that you have no confidence, however If you free self-think, you will accurately understand in reality that your belief creates no confidence!

At that moment you reveal the contradictions in their thinking to ask themselves important questions and eventually arrive at an accurate understanding. Encourage them to do the reasoning to understand for themselves, to change their life and the world for the better in reality, or remain ignorant of reality, by justifying.

All comedians, by exaggerating, are magnifying life. It becomes funny because it creates a more accurate understanding. For example, one day, a mother asked her son, a well-educated young man in the knowledge of words, to watch the front door because she was going next door to a party. The young man watched the door for four hours and got tired of it, so he took the front door off and brought it to his mother at the party. This shows that what is important is the understanding of meaning, not words!

Illusions

As a free self-thinking lifeguard, I tried to keep people away from rip currents at the beach. Strong outward currents seem calm and very appealing. However, calm water is an illusion of the norm in reality because it will pull a swimmer farther out into deeper waters creating a danger of drowning. So do all illusions of the norm in reality, creating danger. However, with a more accurate understanding of the spectrum reality of current at the beach, you will know that calm water could be a rip current that will pull you into danger of drowning!

People must correlate with nature from the reality of science to make everything work and if we don't, we will destroy ourselves.

To be a free self-thinker in wisdom, you must learn from the past. Prepare for the future and do not underestimate the cleverness, charisma and cruelty of hierarchy and their obedient scared illusory followers. The truth is in understanding by debating all books of history, for mor understanding.

People must change and adapt to today's complex world by free self-thinking in search of wisdom to become humane-beings or we will become extinct. So, you have no right to complain if you don't do what is suitable from a misunderstanding of life's reality. Because when you are not part of the solution by free self-thinking, you are part of the problem.

Most important among the personal attributes of a free self-thinker is the willingness to accept the possibility of being wrong, which is essential in science to achieve a universal truth, for that time, You must be strong enough to stop saying, "I am a believer," because saying "I am a believe" is to participate in the comforts of a specific group's illusory knowledge as a sheep that follow, meaning you are not constantly searching in reality for what is right. Once you subscribe to illusory beliefs, you stop free self-thinking and become part of the group dogma. As a free self-thinker, instead of saying, "I believe," say "I am not sure," or "This is what I think." That means you are still free self-thinking to understand better the world we live in. This leads to enlightenment because all beliefs are products of illusions.

To their people, the Pharaohs of Egypt, ancient Greece, and Rome were believed to be gods or, at least, demi-gods. In Britain, on the bottom of the symbol of English royalty is a motto in French, asserting, God chose them to be the hierarchy {royalist), and the house of Lords, is the house of gods, god-players. The fact is that all leaders are neither humane, nor godly, nor chosen by God. They are just people, god-players, intending to have power over people. The concept of democracy, and the 10, moral commandment is nobody has the right to play God or receive something for doing nothing. As people get mor understanding of reality, they will want to free self-think, and they will change everything for the better. The ancient Romans chose free self-thinking Jesus and things got much better. The East chose free self-thinking Buddha and things got much better. However, Jesus and Buddha were hijacked by the hierarchy to create a religion to be in charge of lazy people that becomes an aggressive gang in sheep clos in a herd of grazers!

People must accept responsibility for themselves to be aware of the consequences of their actions and join the rest of the modern progressive world in wisdom, science, understanding, to arrive at a universal truth by debating. It is the future, whether you believe it or not! Today, some people are destroying the environment for their daily needs, while others destroy our planet for profit and greed. Simultaneously, the free self-thinkers and scientific community tells us the truth about what is happening and warns us about what will happen if we don't change. However, scientists should stop preaching and start creating a more accurate understanding from debating in scientific conversation, with all people to get them involved, by seeking more universal truth, we can realize the need to change course and overcome the obstacles confronting us to save Earth. However, today most people do not seek more wisdom as they go about their lives, oblivious to the consequences. Many do not care to debate in conversation because they are all talked out from leaning to preaching beliefs, tradition, and propaganda to stop change. After being taught to listen, believe, and obey, they have no confidence to debate, so they can disagree or even have the confidence to have a conversation of reality.

We have so many nuclear weapons not to scare people; they intimidate other leaders (hierarchy and regimes, god-players). Nuclear weapons let them know that they cannot escape the consequences of using them if they start something.

In this book, I don't write what I believe or what I don't know. I only express what my accurate understanding has made clear through wisdom from debating about reality. Therefore, I never mention angels or spirits or miracles or anything that comes from the illusion of belief.

Free self-thinkers in wisdom desire a democratic government run by humane representatives to protect all lives. Free self-thinkers sometimes need help to protect themselves from gangs and the followers' cruel feared leaders, from their organized illusory belief systems.

Fear makes all beings or animals or people dangerous. Often free self-thinkers encounter people who are afraid of God and god-players. That is why they join groups consisting of bullies and bullies are so scared that they are dangerously aggressive. It is time to be able to change, and the rights of a free self-thinker to be the majority is necessary for a creative world.

Free self-thinkers in wisdom do not compete. They don't want to prove they are better; they know it, by the understanding reality of science, that is the reason they always feel good about themselves, look young and happy, with a smile on their faces, from the joy of a love of life and that is the reason believers are bullies hate them and the answer is to free self-think! The Old Testament was scary, as people free self-think, they created the New Testament that is less scary. So, free self-think to understand reality!

Understanding Right from Wrong

In this chapter, I will prove beyond the shadow of a doubt that free self-thinkers can readily recognize right from wrong; that is why they have the wisdom to create knowledge and the ability to belong everywhere and nowhere in particular. They analyze everything through a more accurate understanding in a scientific way that helps guide them towards the right path.

To prove guilt or innocence, free self-thinkers know that justice must be based on irrefutable empirical and scientific evidence. Unfortunately, today, religious law rules over seventy-five percent of the world's countries. Religious leaders and most judges are positioned to protect hierarchy. For various reasons, 1) they are elected by hierarchy, 2) they become hierarchy themselves, 3) the accused is judged guilty or innocent according to beliefs or prejudices, read your history books. When a leader can get a large group of people to agree with their illusion of knowledge, that is not moral, humane law. Therefore, leaders create many rules, which provide many ways to find the accused guilty. Disagreement with the hierarchy can entail more legal work and that is how lawyers become wealthy—by creating work where none should exist! Understand this because it affects your life.

The really guilty parties are the religious or biased judges who adjudicate based on religion, opinion, or politics to protect their privileges from tradition that is a belief, that they are special, but that is not right, moral, or humane. That is why a free self-thinker in wisdom knows right from wrong better than others beyond a shadow of a doubt.

I saw a conversation on TV between two scholars: one religious believer and one atheist philosopher. They were competing by discussing which is better. While watching them, I realized these speakers were one religious believer and one atheist cross-talking and not listening and learning by respecting each other Based on their knowledge, the atheist spoke, from the philosophy book and the believer spoke from the Bible book, instead of listening to what they meant, not what they said. I saw that each party had different conversations because they were competing and not having a debate conversation in wisdom. Conversations within mixed contexts tend to become circular and lose meaning. I have viewed a few debates between religious professors and atheists and the outcomes were always the same. Both sides think they are suitable for cognitive dissonance. They forcefully defend their beliefs, but unfortunately. Just because you are a professor, or a scholar does not mean you are open-minded and correlate to God-reality of science. Being educated, wealthy, comfortable or religious does not necessarily make you a humane-being. But when you are right, you are right; and when you are wrong, you are in a terrible situation.

Many say the meaning of life is fornication and replication, or to give life meaning for the comfort of body and brain. That sounds great, but life only for comfort provides nothing back to your health and the world, which creates no inspiring life because life is a series of challenges to be met and overcome one, sometimes two, at a time. Comfort and selfishness lead to less understanding, more narrow-mindedness, more fear, less freedom of thought, more depression, more prejudice, and more hate. With all that baggage, is it any wonder some societies and countries welcome war and blame God or someone else, for what's wrong? Ironic, though, because soldiers from both sides fight and die on the battlefield pray for survival or salvation to God, Allah, Rahway to create more hierarchy privileges! The meaning of life is to create a more accurate understanding of reality, as a humane-being, to create an inspiring, joyful, loving life!

OBSTACLES OF THE BRAIN

Doctors and scientists over the centuries naturally thought that the images we see or imagine appear as totally conceived, pictures in our brains, like a photograph or a movie. This is wrong. As we now know from scientific evidence, our brain is a digital computer. However, illusions of knowledge religion distort reality and cause blockage in the computer brain, like a virus in a body or computer.

Scientists now know that knowledge and pictures create digital electrical signals in the brain, cameras, and computers. Therefore, one's ability to correlate facts into universal truths is reality by accurate understanding and utilizing the power of your mind's free will. You can solve any problem or overcome any addiction because your mind is the real you. Still, your brain is just a computer organ. Make decisions that you know are right by **humbling** yourself, being willing to learn from others in a scientific debate in reality, and accepting the possibility of being wrong, because nobody knows everything or will ever know everything! Don't let preachers or memorizing religious beliefs that create tradition or propaganda or knowledge that create illusory obstacles in your brain create misunderstanding in your mind. By aggressive competition to prove that they are better hierarchy leaders, that have more knowledge however, they have no understanding to create the wisdom, to solve problem in reality.

Today, various treatments can be used to ease or erase beliefs and illusions of knowledge, which create fear, misunderstandings, and violence. Thankfully, these problems acting as obstacles in the brain can now be diminished or removed using several techniques, such as hypnosis, neurostimulation, exposure therapy, magnetic transcranial targeting, medication or simply by free self-thinking in a debate conversation to create a more accurate understanding of reality. I prefer free self-thinking in a debate conversation over lasers or medication in my brain!

Sadly, our world is on a course of certain self-destruction. Whatever we are doing to this planet is not working for the sake of our and all life survival. Most people are followers. They are told to obey, no question, no debate, no disagreement, no thinking for themselves. Just do as you're told, follow the leaders, believe in, and obey tradition in blind faith or you are out, to stop change. This to keep you idle, and it is to prevent you from free self-thinking!

A free self-thinker understands that it is wrong for a religious leader or hierarchy to ask for money in exchange for a heaven seat. If someone says, follow me for life and the reward will be countless beautiful virgins in heaven, that is not right. It is like saying: "After I kill you, I will give you time to think and talk in heaven." Or "I will make you a saint and give you a great place in heaven or whatever you want after you are dead."

Why exercise your body? To build strength. Why exercise your balance? To improve equilibrium. Why exercise free self-thinking in search

The Enemy of Knowledge Is Not Ignorance

of reality? To understand more accurately and express yourself more intelligently. These things come from your free will, not from illusion or belief or leaders or being a blind follower.

Let me show you a straightforward way to exercise your mind as a free self-thinker by questioning yourself. For example, why is that you think what you believing your family tradition is true? Where is the evidence? Why is it that others think their different belief in tradition is the truth? Why is it not possible for all beliefs to be true? Why do believers act as if they know everything? Why can't religious people admit that there are things that nobody knows and that are the absolute universal truth?

Know yourself, ask questions, seek wisdom, participate in a debate conversation, and examine everything by a scientific inquiry line. This will help you think, which exercises your mind and facilitates recognizing wisdom and universal truth. Wisdom continually correlates and aligns with the present. Known facts, philosophy, beliefs, and religions are fixed and stand still, but your mind does not. You control it and don't let anyone else control your mind by preaching belief in your memory bank to create obstacles in your brain. Sometimes it is hard, challenging, and exciting to keep your mind and body in shape, it is better for you and for the world.

People need to be empowered to free self-think in wisdom and become humane-beings who are truly free and protected by their elected representatives, instead of being led by leaders who control how and what you have to think. If more citizens worldwide helped us free self-thinking, great accomplishments would occur that are unimaginable today. Therefore, there is no need for leaders! Give leadership to be shepherds of sheep; however, don't give leaders people to create a gang, leaders always seem to find a way to control those lazy people, who give up their free will to free self- think, but people who free self-think in wisdom develop the confidence to stop leaders' greed, for a safer world.

Eventually, people will evolve to make their own decisions via free self-thinking to accept autocratic leaders any longer. Instead, they will want representation for the people, by the people. Today, many lives are in the hands of warlords, tribal leaders, dictators, or kings; it is not all their fault because some are humane-being. However, they obey violent, greedy leaders who make illusory religious laws to protect their privileges by hierarchy laws. That makes the king into a God to make hierarchy In to god-players, not for the people to think original thots. This is not humane law, it is religious and hierarchical law; it is different in every country, not acceptable at this evolution stage. Leaders promote various forms of competition as a word tradition, competing in games, competing in sports, competing in wars, all to justify their existence. This is an animalistic law, not humane-being law that protects all lives for the future.

A representative who truly helps and protects people welcomes brilliant free self-thinkers for their latest wisdom ideas-concepts-innovations. In contrast, leaders do not like thoughtful ideas that threaten the status quo because they want and need to stay in charge to remain in power. Pay attention by free self-thinking to know for yourself? Some say they tried many different jobs but weren't particularly good at anything. However, when they joined the military, they excelled. They were good at yelling and giving orders and thus became officers. What does that tell you? And watch out for that child who is a good liar because he probably will grow up to become a leader in the hierarchy someday. Most people understand that politicians are excellent "stretchers of the truth." We know that God does not choose leaders; they play "god" (god-players), we reap war, murder, rape, genocide, torture, mutilation, and other atrocities.

They do this to stay in power and preserve their hierarchies, bloodlines, and red-carpet treatment. Just as a gangster must use guns to rob, maim or kill, a leader must play god, be a good manipulator of meaning, be a good liar and give orders. For example, former President Obama made a speech in Egypt and said, "You have the right to your religion." The speech created a fanatic Muslim riot against Christians worldwide, killing many people because all leaders need a religion, making Obama a powerful hierarchy to make war for-profit and more privileges. Leaders' hierarchy will never have the privilege to understand the wisdom to enjoy the love of all life, which is more joyful than all privileges!

Hierarchy makes a pact with religion to gain the support of its obedient followers. Therefore, leaders are evil, not humane-beings. It is the reason that today's modern civilization is so slow to change and adapt to current existential threats! will eventually destroy us all because politicians that have been in the house of representatives as Democrat or Republican more than four years become part of that gang of believers for their movement and preach half-truths to stay in charge because it pays to advertise illusion of knowledge to believers and are not representative of all the people. Read your history books of democratic Athens, and debate in a scientific method for a more precise understanding of reality, so you can be a thinker humane-being to protect life and not be scammed by belief! Former President Richard Nixon was a liar but not good enough to become a real leader.

The Voice of Europe took this picture of President Richard Nixon.

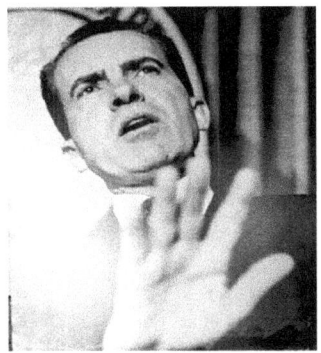

Voodoo Zombies

An extreme example of how leaders stay in control and prevent change for the better can be seen in Haiti, with voodoo religious priests who practice zombification, to protect hierarchy privileges.

I am talking about live walking dead people or so voodoo religious priests who practice zombification, to protect hierarchy privileges. **This is not a joke!** It would seem. In 1981, an article came out in *Harvard Magazine* called "The Secrets of Haiti's Living Dead," written by Gino Del Guercio. Haiti's research by an ethnology-botanist named Wade Davis regarding voodoo and zombies' supposed existence. What Davis found was an underground society of leaders utilizing brainwashing tactics to dominate and control the community. Voodoo priestesses told the people that they would become zombies if they were to go against or disagree with their religious teachings. The community believed them for a good reason. When a person acted against a voodoo leader's laws, the priestess could simply take that person aside and blow a poisonous powder harvested from pufferfish, into his or her face. This neurotoxin would subdue the individual long enough to be presumed dead. The person would then be buried alive. A brief time later, the priestess would exhume that person from its grave. With nerve damage from the poison and brain damage from a lack of oxygen, the person would continue living in the community as a bona fide walking zombie. All this tragic manipulation of men and women is designed to stop free self-thinkers from enabling change for a better future! No country interfered because all leaders are terrible and **protected by the united nation (united hierarchy). Imagine this for yourself?**

Using voodoo techniques such as this, accompanied by properly controlled "living-dead" examples, priests and leaders render people to be terrified to believe nearly anything. All religions, in the past and present, utilize underground (gang) societies that use force, torture chambers and brainwashing lies propaganda. In 1804, Haitian voodoo religious leaders created a revolution that killed and expelled all the white people on Haiti's island to protect their privileges. All voodoo religious leaders are still in charge today and no country interfered **because all leaders need religion and tradition to exist; leaders create all violent revolutions**. However, all peaceful evolution is made by the people's representatives. **Unfortunately, most people's representatives are assassinated to keep people from having the power of freedom and utopia to be creative.**

Here is another example of a hierarchy of destructive greed. In Muslim countries, women are for sale as a religious law, which creates the hierarchy with money can have over 50 women and 50 men will never experience a woman. However, "nature" makes 103 women for every 100 men. One man cannot satisfy one woman; if a man experiences many women, it is okay; however, if a woman experiences many men, she can be stoned to death. That is the reason it is religious law, not *humane* law.

In 2018, two women from the north of Europe who enjoy sex went to North Africa to satisfy depraved Muslim men; the women were arrested and killed by Muslim law. Throughout history, leaders have incited followers into killing free self-thinkers. If someone were not obedient to their doctrine of spreading illusions of knowledge, and tradition, leaders would label the disobedient ones with various names: pagans, heretics, witches, demons, Satan, Lucifer, traitors, communists, and infidels. Leaders created scary books, ugly and scary drawings for the unbelievers and pictures of hell. To show what will happen to you if you don't believe! Imagine this?

Indeed, what exactly was the practical purpose of human sacrifice? Did the blood of disembodied beating hearts guarantee plenty of rain for a good harvest or superpowers on the battlefield? Human sacrifice was a means for those in power to stay in control. Leaders sacrificed many free-self-thinkers who would not follow them. Without courageous free self-thinkers, the community's potential for betterment became less likely. When the ancient Romans converted England to Christianity by war, the Druids lined hundreds of innocent civilians to sacrifice their old illusory gods, so the Romans would not win. **It didn't work** and religious leaders destroyed all those lives. To protect their privileges Because they can! All today's humane changes are created bay books of wisdom, and by debating in God reality!

That event took place about 1,000 years ago. When Spain was going to war with Portugal, the Pope created a peace treaty by giving the north part of America to Spain and the south region to Portugal, in return, a promise to make everybody Christian, that started the justification for exterminations, that have occurred throughout America and Europe even to this day. Look at the widespread slaughter and torture imposed by the Spanish Inquisition and the cold-hearted efficiency of the Holocaust perpetrated by Hitler. So be a humane-being, free-self-thinker and wake up from your illusion into reality to protect and create safer, better government better country and a better world in God reality of science. Be a humane free self-thinker, to enjoy, the love, of life!

PART TWO

You Are What You Do, not what you believe you are!

This is a statement of wisdom. If you believe you are entitled to your exalted position "chosen by God" or feel special because of your ancestors, you expect something for doing nothing. That is not wisdom; it does not correlate to a universal truth. It is created from illusions of knowledge and a hierarchy to want something for doing nothing by hook or crook that is a parasite. However, if we free self-think, we will understand that people from all walks of life have generated all knowledge from wisdom; you should not be remembered for what you did not do, only for what you did do!

Just believing that you are the right person does not necessarily mean you are humane. It is the actions that you take and the challenges you overcome that define you as an individual, from the action of your free will, which exemplifies your humaneness. Then you will understand that you are a humane person and knowing this reality for yourself will give you self-confidence.

Let me tell you a story: At one time, I lived on 4th Street and 9th Avenue in Los Angeles, California. A neighbor would walk his pet pit bull and I heard from others that his pet pit bull killed numerous cats and dogs. So, one day, I confronted the pit bull owner and asked, "How do you feel about walking your pit bull?" His response was, "I feel great when I walk this dog. Because I see all the other dogs and cats are afraid of my pit bulldog. They recognize he is dangerous." So, I said, "Next time you walk your dog, put a spiked collar on him and a scary mask on yourself and I will guarantee that not only cats and dogs but everybody else will be scared and you will finally get the help you need for letting your dog kill other animals as fun. So next time you decide to be a follower of a person who enjoys power over other living things, free self-think about it first. Then, discover wisdom to do what is right and what is right is not to be a follower!

The entertainment industry could be helpful to help people understand the importance of thinking out of the box. The media can illustrate the positive impact of an accurate understanding to embrace the magic reality of life, that will create wisdom in their entertainment stories; however, the media are in it for money and leaders are the ones with your money, to pay for propaganda because **it pays to advertise if people don't free self-think in a debate.**

A free self-thinking representative of the people would not tell you that you are born a sinner. They would not command you to kill non-believers. But unfortunately, most leaders will say or do just about anything to maintain control to protect their privileges.

The individual's rights are the most important ones, above any rights of gangs, religions, and leaders in government, because the government must be for the people to create great minds for a safer world!

ALWAYS IN FRIENDSHIP

Always in debate conversations, maintain friendship and civility. Believers in a conversation will try to justify anything that does not correlate with their illusion of knowledge; and attack by competing. However, justifying is not an answer, it is an excuse, and competing is not a debate! Eleven thousand years ago, most people were nomads wandering in small tribes or clans. They came together for safety and to share their experiences and knowledge. This started the practice of hospitality. In search of wisdom, people pondered the thought that some power or force of nature created everything. This was the first universal truth for that time, that united all people, and they named it God. However, since creating significant competing powerful gangs, they created religions with different illusory traditionary beliefs, to unite the gang. The gang's hierarchy made privileges for themselves. And that's started nature's competing animalistic laws, and only competition creates ego; ego creates hierarchy; hierarchy creates religion; religions create tradition, that created obedient followers; obedient followers create a gang in blind faith: and blind faith creates ignorance of universal truth, and **the absence of truth is a lie**! However, some free self-thinking people did not think from an accurate understanding, debate in reality all writing, they became united humane-beings to create all knowledge, that create a humane utopian better world for life, because violence or competing religions (illusion of knowledge). create **nothing.**

Galileo was a free self-thinker, not an obedient believer. He worked to end Ptolemy's geocentric model of the cosmos, which said all the heavens and stars revolved around the Earth, and the Earth was flat. That model made people feel special because they believed from their religion that they were the center of the universe, and they were born humans. This earth-first model was a standing conclusion for hundreds of years, until Galileo revealed the universal truth about how our solar system works. Even in the face of imprisonment and torture because the Catholics hierarchy said, he was lying? he pursued his path, using his mind in a scientific method of thinking. He created the new scientific knowledge that unites all of life. Because when you free self-think, you will understand what is right, you will do what is right even in the face of torture! What if Galileo and all other great free self-thinkers in science obeyed the hierarchy's religion and tradition? They would have been just like most folks who follow like sheep. Then, where would we be today? Preaching is propaganda, not reality.

I ask, "Why be a believer when there is evidence of truth available? Why not analyze life through scientific inquiry and research for a better world?" The response is, "If I leave the religion, and tradition; I will lose the support of my congregation, my friends, and my family. Do you think it is easy to renounce my religion? I won't be able to get a job or receive help from my religious members. I will be ostracized." A person who responds this way is weak and has bought into the idea that comfort, status, and money are more important than doing what is right. That is not wisdom but rather a form of greed that comes from an unhealthy brain full of illusions.

Greed is the enemy of wisdom. A representative of the people should focus on making the government function better for all the people, not just for the regime and by assisting the needy, providing wisdom to govern the country and not be divided by religious sectarianism and political corruption corporate greed. It should not be a government full of leaders controlling everything by creating laws to benefit the powerful corporate and political "gangs" that essentially run the country. Lobbying that represents an influential leader should not be allowed in government. Instead, they should have a debate to arrive at a more accurate understanding that this country and the world should be by the people for the people, not by the gangs for the gangs followers of laws, to create a safer world for all lives! Because the grates minds that created all scientific knowledge hath the freedom to free self-think to disagree with making a better world, that is the reason all people need **to have the freedom to free self-think and disagree in a debate to create an accurate understanding of reality to do what is right.**

THE PURPOSE OF LIFE

When we are born, we have much to learn. If it weren't for our humane parents, teachers, and representatives in debate conversation, we would remain savages, just like wild animals. Unfortunately, for an illusory reason, many homo-sapiens are not humane. Therefore, it is necessary to have humane-beings exemplify living by doing what is compassionate.

In the first hour of life, you have a name, a nationality, a religion, and a tradition. After growing up, some people might spend their lives fighting and killing or being killed for a reason they did not choose.

The purpose of life is: To create free self-thinking and, challenge yourself in debating, create a more accurate understanding of the spectrum of life magic reality, to understand God universal truth of that time, to know t to have the wisdom and the will, to become a humane-being and be able to enjoy life fully, **in a utopia living with humane realistic people!**

No excuses allowed! You must give up all your paradigm that make you fill, from believing you are special, to advance to the next level of attaining new realistic understanding by free self-thinking, you will see that all problems can be solved through understanding God reality of science.

HIPPIES

When new scientific knowledge arrives, we must abandon our previous understanding. That is progress. For example, the "hippies" of the 1960s were free self-thinkers. They were the most significant movement of independent-minded people in the twentieth century. They were not interested in war, money, or power (except "flower power") but instead sought peace, harmony, and love. That is the wisdom of being a humane-being. Hippies understood that control by leaders, gangs and authorities that created war was wrong; they invested their time in being creative. The status quo community of believers did not think hippies were right. And yet, it was the hippies who invented desktop computers and created the internet. Hippie's interest influenced Steve Jobs in Eastern mysticism and the underground movements commonplace in the 1970s. because the hippie was interested in the God-reality of science.

The invention of the internet empowered the individual by instantly opening a world of all knowledge and information at one's fingertips. This made knowledge available without spending a lifetime memorizing knowledge and made some influential leaders and businesses obsolete. Some former hippies helped develop DNA research. Before the hippies, a highly contagious, deadly disease called smallpox killed millions of people worldwide every year, until the late 1700s when English doctor Edward Jenner created a successful vaccine that eliminated most smallpox in developed countries. However, smallpox lingered on, killing millions in poor, undeveloped nations for three more centuries until the 1970s, when a former Israelite hippie, the son of Jewish immigrants from Eastern Europe, became a doctor United States and changed all that. His name is Dr. Larry Brilliant, who, after earning his degree, spent several years studying in India at a Himalayan Hindu Ashram. Back in America, he was chosen to spearhead the World Health Organization's campaign to vaccinate over three million people in Africa, Asia, and South America, which resulted in finally eradicating that deadly disease from our planet because he was a free self-thinker humane-being. All hippies were also non-religious. They loved everybody and everything in life. Their motto was peace and love of life, **is a utopia**. They loved Jesus too, not because he looked like a hippie, but because he was a man of wisdom and a very humane-being. Hippies allowed themselves to be creative and think original thoughts in a friendly debate. They presented opposition to war, governments, leaders, and religions because those forces fear change. President Lyndon Johnson did not think hippies were fellow Americans. Hippies understood we have too many laws that merely serve to prevent the progress of free self-thinking and enrich people in power. This change scares the obedient followers of the illusions of knowledge. Too many scary laws and scary gods are obstacles to free self-thinking. At the same time, all the leaders, scrollers and followers in the world were saying that it was not possible to eradicate smallpox. **What do you think of those knowledgeable leaders and their followers now?**

Today we have the 2020 pandemic is just an example! By religion law and hierarchy law, as created a society of people in this twenty-first century that have the largest population of illusory religious followers and the largest population of very wealthy hierarchy leaders. However, because of all these laws, we don't have a massive movement of independent-minded people. **It seems that we cannot fix anything.** The hierarchy is perfect in creating new laws and rules that lock up one million people in jails and the rest of the people locked up at home has a Curfew.

FROM DEBATING IN THE SEARCH OF A UNIVERSAL TRUTH ABOUT GOD

God is life energy; everything is energy and not only crystals have memory; everything in the universe has memory. If it is, then the universe is an infinite computer that memorizes to do what is right. If it is, then nobody or religion is superior. Get over it! God unites us, in reality of science, not separates us in illusion fairytale created by inhumane cruel leaders, to create gangs of people. Only by free self-thinking, debating in the search of universal truth, all the people of this planet will arrive at a more accurate understanding of God-reality, that will unite us, to do what is right, for a better life, a better government, a better country, and a better world.

SATAN, LUCIFER, AND THE DEVIL

People have been writing books and scrolls for over five thousand years. Seven hundred years after the death of Jesus, Christian scholars collated some ancient imparting wisdom stories into two books, the Old Testament, and the New Testament. Meanwhile, hundreds of other books and scrolls were destroyed, including books of Plato, who wrote about Socrates' wisdom and democracy, because these books did not create ignorant obedient followers of religious believers for hierarchy.

Mohammad, who founded the Muslim religion, considered himself the "last prophet of the Israelites," whom he called "the people of the books" because they wrote all books of wisdom for a better world. In the face of torture and even death, the Israelites continued to pursue the search for wisdom. They are still here because they understand the necessity to love all life and understood that wisdom from free self-thinkers would prosper, while the illusions of knowledge will be forgotten in the future. Wisdom creates universal truths to unite, and help people become humane-beings. In the original Hebrew books from which the Old Testament was written, there is no Devil or Hell, only Satan/Lucifer, who Christian and Muslim hierarchy grossly misrepresented, **to protect hierarchy privileges!**

Satan is not a devil. In Hebrew, his name means "someone who disagrees with you in a conversation." To enlighten, Satan's other name is Lucifer in Latin, which means "a bringer of light" in conversation. His names become synonymous with evil and the "fallen angel" because the religious hierarchy did not like anyone disagreeing to protect their privileges. Socrates was condemned because he was a Satan/Lucifer.

Leaders used the imaged hell with Satan to warn their flock what would happen if anyone disagreed with the religious leaders. Followers that disobeyed were told that they deserved to die and burn in Hell forever. Essentially, the words "Satan" and "Lucifer" have been hijacked by religious leaders that created a power by illusion of knowledge from believing in blind faith, to protect hierarchy privileges, prevent change, to stay in charge.

A vicious God as a terrifying animal describing God by the hierarchy describing themselves. Religious leaders who describe God as terrifying are expressing themselves because they are terrifying who play God. Hippies and free self-thinkers prefer to morph the word "terrifying" into the word "terrific." Life is not terrifying; it is terrific. Leaders-god-Players are terrifying. Everyone should have Satan/Lucifer's friends in their lives to challenge themselves and let go of biases, beliefs, fears, that impeding their understanding of God reality, it is important to accept the possibility of being wrong when debating with Satan or `Lucifer. However, such conversations are essential to finding a consensus leading to the understanding to be better today than yesterday.

COMPARING CULTURAL CONTRIBUTIONS OF RELIGIOUS FOLLOWERS AND FREE SELF-THINKERS

Did you know that 66% of all named stars in the night sky come from Arabic? A thousand years ago was the Golden Age of Islam. During this period, great leaps and bounds were made in mathematics, engineering, agriculture, and seamanship. Star maps were made to improve navigation and mathematics rapidly advanced. The word "algebra" derives from the Arabic "al-Jabr." "Algorithm" is Arabic, and algebra uses Arabic symbols.

However, if you look at the middle east today, you will find many people out of touch with current scientific knowledge and reality. Why is this? A "religious leader" Imam Hamid al-Ghazali (1058-1111 A.D.) was a Muslim religious cleric leader and preacher. He is to Islam what St. Augustine is to Christianity. The Imam created a revised, "proper" interpretation of the Koran—a new guideline for all Muslim people to follow as "religious law **by extreme violence punishment."** For more hierarchy power. When this obstacle from religious law happened, Muslim innovation almost completely ended, because of fear from religious law.

Innovation by free-self thinking dramatically decreased when Muslim clerics forced people violently by killing the free self-thinkers to create ignorant followers of religious law by Imam Hamid al-Ghazali's doctrine, stating that manipulating numbers and mathematics is the Devil's work. But math is a universal language. Without understanding the language of the universe, how can science make progress? It cannot. Yet this happened to Islamic culture a thousand years ago. Today, it is greatly affected by still following religious leaders, who proscribe strict rules of law based on illusions and kill the free self-thinkers that did not follow and obey religious laws to protect leaders' privileges.

There are approximately 1.5 billion Muslims in the world today. How many of them are among Nobel Prize winners in the sciences? The answer is 0.%. One-half of one percent for peace. How many Israelites are there in the world today? Approximately 10 million. What percentage of all Noble Prize awards in the sciences would you think free self-thinking Israelites are responsible for? The answer may surprise you. It is 25%, one-quarter of the world's Nobel Prizes in science. Plus, Israelites are responsible for 25% of the Kyoto Prizes, 34% of Wolf Foundation awards and 38% of the National Medals of Science. Medical and scientific advancements have saved an estimated 2.8 billion lives by Israelites (free self-thinking nomads individuals searching for wisdom), a scientific method of thinking.

Look at the difference between the Muslim religious culture of 1.5 billion Muslims and 8 billion people globally, with only 10 million Israelites. This means the Israelite scientific method of free self-thinking is empowered by debating a more accurate understanding of reality. These people who are not followers of leaders of religions, tradition or philosophy or hierarchy are why the Israelites have been mor then **500 times more effective in making scientific breakthroughs for a better world.**

The concept of being an Israelite in the 21st century is free self-thinking. It is a mind-blowing thought to understand that the Israelite movement is responsible for so much scientific knowledge. Imagine what discoveries the world could have today if Islamic culture had continued its earlier scientific inquiries. This is the difference between free self-thinkers with the representative government of the people, versus followers of aggressive religious and political leaders (God Players) with no representative government. It's either the search for wisdom way or the followers of illusion of knowledge way. Pick one. The difference is not between Muslim people and Israelite people. Because you don't compete in wisdom or science, you try to find the best path to better yourself and the world as an individual, because, it is not what Gad can do for you, it is what you can do for God as a humane-being.

This book is not preaching to tell you what to think but to think for yourself. Its purpose is to empower you to ask questions and, in a debate, conversations God reality of science create a more accurate understanding of the spectrum's magical reality of life, be creative and do what is right in God reality by your free will, from loving yourself and all lives.

PUBLIC COFFEE SHOP OF WISDOM

It is time to consider my proposal for a coffee shop named "Public Coffee Shop of Wisdom." To make America great again. It's based on King Solomon's temple of wisdom. It's a public coffee shop dedicated to debating conversations for a better understanding of reality. This coffee shop is a place for all individuals to be heuristic; it encourages people to understand more and learn from each other so they can create more wisdom for life.

A democratic coffee shop that welcomes all people regardless of race, creed, or national origin. A place for social networking, making world friendships and create free self-thinkers that love all lives from an accurate understanding of reality. In the coffee shop are books of inspiring humane stories of the past, science, literature and in all book's empty pages, so readers can write a comment about what they like or dislike about it, no beliefs or opinion allowed. And as with a library, if you want to sit next to someone, you ask permission. You are not to raise your voice, use fighting words or compete, because competition is for animals and preaching creates belief that creates tradition, in blind faith. **This coffee shop works!** it will unite all the people of this country and the world, for a humane future!

The following picture shows an Israelite from the Cohens Tribe in a square setting for debating, inside the temple of wisdom, on Djerba's desert island, and reading, Ancestors' humane inspiring stories. No preachers, no alter, no holy water, and no confessions room, just a place to sit, read or debate, learn by a scientific method from others to discover for yourself right from wrong and create a more accurate understanding of all the spectrum reality of life magic in your mine, to be creative, so we can solve, all problems!

Leon D. Halfon

GREBA TEMPLE OF INSPIRATION AND WISDOM

The oldest Israelite temple in the world is on Djerba's tiny desert island in the Mediterranean Sea off the coast of Tunisia. Moses himself designed it for free self-thinking and debating conversations to help attain wisdom. Built by individuals, for individuals, but not for preachers, it has 3 three names: the House of God, the temple of Wisdom and the Greba Temple, and Greba is a name of a cake to eat, with coffee and debate. The temple's cornerstone came from the original King Solomon's temple of wisdom. All the 20th-century woodwork in the Greba Temple was built and donated by my father, Mero Halfon Dula, a great free self-thinker. He did it to inspire other people to think for all their lives.

During a conversation in the Greba Temple, you cannot preach, raise your voice, use fighting words, compete or be violent. The seating arrangements do not face an altar or dais for a preacher or a sermon. The seats are arranged in squares, like a coffee shop, for reading books of wisdom or conversing to debate to understand the meaning, for the search of universal truth and create free self-thinking teachers of wisdom. That is what democracy is about. Get everybody involved in the movement of free self-thinking in wisdom. The Greba Temple is not a religious temple; it is a democratic temple, by the people for all their lives! Freedom of religion isn't democracy, because it cannot create free self-thinking in wisdom!

The Enemy of Knowledge Is Not Ignorance

The difference between a teacher and a preacher is that you can disagree with a teacher, but you cannot disagree with a preacher. Teachers shod promote free self-thinking for wisdom to be creative for a better world. Preachers promote propaganda to create misunderstanding to build a united gang to protect the hierarchy`s control. However, today some teachers are preachers that represent leaders and leaders worldwide hate-free self-thinking Israelites or Zionists. Still, they like the religious tradition Jews because they have made their temples look like Christian churches or Muslim mosques to be safe from other hierarchies.

Jews from the Island of Djerba 1960

PEOPLE OF THE BOOKS

In the above photograph, the Israelite free self-thinkers humane- Cohen people on the desert island of Djerba dress in robes as Jesus did, but not alike and are not hugging each other because they are not part of a gang, but rather free self-thinkers, individuals in search of wisdom for a better world. You cannot tell how they dress who represents the people because they are all individual free self-thinkers and don't compete. **They are selected by the tribe of Levi, the direct descendants of Moses as the most humane**. If you strike them, they will turn the other cheek, just as Jesus taught, because violent people are animals, not humane-being!

Unfortunately, it seems like people have fought wars and been cruelled to living things forever. We are still cruel to living things today and many people blame God for it. However, these teachers of wisdom, the Israelite Cohens, are examples of humaneness. They've lived on this island for 2,500 years, didn't overpopulated, had no weapons, wars, jails, lawyers or judges or any violent quarrels and disputes would be settled by a wise man representative of the community, in a realistic debate for the wisdom of universal truth **and that is utopia!**

These people are known as the "People of the Books." Their ancestors wrote the books of the original Bibles, the books of the New Testament, the Old Testament, and many other books of wisdom. Today the Bible is found in hotels, motels, and homes around the world. Over time, the Bible was used to teach people how to read and write, which promoted a more humane and more scientifically educated world. The "People of the Books" were the original recordkeepers of ancient wisdom and are still searching for more wisdom, however, all books of wisdom are stories that promote wisdom!

These Israelite Cohen people work as masons, carpenters, and jewelers because they **did not want anything for doing nothing**. The difference between them and other groups is that you cannot distinguish who is rich or poor or even who is in charge. They have the wisdom to be humane with each other. They do not value the power of money, hierarchy, or competition that creates the ego.

When the ancient Romans ruled, they grew wheat for their Army in North Africa and lived on my native desert island of Djerba. At that time, the Romans had conquered most of Europe, North Africa, and the Near East, including present-day Israel and King Solomon's Temple. That is where Jesus kicked over the "money table of the religious hierarchy" because the people were greedy for Roman money, by competing for an ego.

John the Baptist and Jesus told universal truth wisdom and for that, they did not deserve to be killed. Unfortunately, leaders do not willingly give up their power and privilege, no matter who or how many, or how much they destroy. Do not blame anybody else but the hierarchy in charge because the people are just followers or free self-thinking humane-beings, that many of them wore crucify. By crucifying the man Jesus, the pagan Roman rulers turned Jesus into a god and in effect, set up the hierarchy of the early Christian church that Jesus disapprove of. Regardless of the name, cruel religious hierarchies run most of the world today using propaganda and enforcing religious law. By the time people begin thinking for themselves, it is often too late. The hierarchy becomes self-propelling and maintained by their tradition, and ignorant followers that believe in aggressive inhumane obedience and the power of money. However, the Cohen tribe survived because of their wisdom by pretending to be religiously tolerated by world power's hierarchy. My grandfather and uncle were the representative Rabbis of wisdom for the community on Djerba's island during the 20th century. Since Djerba was unknown, no hierarchy came to destroy the ancient books of wisdom in the extensive library that my grandfather owned to control the world. All the books were handwritten and rewritten because these originals were thousands of years old. From these books, I learned all I could think about the great wise inspiring men of ancient history: Moses, King Solomon, John the Baptist, Jesus, the Night Templar, and many others.

All these free self-thinkers understood that "you are what you do"! My grandfather's name was Simon Cohen. He wrote the Glat Kosher book, which admonished people to treat animals humanely. If an animal is killed for food but dies in pain, then it is not fit for consumption because it suffered. To be considered a Glat Kosher food, the animal must be slaughtered painlessly with kindness and respect. Initially, the Jewish leaders did not accept the Glat Kosher killing method because it was not economical. However, more people are humane today and often demand that their food be Glat Kosher. They want a healthier mind and body because **it creates meat, with no adrenaline** and to be humane toward animals all their lives or become vegetarians. These people of the books paid a bribe to the Muslim hierarchy and paid sixty-five million dollars in gold to the Germans to be left in peace! Because free self-thinkers are a minority.

After World War II, the Cohen tribe and the Israelites departed Djerba to Israel. They wanted independence from the Muslim hierarchy and religious fanatics gangs who bullied and attacked defend last innocent people. These murderous thugs bombed the Greba temple, killing fifteen people and they are still killing today. Remember that violence is for animals and debating conversation is for humane-beings that create a safer future. The Muslim hierarchy and their religious obedient followers are a gang of bullies because, they are inferior beings; the cause is from their leader killing all the free self-thinkers that disagreed, to protect their religious privileges.

COMPETITION

Ever since I was young, I have never enjoyed competing with other people because of my accurate understanding of reality. I concluded that competition enlarges the ego of the winner and creates inferiority for the loser. On the other hand, I have constantly challenged myself to become better and better at everything I do. For me, this understanding helped me grow humanely. It may seem that competition brings out the best in people to be useful for hierarchy. However, if you free-self-think in wisdom, you realize the universal truth is that the greatest humane-beings in history did not compete against others. Instead, they challenged themselves to be better and received boundless joy from the inspiring journey of life. They did it because they were free self-thinking humane-beings, with a more accurate understanding, of what is right from God reality of science. That is what makes the world a better place, for example, **Jack Lalanne did not compete, he challenged himself to become better and better at everything he did; and help everybody free self-think, to challenge themself to be healthier. He did it from his love of life as a humane-being. I don't care how big of a competing champion you are, you will not be as powerful, and help as many people as Jack Lalanne, because you are selfish from competing ego. Another** example is. **My friend Henry Lamothe , performance, was, to jump from, 35. Feet hi, into a pool of water, 14. Inches deep, 10. Feet wide. He said that if thy introduce this sport in the Olympic, it will get reed of all the egoistic competing champion. You are what you do for the love of life, not from believing you are a winner. However, most people are brain-washed by leaders that the word I, is ego. However, ego derives from only winning**

the competition. It does not derive from the word I, or from what you did, or what you do. Our competitive behavior is the reason we are here; it comes from nature's animalistic law. Nature's law is cruel and arbitrary for humane-beings, but it is not too cruel for inhumane-beings who act like animals. People are corrupted by aggression, which derives from nature's competition. It seeks only to dominate and survive. It is a result of this awareness that, over time, people have made strides by free self-thinking in search of universal-truth to become more humane, for a better world.

In New Guinea, tribes conduct annual war "competitions" against each other's tribe." If tribe A kills more warriors than tribe B, then tribe A wins. The chief says it's just like a football game, it is tradition. Then losers will feel inferior and inferior people become bullies to feel superior. In nature's law, the loser ends up being eaten by predators. In wisdom, you don't need to compete or prove anything to anybody but yourself. Free self-thinking in wisdom enables us to understand that competition, religion, tradition, gangs, and greed do not correlate with the environment or democracy or God reality of science. We know this is true because the homo sapiens hierarchy has destroyed every great civilization in history by wars and environmental degradation. Unfortunately, by competing and polluting, people are still doing that! Nature needs humane-beings to protect all life and the environment. So, for example, if someone is humane, they would raise a dog to be compassionate. But, unfortunately, not all dogs are raised humanely because they are bred to compete, fight, and kill other dogs. One of God Commandments is "Thou shalt not kill," but that humane law hasn't stopped people for thousands of years from killing by believing in blind faith. Per my grandfather, free self-thinking is a scientific method for a more accurate understanding, which leads to wisdom, which creates a love of life, which evolves people into humane-beings. This movement has been at work back to the homo sapiens that are free self-thinkers, not followers of hierarchy. This is the only way to attain a utopian democracy. A hierarchical system does not create a utopian society because it is based on competition. Many people have persecuted others throughout history, believing they were human, and others were not human. However, persecutors were the ones who were not humane-beings, and the word human is created by religions, You must give up all your paradigm that make you believe you are special, to advance to the next level of attaining new realistic understanding by free self-thinking and debating to become a thinker. Not a stinker!

TO BE A HUMANE-BEING OR NOT TO BE A HUMANE-BEING - THAT IS THE QUESTION?

Not all people are humane-beings. However, all PEOPLE ARE borne free self-thinkers with common-sense, AND SOME people, are encouraged, by the adults, to search for universal truth in reality, and by asking QUESTIONS, created the accurate understanding to love everything in life, and evolve into a creative humane-being to create wisdom, which makes all knowledge, for all lives. This scientific SYSTEM IN GOD-reality is proven to work. However, the majority of the people, that are borne free self-thinkers with common-sense, are obligated by the adults to believe religion tradition to fill special to unite from filling special that create inhumane people, that Tortures and kill, free self-thinkers, humane people that are, and will make a better world to protect hierarchy, It is wrong when obedient followers are found not guilty of carrying inhuman orders and doing inhumane acts. Regardless of the justification for fighting and killing, it is doubly wrong to be inhumane of humane people.

A free self-thinking humane-being would never be proud of hurting anyone, even in self-defense. You should only be proud of the lives and the environment you nurture. Ignorance of reality is wrong for people, no matter how you justify it. Because it is proven not to work, in-reality of science.

On the other hand, free self-thinkers should never trust or underestimate the majority power and cruelty of ignorant, fanatical in illusory knowledge people. Read your history books in a scientific debate. The right of an individual or an animal to humane treatment is the most important for humane-beings. Today, we have the United Nations to protect countries (hierarchy) because hierarchy created it. However, we need a global computerized high-court program run by humane-beings to protect all individuals' lives and the environment from the United hierarchy. To become a world **of humane-beings or not to become humane-beings, which is the question?**

It doesn't matter where you come from, your background, or your skin color. You can become a humane-being, through thoughtfulness in a scientific method of debating conversation in God reality to unite, and better your family, your country, and the world for all lives.

CHOOSE CONVERSATION IN REALITY INSTEAD OF VIOLENCE

As an animal trainer, I understand that the animal's wilder he is the more the animal behaves by aggressive instinct, the more they misunderstand you. The more they become frightened and more dangerous. This is nature's survival technique.

I grew up with the People of the Book on the desert island of Djerba; they experienced no violence among themselves for thousands of years. When people understand the importance of a scientific method of debating to find wisdom and become a humane-being, it will enlighten the rest of the world to solve all problems because it works in reality of science.

In real estate, it is all about location, location, location. The People of the Book decided to separate themselves from the rest of the world that lived by natural law, which naturally creates a balance of overpopulation by violent competition of wars. The people of the Book chose to live on the isolated location of the desert island of Djerba. They made a peaceful existence (utopian) by utilizing debate conversations to discover more wisdom from universal truth and are an example for the rest of the world!

About 2 million years ago, people and chimpanzees had the same ancestors. One group of ancestors made-up words for conversation and evolved to take over the world. Unfortunately, the other primates group was unable or didn't want to communicate and remain, a gang of chimpanzees still living in nature's violence law.

Today people are divided into two camps: The believer's followers of illusion hierarchy gangs that handle life with natural law, as chimpanzees do, and others as humane-beings, solving their problems with scientific minds by debating conversations.

One solution is to separate the two groups with walls, people in illusion on one side and humane-beings on the other side, to avoid bullies, confrontation or create a separate part of the city as a Ghetto, to create a safer location for humane-being and that will eventually create a revolution or riots for more demand from bullies by leaders. Another option is to bring people together in harmony by learning to use conversations in a scientific method to create universal truths for an accurate understanding of reality, which will make all people know right from wrong, in a public coffee shop to search for reality. Only then will we be able to co-exist, to be humane enough to save them, all lives, and the environment. In this way, we can convert problems into solutions, because all solutions are solved by an accurate understanding of reality, not religion, opinion, philosophy, or propaganda that are obstacles in the brain to an accurate understanding.

DAAA

Because we are homo sapiens, we can use many words to talk; other animals cannot. So, when we have meaningful scientific debate conversations searching for wisdom, we evolve into humane-beings, not just animals that can speak. We are more advanced than animals because we can use thousands of words to understand a conversation's meaning. But even so, people often misinterpret the meaning of words. In the future, our languages will evolve to give every word only one definition, one specific meaning, like mathematics, for a more accurate understanding of meaning in a conversation.

The Enemy of Knowledge Is Not Ignorance

If someone attacks you in a conversation, it is because they don't understand what you mean. They get this feeling that you are talking over their heads. For example, suppose two participants are talking about something you do not understand in a conversation. In that case, you might ask them to stop because it creates zero thinking, zero learning and zero understanding. If you want to learn, it is up to you to free self- think and ask questions to develop a more accurate understanding.

In today's world, dictionaries and leaders give many meanings to a single word. This creates misunderstandings of reality in a propaganda program to making people uncertain and that creates no confidence for more power over their followers. Leaders love personal profit at the cost of their deluded believers in illusions of knowledge and opinion. Dictionaries and religious books are complicated so that you will need help from a leader or a preacher.

However, the true meaning of words should be simple in knowledgeable debate for an accurate way to understand. That is why I create new words to give more precise meaning and interpretation. I introduced unfamiliar words in this book that you won't find anywhere else to clarify this book's intentions. For instance, my books are the only books that are using the word "Daaa."

On the other hand, people who establish their thinking for themselves and get their independence call themselves free self-thinkers. Throughout history, people moved to new locations to establish themselves and then declared their independence. For example, the United States declared its independence from England. Then Texas, California and New Mexico declared their independence from Spain. And Israel declared its independence from Jordan; Also, part of Scotland wants independence from England because they understand the illusion of divine royal leaders and the Scots do not want any part of it. They recognize that independence should be available to all people. However, some people don't want their independence because they are insecure from lessening to scary preaching, propaganda so they need to be cared for, in exchange for a vote.

People who did not get their independence and are part of a collective influenced by religion, tradition, blind faith, propaganda, a dominating family, or a gang are called "Daaa." In the television show "Star Trek Next Generation, created the word" Borg", because they are boring people in a box, ore by believing in a square book, part of a collective by tradition, they are created by parasite leaders in power that need Daaa and despise free self-thinkers and the countries they live in, rulers hate the fact that free self-thinkers cannot be controlled and influence the people that are Daaa. To maintain power, leaders must destroy free self-thinkers by creating hateful propaganda, to protect their privileges. In the mid-20th century, Stalin's communists (atheists) killed over 50 million free self-thinking people in Russia to stay in power. Stalin said, "What is important for me is my family (his gang of henchmen)." He was not a representative of his people. He was a murderous tyrant. Hitler, the mid-20th-century German Fuhrer, had his followers kill over 30 million people to stay in power.

Similarly, Turkish rulers killed Greeks, Muslims, Kurds, and Armenians to maintain power. They did it with the help of ignorant competing mobs of followers who were Daaa. China's huge population was peaceful until the Chinese communists (atheists), led by Chairperson Mao Tso Tung, killed over 70 million of his people. The average Japanese individual before World War II was not warmongering. Yet Japanese leaders ordered the murders of over twelve million Chinese and Filipinos. In Africa, e government of Rwanda conducted massive genocides as well.

Today, there are too many free self-thinkers to kill them all because of the American Constitution's wisdom: By the [people for the people from the people. Not for hierarchy, or religion, or tradition. However, we need a lot freer self-thinkers in wisdom to stay safe from leaders with are Daaa people.

Peace-loving religious people have been made irrelevant by their silence because they are not free self-thinkers. They will be awakened one day in the future and find out that the ignorant, leaders-hateful, fanatical bullies have taken over their world and their nightmare will begin! Peace-loving religious, Syrians, Koreans, Germans, Japanese, Chinese, Kurds, Russians, Rwandans, Serbs, Afghans, Iraqis, Palestinians, Somalis, Nigerians, Algerians, Jews, and many others, have been killed, they did not speak up until it was too late! They followed leaders blindly instead of thinking for themselves in a scientific debate to know right from wrong. And that is still happening because they are Daaa and obey.

Christians, Muslims, and Israelites started as nomads searching for wisdom, but today many are Daaa because they are no longer nomads searching for wisdom, and are religious peace-loving, obedient believers seeking comfort by praising other men (God Players) and blaming God for all atrocities, because they did not understand reality! What are they on this planet for? just to complain to God. For example, When the ancient Greeks were contemplating going to war against the Persians, the people wanted to know from the Oracle at Delphi who will win. The Oracle's prediction was, "If Greeks go to war, you will destroy a big country." With this prediction in mind, the Greeks confidently went to war and were defeated. The Greek people complained that the prophecy was wrong. The Oracle (religion) responded, "You had a big country, you fought a war, and you destroyed your big country." The prediction was correct; the Greeks just misunderstood the message because they could not ask the Oracle, or preachers any questions or debate which big country, they were talking about. When in doubt, always ask questions and if you do not, you become a believer in an illusionary knowledge, scam.

VERIFIABLE CONCLUSIONS

Another phrase I like to use is "verifiable conclusion." In a scientific method, a verifiable conclusion becomes a universal truth for the time. This represents a scientifically proven theory. It is not blind faith, a belief, an opinion, or an illusion. As an example, Darwin's Theory of Evolution is not a belief; it is a verifiable conclusion, is about all lives including people evolving into differently to adapt to nature or be extinct, because nature don't adapt to life. Why should anyone mast be prejudiced against others who have a different skin color? Do you know what causes various skin tones? The cause is vitamin D. For example. If you live in a sunny area, your skin becomes darker to protect you from too much vitamin D. If you live in an area that is not sunny, your skin becomes lighter to absorb more vitamin D. Similarly, my horse grows longer hair in the winter to protect him from the cold. Shorter hair in the summer to protect himself from the heat. Also, if you don't get enough or too much vitamin D, you will get sick! I am telling you this because it is wrong to be prejudiced against people just because their ancestors had different levels of the sunray or having a different point of view of the spectrum of the life magic and by not being hierarchy and by not competing, you will create a more accurate understanding of reality for more scientific wisdom. Yet, some skeptics still think Darwin was wrong because of the cognitive dissonance in their brains from believing in illusion refuses to accept God science's reality. However, people that memorize science to create from science a religion from competing greed they justify their illusion and justifying is not an answer, in reality, it is just an excuse!

THE UNDERSTANDING MOVEMENT

If you want to get elected in America, you must seek religious leaders' support because they can influence their followers' votes. This is tremendous power for preachers who tell their flock what to think and do. This is influence peddling and it is wrong. In a real democracy, people are supposed to free self-think and debate to create understanding! Not follow and obey! Ironically, every living American president, because they are a hierarchy that needs religion to stay in power, which is the only reason they attended televangelist Billy Graham's funeral because, he could make 2,000,000 people vote one way, except for Donald Trump, who did not participate in the funeral. People who record ignorant obedient followers are leaders, not representatives of the people, imagine this!

Abraham, Moses, King Solomon, John the Baptist, Jesus, Buddha, Socrates, Archimedes, Newton, Galileo, Einstein, Martin Luther King Jr., Rosa Parks, Steve Jobs, and many more were free self-thinking humane-beings of different eras, various places, and various skin color. They did not align themselves with religious leaders and hierarchy to become more powerful or improve their lot. They were not followers or fundamentalists. Instead, they opposed religious autocracy and helped humanity adapt to change. I hope more countries choose to be governed by equitable, humane laws without dealing with radical fanatics who overpopulate their own countries for power and money to become detrimental to the environment necessary for all lives.

In today's world, cruel religious armies are not needed. That is the government's job that represents all the people's inhumane laws and fosters all the people's movement towards fixing all problems. But, unfortunately, in religious countries, some people think they are Gods or can speak to God. But what kind of God would allow billions of people to be enslaved by force or poverty or famine due to overpopulation for power and the overuse of limited resources? Do you expect God to fix everything? Besides, the god-players on earth are not real gods. They are inhumane, greedy leaders that create ignorant followers. This is the age of the scientific way of thinking, in the wisdom that works, with instant access to information about our interconnected world, to accurately understand God's scientific reality.

The word "ignorant" derives from the word "ignoring scientific reality." It is not meant to be an insult. It simply means you are ignoring the God-reality of science, which is out there. The term "knowledge" comes from "knowing," not from the word "believing or opinion." Because if it is only a belief or opinion, then it means you do not know. Bibles say God created man in His image. What the bible writer meant is that God is energy. Man is energy because what is essential is meaning, not words. In the scientific debate, factual scientific knowledge is necessary, not belief to create parasite destructive greedy inhumane hierarchy.

THE ONLY BIBLE STORY ABOUT SATAN IS IN THE BOOK OF JOB
This wisdom story is created by realistic debating!

What is the real meaning of the Book of Job in the Bible? When was it written? Why was it written? What the writer meant? Ask yourself and in a debate, these questions to learn from others will create a more accurate understanding of meaning. For example, when the story was written, pharaohs and kings were believed to be gods. But the god of universal cosmic energy is believed to be the God of all Gods.

The man Job was a good and prosperous father living in Egypt thousands of years ago. He had property, animals, and children. He prayed ten times a day to show his love of the Pharoah "god-king" and praised him for his wealth. In those days, Pharaohs had advisers. One adviser was a Satan, meaning in Hebrew, someone who disagrees in a conversation. To prove his power; the Pharoah egotistically boasted to his advisors that Job would love him no matter what. Satan disagreed with god-king and said that Job would stop praying and loving you if you take all his wealth. Despite this advice and to make a point of his ego. The Pharoah god ruined Job by killing his three daughters and seven sons and confiscating his property, animals, and valuables. Afterward, at first, Job continued praying to the Pharoah god-king, saying philosophically, "The Lord gives and the Lord taketh away." Then Satan pointed out to the Pharoah that Job was not physically hurt and advised him to stop loving you if he hurts Job or sickens him. That advice challenged the Pharoah's ego, so the god-king proceeded to violently inflict painful boils and open sores all over Job's body. His neighbors and friends believed that Job deserved this punishment because he didn't pray enough to show his love of the Pharoah god-king. Job reminded his neighbors that he still prayed ten times daily to the god-king.

Later while Job was alone and full of pain, he supplicated to the "God of all Gods, "the energy of the cosmos. "How could you let this happen to me? I kept praying to the Pharoah religiously every day?" The cosmic response was, "I am the life energy of the universe that made a Goldilocks atmosphere for life to flourish and gave you higher consciousness, for you to appreciate all the beauty of living things and instead of being grateful, you expect me to listen to your prayers and complaints. Life is not about what I can do for you. It is what you can do for life. Kings and religious leaders (god-players) who control others, need for their ego, to be worshiped and pray to feel good about themselves. However, I am the life energy; I do not want or need to be praised or worshiped or prayed to. I gave you a higher consciousness to understand, enjoy and have the wisdom to take the responsibility of protecting the Goldilocks life for your own good. Use your higher consciousness and the cosmic energy inside you to challenge yourself, improve the world and enjoy life spectrum magic reality.

Do not blame the universe's life energy because all the problems are created by people believing (god-players). For example, all religions believe in a God in the sky that is a man or a woman because it was created by a man or a woman (god-player); however, by free self-thinking, you will understand to find the universal truth that unites all people to do wot is right.

In the city of Jerusalem, there is a place called One Hundred Doors. Behind each door is a small shop and, in each shop, a woman is selling small items to make money to feed her husband, who does not work or do anything profitable. He prays every day to keep God from destroying the planet, but he is deluded by religious beliefs and their illusions of knowledge. This is not wisdom. It is a man's religious law to control and abuse women!

A Hindu friend of mine from India named Gar, who I met while doing a construction job for him, was having domestic issues with his wife, so I invited him to live in my house in Los Angeles while I went to Texas. Gar watched over my house, and we talked on the phone about everything. He would tell people, "Leon is my guru." Likewise, I thank all my friends for being my gurus (my Satan). It is all about the importance of knowledgeable, meaningful realistic debate conversation. **You must give up all your paradigm that makes you believe you are special! to advance to the next level of attaining new realistic understanding by free self-thinking, to become a thinker, not a stinker. For example, my friend Jhon Niemans in a debate searching for universal -truth, is my Satan. for example, if you are searching , for your cat. Do you tell what the cat looks like in reality or, what you tell what you believe the cat looks like? That is why People in the search of universal-truth, will always tell you the truth.**

DISCOVER IF SOMEONE IS A FREE SELF-THINKER IN WISDOM

A free self-thinker in wisdom will respond in conversation by telling you what they know, understand from their conclusion, and, if they do not know how to prove their conclusion, they will not say, I believe or lie or compete, because it is against the search of universal-truth. A believer will respond by telling you what someone else has spoken, written, or believed. For example, Jehovah's Witnesses will not tell you what they think or understand; they want you to read the bible and believe in blind-faith, or if you won't to save the world from parasite hierarchy, you have to be anointed with oil, by a religious hierarchy to be the savior. or if you to be, the president of the country, you need the blessing of a religious hierarchy. How convenient it is for parasite hierarchy to stay in charge by keeping followers ignoring, the universal-truth for that time, in God reality of science! So, free self-think to save all lives, from hierarchy leaders propaganda!

Gather ten people and ask them to produce one answer, to solve all our problems. They will produce different answers, but a single answer is alone to solve our problems. Universal-truth wisdom for that time incorporates all solutions into one correct answer. In the scientific debate, free self-thinkers combine the answers to know the right things for a better world. That is free self-think in debating, a scientific method to find the universal truth wisdom for that time, that will unite all correct answers and solve all problems. Today people have answers that justify their standard way of life and justifying is just an excuse; it is not an answer; it is a waste of time. A solution is a direct response to a question by agreeing or disagreeing in God reality of science so that you can debate creating a universal understanding.

PEOPLE WITH LITTLE OR NO FORMAL EDUCATION

Richard Branson—One of the most recognizable billionaires today, struggled with dyslexia and dropped out of school when 16. He founded his first business, a mail-order retailer called Student Magazine. That company would become Virgin Records and its retail stores. During his career, Branson ran approximately 500 companies.

Thomas Edison—America's most prolific inventor, did not graduate high school. Instead, Edison's family moved to Port Huron, Michigan, where he attended public school for 12 weeks. He was a hyperactive child, prone to distraction and was deemed "difficult" by his teacher. **His mother quickly pulled him from school and in a debate, realistic, conversation taught him at home, whereby scientific debating in knowledge conversation. Thomas Edison became a genius.**

David H. Murdock—After dropping out of school in the ninth grade and working at a gas station until he was drafted into the Army in 1944. After returning from World War II, Murdock purchased his first business, a diner in Detroit. He sold the restaurant several months later and made a $700 profit. In 1985, he acquired the Hawaiian real estate outfit Castle & Cooke, which owned the fruit company Dole. As a result, Dole became the world's largest fruit and vegetable producer.

Steve Jobs—He dropped out of college after attending for a short time. He started and developed apple computer products.

Robert Riley was born as Irish catholic, **did not graduate high school. Instead, wrought article of a new design of cars and boats for Popular-Mechanic books for 30 years, is last car design, did, 225 miles per one gallon, in a world rase of the most economical car of all cars**. This result is in search of universal truth reality, he become a genius, not from illusion!

Orville and Wilbur Wright—Neither one graduated high school but started building bicycles. Then they decided to build a motorized glider. They designed the first propeller for flight, by debating for 4 years they built real airplanes, not gliders and founded the Curtis-Wright airplane manufacturing company.

QuintonTarantino—Movie, Director. Vidal Sassoon, Famous Hairdresser

Albert Einstein left school at the edge of 15 years old and received his doctor's degree, at the edge of 60 years old, with no education for it.

Other famous people with little formal education who created wisdom by free self-thinking are **Benjamin Franklin, John D. Rockefeller, Walt Disney, Charles Dickens, David Karp and many more. All these people**

were into scientific accurate understanding, in search of reality, to become creative from their wisdom, not schoolers.

It seems that the most creative people are not schoolers because knowledge cannot create new knowledge! On the contrary, they are free self-thinkers searching in the spectrum magic reality for universal truth in scientific knowledge, for new wisdom in God reality of science to creates new knowledge! So please don't compete with your knowledge because your knowledge can't come from illusory religion or propaganda and tradition, to create fear, jealousy, hate to separate people, because you are looking at the magic of life from one direction, that creates an illusion of knowledge that create obstacle in the brain, to promote parasite hierarchy with no wisdom no reality, only by the scientific method of debating to understand from others the spectrum magic of life reality, to arrive at the universal truth that unifies, all the people and creates a utopian world.

Two friends in a coffee shop in America, one friend tells the other, my son memorizes knowledge like a computer, now by competing, he became a senator. By more competing, he can become the president, the second friend said. My son debates in a scientific method of thinking to understand the spectrum reality of life. He became a humane-being. And one humane-being called Jesus was selected as a God by schooler hierarchy because of his wisdom!

People believe that affiliation with their gang, tribe or religion, tradition, or philosophy, gives them an identity, but it is only an illusory one. By free self-thinking in search of reality, you will not lose your identity. On the contrary, it gives you a truthful realistic personal identity, because you are only what you do. When you do nothing, in reality, you are nothing, only people who make a better world deserve it all! Because this is what we all need today, creative free self-thinking people for a safe world. **Why don't you get over it and get real**?

When children are repeatedly told something at an early age, they believe it. Therefore, some people who have been encouraged become athletes, artists, scientists, and other vocations. On the other hand, if you are told by your elders or a preacher to believe that some people are crooks, you will grow up to believe that day are crooks or sinners or inhuman. Only by free will and determination will you achieve goals to overcome challenges.

So, tell your children to think for themselves and debate become a free self-thinker in reality that creates confidence from more accurate understanding.

Since the beginning of recorded history, people have gathered together to avoid predators and other large groups. They knew it was wiser to be part of a collective for security. Nowadays, it is wiser to avoid big groups and stay safer as part of a smaller group of people you know, enjoy and trust. In scientific debating than being in a mob with a leader! It is time to change with the times, from new wisdom.

To make a better America, we should encourage free self-thinking for all people to "get out of the box" of their restricted precepts. This will adjust the way people see things and help them make the right decisions. We should all be grateful to live in a country that allows us to experience and enjoy the full spectrum of the magic of life and live among creative, free self- thinkers as an example to the rest of the world.

People must live by humane law and the highest achievement of life is to be a humane-being. Wisdom and universal truths are attainable by your love of all lives as a humane-being, learning from each other without competing. Competition is an old pattern in nature's laws from the past when people acted more like animals and still do because they don't know how to learn from each other**! For example, in a debate, you must treat each other with respect, so you can learn something brilliant.**

DISCOVER A NEW MEANING AND NEW WORD

If you discover a new species or find something new and there is no word for it, you give it a name. That's how all words are created. Explain the meaning and it is understood. Only then, meaningful conversation and clearer communications are possible. However, suppose you are reading law documents, books, or any writing that you don't understand and there is no explanation for that word. In that case, dictionaries and research may be necessary if you wish to be more accurate in reality, during a debate conversation; keep on researching and asking questions.

All Bible stories are just stories! That are written to create a mor accurate understanding of life reality. However, many of their meanings have been modified to create obedient followers for leaders to control. However, in a scientific debate conversation searching for wisdom, you will find the story's original wisdom for a more accurate understanding.

If the Bible is the greatest story ever told, then Babylon's story is the greatest example of a universal truth! The story is about a group of people who created a task to build a tall tower to reach God. The God in this bible tale did not want living people invading his heaven. When the Babylonian builders completed their mighty task, God made each of them speak in different languages, causing confusion and misunderstanding. The workers began babbling incoherently and failure to communicate caused the building to tumble down, killing them; this kept them from doing their tasks. The wisdom here is if you don't communicate clearly and understand each other accurate meaning from believing in illusion of knowledge, religion, tradition . We will never arrive at understanding of God universal truth of science, and **never succeed! At a better life, a better government, a better country, and a better world, a better environment for all lives!**

At the end, from babbling in beliefs, we will destroy all on this beautiful planet. So, please debate in God universal truth of science!

Believing this religious story in the Bible, as fact, is ridiculous It couldn't happen. However, if you look at it as a free self-thinker, you realize **it is the greatest wisdom story ever told. Because by changing books, for propaganda from hierarchy greed, and without communication and accurate understanding, we will never succeed in our task!**

If you accept from your illusion of knowledge that God punished people trying to reach is heaven, this information will create obstacles in your brain; it is like eating food that will make you unhealthy when there is plenty of healthy food today that's better. For your body and mind! So free self-think in a debate for a better body and mind.

New knowledge is not created by belief or religion or illusions or propaganda or philosophy or knowledge!

"Learn from yesterday, live for today, hope for tomorrow important thing is not to stop questioning." -Albert Einstein.

POLICE SHIELDS

The first policing armor shield had the symbol of a six-point star on it. In search of wisdom, the symbol originated when the People of the Book wanted to find a symbol of God to put on David's shield to protect him from the Philistine warrior Goliath. **The Cohen people of the book, understood from Moses that God was Energy.** As they looked at the sun shining on a bush, it created a six-point energy spark. They understood that this was the fingerprint of life energy God. What we know today from science is that most snowflakes are six-point stars. And all building blocks of all living things are SIX POINT STARS.

This is not a religious belief; it is a realistic scientific method of searching for universal truth by free self-thinking. That is why they put that star symbol on David's shield to help protect David from Goliath by the fingerprint of life energy.

The first police badge was a six-point star that sheriffs wore. When officers wear their badge, it represents God's symbol, the Energy of the Universe, to create humane laws of wisdom to protect and serve the innocent free self-thinkers from aggressive, violent, inhumane bullies' gangs and their greedy leaders!

The idea of a star-shaped badge as a shield still exists worldwide, making police officers wearing it know that they are doing God's work, which means doing work in scientific reality to be humane officers, to save free self-thinking humane-being individual, from competing believers followers of a gangs.

PART THREE

Evolution

The truth about nature is that it requires a sense of dynamic equilibrium in the natural world. However, science accepts that all systems are in a constant state of flux. People evolve on this planet and as we continue to uncover new wisdom to create new knowledge, we must adapt our conversations and theories to adhere to today's reality by debating, because in today's age, old religious, and tradition keep people idol, they are illusion of knowledge that will not lead people to evolve with the time, because they have no accurate understanding to be scientific or realistic!

An old saying: "If you give a man a fish, you feed him for a day. If you teach him how to fish, he will eat for a lifetime; another outlook, if you fix a problem for people, you will help people for a time; if you teach people to fix the problem, they will fix it for a lifetime." To that, I would add, "If you teach a person to free self-think in a scientific debate, he will create new knowledge to fix problems and will teach people to free self-think in a scientific debate to create new knowledge to fix all problems for a safer democratic joyful world. By challenging yourself, you will always feel good about your life and all lives, which is the path to the joy of living!

Free self-thinkers can handle a leader, but they cannot handle a gang of ignorant, fanatical followers or an obedient professional authority paid by hierarchy. Therefore, I propose that all police officers and soldiers pass a humane test in a debate conversation in God reality of science, before joining the workforce if they are by the people for the people!

Your brain is a computer when you search in it. Would you instead find the illusion of knowledge or realistic knowledge? For example, when your computer is full of useless files, they slow down and hinder your work. What do you do? You delete, delete, delete and you should do the same with your brain by knowledgeable debate for a better computer and a better brain!

Shifting your focus away from certain long-held traditions and beliefs in the illusion of knowledge may be frightening and challenging, but it is essential for change for the better. You might feel more comfortable in the darkness in the illusion of knowledge rather than turning on the light to see God reality that is there. But once you switch on the light it reveals the universal truth of the time, you will see there is nothing to be afraid of. At that moment, you will accurately understand that it is more frightening to live in a dark, blind-fate illusion of religion than in the light of God reality of science. You will be excited to realize you can free self-think to see the light of reality, instead of believing what someone else tells you is there in blind faith in the dark, instead of free will and freedom of speech, in debating, because both are essential to better yourself and the world! In the past—and still today—governments and religions want to do all the thinking and want you to do all the obeying; they want you to be "moldable." However, it should be the other way around because ordinary people are the creative ones, but the hierarchy will not let that happen because they are greedy and want to control others by their ego from competing, to feel good about themself. Therefore, the government is the entity that needs to be moldable if it is to represent the people. That is the democratic way to find universal truth that will direct this country—and the rest of the world—in the right direction in the shortest time, Isaac Newton was a self-thinker in a scientific method of thinking, Newton saw an apple fall from the tree. He knew it was a reaction to a force that made the apple fall, it creates understanding of reality physics and science, that's how he discovered the force of gravity. Gravity became a new word to name this further action. Newton did not know how gravity works. Letter Albert Einstein discovered how it works in a scientific method of debating, research, in physics, and mathematics. **Billions of schoolers with knowledge have seen an apple fall, however. They did not search for understanding in God reality, because they are followers of illusion, and memorizing knowledge to become Sheep in a herd of grazers.**

Newton also knew that the actions made by the universe's energy caused the reactions that created the universe and made life possible. He called that action God. God is a word used to name the unknown., Newton did not know how God works. Newton wrote about his discovery but had to hide it because he was afraid of being persecuted by religious leaders and their ignorant mobs of followers. It took 200 years after Newton's death for someone to find his book. Regrettably, today and in the past, some of our most extraordinary humane-beings were tortured, killed, and by scaring, and by preaching illusion brainwash their followers, to be in charge.

I do not blame anybody who wants to live in a better world. Sadly, people are still at each other's throats over illusions of truth from their beliefs, and tradition, some may not be willing to acknowledge scientific proofs, historical facts, verifiable conclusions, physics, and mathematics. However, these all contain universal truths that are not subjective to each person. It would be funny to see Einstein argue or compete or be violent with Newton about science because the universal truths they both discovered are not subjective to each person; they are verifiable conclusions. People fight over beliefs, religion, tradition, and that creates the philosophy of the atheist! because they are all not universal truths; therefore, they are subjective to each person because they are illusions of knowledge, not God reality of scientific thinking. **It is time to stop fighting and competing because it does not work for humane-beings, or democracy.** Use your mind's resourcefulness by a scientific way of debating for a more accurate understanding of God spectrum reality of life magic, for a safer life!

FREE SELF-THINKERS ARE PROBLEM SOLVERS

I have a friend who likes to talk about scientific theory. It is fun to discuss subjects that we currently do not understand completely. One day we discussed deep space travel and how it could be possible to travel the great distances of the universe.

By using our imaginations and engaging in critical free self-thinking, we came up with some interesting theories. But, of course, theories are just self-understanding ideas; they are neither verifiable nor universal truths unless proven as a universal truth.

When you electrically stimulate particles around an atom's nucleus, they jump from one orbit to another faster than light speed. Nobody knows how this happens. However, it is a magic reality, So I theorized that alien spacecraft could change directions instantly and travel faster than the speed of light. This reminds me of those atomic particles that jump faster than the speed of light, from one orbit to another orbit.

I theorized that we should somehow imitate the particles traveling around the nucleus to jump from one orbit to another through space simply, but how? Since orbits in a nucleus can be altered by jumping atomic particles.

The universe contains the magnetic fields of stars, planets and asteroids traveling in orbit. These are like the concentric circles that occur when throwing a stone into a lake, creating rings. In our solar system, the forces of gravity create these permanent orbital rings in space. For example, the Earth gets caught in the Sun's magnetic spiral, which we call our orbit, while our Moon orbits in the Earth's circle. I share these thoughts because it demonstrates that you can develop theories that might eventually uncover new knowledge when you are free to self-think and use your imagination.

Science unifies us. The thirst for knowledge drives scientists to explore and discover new, universal truths. In the same way, it would be beneficial if more people aimed to solve societal dysfunction through scientific methods by free self-thinking. We would discover more answers and uncover more perspectives on subjects that will solve global problems. When everyone gets involved, we are more likely to succeed. As the saying goes, two heads are better than one. It would be great if people utilized their imagination to discover more ways to do things that will unify the world! When theories work, they are called "verifiable conclusions," a universal truth that leaves no room for illusory justification. That is problem-solving. Imagine no preachers worldwide, no followers, leaders, gangs, organized beliefs, hierarchy, and criminals. Instead of violence, we will have the freedom to free self-thinking in a debate searching for utopia.

My friend Dan always talks to me about space aliens. He says they are all around us and have been around for thousands of years. He says leaders of countries already know this and are worried about it. If this is true, then the aliens must be brilliant at traveling such long distances to this planet. The aliens must have scientists in wisdom that is smarter than ours. If so, this super-advanced outer space intelligence poses a threat to hierarchies all over the world. Hierarchies worry that aliens if they exist, might usurp their powers by winning a war and they will lose their privileges. Government leaders tell their followers that space aliens do not exist, so don't believe your eyes if you see a UFO in the sky. Most preachers state that in the entire universe, only planet earth hosts intelligent life. However, I am not a believer either way. I do not know if aliens exist or not. The hierarchies think they will have to fight the aliens to protect themselves. But only scared, ignorant, violent, greedy leaders fight to protect their privileges. Why not work with these intelligent visitors from the galaxies, if they exist, learn from them? Why would anyone have a problem with intelligent scientists in search of wisdom? I don't have a problem with scientists; I have issues with preachers of illusions for more privileges from greed and lack of understanding reality!

If an alien astronaut space traveler knocked on my front door, I would welcome "him" and ask, "What do you prefer, coffee or tea?" I don't worry about intelligent aliens because I know that if we can communicate and carry on an intelligent conversation searching for wisdom, we will learn much from each other and arrive at a new universal truth. After all, science is not subjective to each free self-thinker in this space or in out of space. Instead, I worry about the scared, criminal leaders and their fanatical dangerous followers on this planet who live in the illusion of knowledge, religion, and tradition with many atom bombs in their possession.

Here is another wisdom; we know that germs protect your body! So why don't we modify germs to protect us from viruses?

This is my question? Are leaders using viruses to scare people and give them the power to stay in charge?

FREE SELF-THINKERS
NEED ARTIFICIAL INTELLIGENCE

People use computers to speed up their work. In the late 20th century, Garry Kasparov was the best chess player globally. Still, at one time, the 34-year-old Russian was defeated by 9-year-old Deep Blue, a computer built by IBM with artificial intelligence. Many people did not think a computer could be better at judging chess moves or judgments in life. Still, computers are more accurate than people and have no illusions of knowledge, prejudice, hatred, ego, and fear of dying.

The Enemy of Knowledge Is Not Ignorance

Since computers lack ego, they would be better than people to assess a case's facts and impartially judge guilt or innocence. That is why computers are used in mathematics, research and storing data. During trials, computers could replace judges, lawyers and jurors who may be biased, prejudiced, or create work where there is no work influenced by their beliefs, not the facts. For example, some criminal justice-related employees accept bribes, some fear criminals, some are hanging judges, some enjoy playing God over others, some are religious believers, and some are criminals themselves, trying to get away with corruption throughout history.

On the other hand, Artificial Intelligence (AI) has no fear, no bias, no hidden agenda, and no sin. Also, AI doesn't compete for power and can be provided at a much lower cost to the taxpayer! AI does not have to be connected to the internet, where it could be hacked by hierarchy. Using AI, people will get a fair judgment, not like the O.J. Simpson trial, a bad joke, and a travesty of justice. AI should be used because I do not know of anyone who likes judges and lawyers. People should have the option to be judged by a computer. This would also unclog the justice system in a democracy.

Jesus said, "He who is without sin, let him cast the first stone." Moses and Jesus knew that people are not perfect, so they did not want leaders, hierarchy, or judges. Today, Jesus and Moses would prefer computers to make judgments because he knew there are no judges, lawyers, or jurors without a sin. That is why I agree with Jesus and Moses that imperfect people should not be judging other imperfect people. For example, the Constitution was created to provide equal rights for all of us under humane law. But women have more rights in this country than men because it is a billion-dollar business for divorce lawyers to represent men and women. And some lawyers create work when there shouldn't be. Some men and women get married to profit from a divorce. The result is, 50% of all marriages end in divorce or separation.

Meanwhile, most men and women in that situation conclude that marital sex was not worth it and was not a wise idea! Women should get 50% and men should get 50% of what they accumulated together by a computer. There would be no divorce for-profit, and couples would be motivated to stay married.

Today, there are more rich people in America than ever before. Ten percent of America's population owns ninety percent of the wealth in this country. With creative tax-avoidance loopholes and lobbyists pushing laws to secure more money and stocks for the wealthy, rich people created a system so their families will forever remain rich. That is royalty; they are "too big to fail." Why did we fight the English royalty, then? When you mention the Rockefellers, everyone will say that family represents American economic royalty. When you mention the red carpet in Hollywood, it represents media royalty. You are what you do, everyone is unique, and everybody should challenge themselves to be more realistic to today than yesterday, for a better life for all, that's what is by the people, for the people, from the people, not for creating parasite hierarchy,

All great civilizations vanished because they expanded the rich, creating a world of gangs, royalty, parasite hierarchy, peasants, servants, and slaves, but no middle-class. The importance of a middle-class is undeniable because it is creative, hard-working, which stabilizes civilization. That is why hierarchy supports overpopulation to serve and sustain them in their luxury, reinforcing their belief that money, wealth and power are the goals and God of civilization. However, overpopulation increases pollution, diminishes natural resources, contributes to global warming, and ultimately destroys our planet. It is foolish to deplete all of our natural resources because of too many people. The only solution is for the government to pay, as a free educational for all the people on this planet, to free self-thinking in a debate to create more understanding to not overpopulate and become creative humane-being, to understand, right from wrong, and do what is right.

Religious leaders tell their flock that if someone is lucky enough to have mineral riches on their property or win a massive lottery jackpot, it means God loves them more because they are good obedient followers. Religious leaders tell these stories to entice followers to obey the illusion of religion, tradition law. The Universe's Energy created everything for life and God does not love some people more than others. Only a certain percentage of people have oil under their land or win the lottery. That is just a %. a percent of people wins the lottery, not God's blessings upon you!

The Enemy of Knowledge Is Not Ignorance

The purpose of humane law is to protect the innocent from the power of judges and other decision-makers who fail to do what is right in God reality, because they are corrupted by those who put them in their authority positions. They are the bullies of a regime from illusions of knowledge. It is not wise to have hierarchy judges with power over others. However, if the authorities treat people like sheep, they end up with a country of **sheep in the herd, of grazers**. Many of these individuals will rebel and could be killed or incarcerated in costly jails because they are not sheep and are meant to free self-think in search of universal-truth from the day they are born.

My suggestion to ensure true justice is to have our computer geniuses devise a program that can judge truth, innocence, right and wrong impartially and rationally, without prejudice or ego or belief from the illusions of knowledge. Use it to resolve all criminal cases and legal entanglements. After all, if a computer can detect a lie, or with MRI, indicate whether he meant or not and win a world best chess player in a game, then a high-tech intelligent computer can better determine the truth or innocence than a person. This would make life less stressful for judges and juries.

No laws should exist to protect the individual from himself or herself. If someone wants to harm themselves, that is their right to do so. But it is not their right to hurt anyone else. This is as fundamental as freedom of speech. Preachers say if you commit suicide, you won't get into heaven. Well, do we know if heaven even exists? It is your life, do what you want with it because no one can own you. No leaders or gangs have more rights than the individual and we all are individuals first. The truth is that many scientific achievements were accomplished by humane-beings who risked their lives, such as Madame Curie, who died after discovering radiation and Louis Pasteur, who saved millions of lives by developing the antibacterial process called pasteurization and the world's first rabies vaccine. They would never experiment with someone else. Such scientists used knowledge and free self-thinking to help life, and that's what humane-beings do.

Only accessible self-thinking humane-beings can create humane law! However, many rules do not make free self-thinker because they are written by hierarchy, a law designed to remain in power. When innocent people are treated as criminals, it is due to too many laws: opinionated law, religious law and unfair laws written to have power. All countries should be a country of humane laws, not a nation of laws made by kings, autocrats, religious leaders, or corrupt politicians. Capitalism is a balloon, and inflation inflates the balloon, eventually the balloon will blow up. That Is not utopia democracy!

It is like swimming: when you first learn to swim, you wear a life jacket and when you know how to swim, you will not wear a life jacket if you don't want to! However, the leader says wearing life jackets saves lives. Staying home saves lives too. **Being afraid to die or being afraid of reality. stops people from living, and free self-thinking!**

Here is another ridiculous law: you must have a life jacket on a paddleboard or wear a life-Jacket wild paddling, that will not work. However, if the board is attached to your ankle by a strap, you would not need a life vest because getting back on the paddleboard keeps you out of chilly water and it is a much safer flotation device than a life jacket. No matter, you have to make the that should decide to stay s safe , by freedom of the mind, not your leaders; this is an example of law just to have power over people. That is why I invented a floating paddle with buoyancy equal to a lifejacket, so if you fall in the water, the paddle will keep you afloat. I patented and built the catamaran paddleboard, called the Malibu Paddle Cat, safer, more stable, and healthier to use than a standard board in conjunction with my floating paddle. It is unsinkable and practically indestructible, easy to use; anyone can do it the first time without lessons and even getting wet. The deck of the Malibu Paddle Cat rides five inches above the water for more stability and safety from marine life. Mature, responsible adults should have free self-think to decide what serves them best, by freedom of the mind, perhaps there should be laws that ban biking, surfing, or motorcycling.

Leaders are fearful of dyeing, because they have vast knowledge, but no understanding of God reality of science, therefore write many laws. There should be only humane laws to have power over me; people evolve into free self-thinkers need freedom. People are born and die every day. **Being afraid of hierarchical laws or religious laws, you become an obedient follower of orders that stops people from free self-thinking. Any fool is meant to be born and die. However, the concept of humane law is to give life the liberty for a more accurate understanding of right from wrong to be creative as a middle-class, and fully enjoy life.**

WHAT IS LOVE?

Love of a woman, a man, a country, a race, a God, a religion or Jesus or Muhammad or Buddha or King David or anyone who seems so right. However, sometimes the feeling of love is just infatuation; it is not true love. It is an imaginary illusion if it does not come from free-self thinking accurate understanding. Sometimes infatuated love will make people act irresponsibly insane. For example, an infatuated person might love a murderer and still ignore all the evil deeds committed and inhumane. That is blind love, which causes people to lose their sense of reality and hinders them from understanding the way they indeed are, and that kind of love comes from illusory belief! Free self-thinking in a debate in the search for a more accurate understanding of reality creates healthy love. It is based on a scientific method of your one result that creates true love for others, loves yourself and all lives and becomes a humane-being.

Sex is great for a being, but healthy love is better., for humane-being. People in illusory love get emotional and can't control their feelings. That's why if a person kills their spouse for cheating with another lover, some courts will accept an insanity plea. The same is true with terrorists who are willing to die for their love of illusory beliefs. They are captivated by an illusory bond with their religion and are blind to logical thought reality. Only by a scientific method of debating will you create a more accurate understanding of the spectrum magic life reality to love all lives. Only then will you love yourself; however, if you first love yourself, that is ego!

Musicians write songs and sermons in all religions about their love of all their religious leaders; King David empire ,became famous because of his emotional poems about friendship and God, create a religion and tradition to unite a gang of obedient followers.

This gives people a false sense of belonging, causing them to be in love with something that makes them blind, because these songs and poems are preaching, and they don't create a self-understanding of reality. It is not healthy to love someone who says, preach, that they love you but doesn't act like it by disrespecting or physically abusing you. On the contrary, healthy love is raising the other person. It is respecting and appreciating them. When two people have a healthy love, they must treat each other fairly. When one party only takes and the other only gives, it becomes unhealthy love. The greatest love derives from the wisdom that comes from an **accurate understanding of life's realities** as a humane-being!

Each person must be humane to accomplish a higher goal, such as raising children and caring for the elderly. to It is like a business and each person must communicate and debate regularly , to do what is right. If a person does only what they want, without regard to other people's needs, that is not healthy love! Love without affection is a word without meaning. Dictators, royalty, and religious leaders keep taking and taking from their people, yet those same people still love their dictator, country, and religion. This is not healthy love, and it is not a pearl of wisdom.

Healthy love creates the most joyful, long-life force, it is created by free self-thinking accurate understanding of life reality. Hate creates the most destructive, sort life force in the universe. Hate is created by illusionary, belief, tradition, philosophy, propaganda, and justification. If you want honest and kind friends, you must start with yourself. Always tell the truth, speak up when you know someone is lying, from greed, and stand up for , God reality of science!

From an accurate understanding of love, love is in all living things, it creates a more beautiful species, and a beautiful world, for the love of all lives, and the joy of living, it is a good reason to be a humane-being.

The reason people sometimes have problems in their marriage is that they compete, and competition creates the ego. When couples or kids fight, it is because they want attention and affection from universal love. If they don't get it, they become unhappy and will fight. However, parents must communicate with everybody and teach them to think for themselves. You should give everybody the right to disagree.

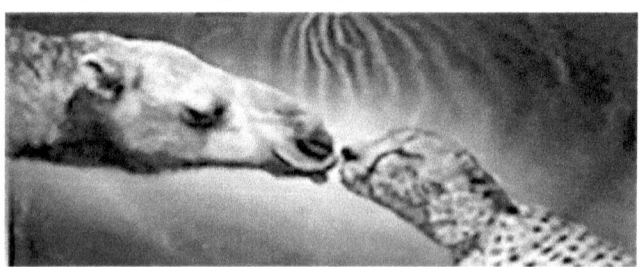

THREE STEPS TO REACH UNIVERSAL LOVE

<u>Step 1</u> When you are born, you need the experience of being cared for, nurtured, and loved to get to Step 2.

<u>Step 2</u> When you are a teenager, you need the experience of loving and being loved by a stranger to get to Step 3.

<u>Step 3</u> Only then can you represent any life. When you love your life , and others, because you have the joy to love all life.

However, if you are not loved or love others, you will want to become a leader, by creating money, by hook or by crook, and by becoming a member of a hierarchy so that your followers and your family will have to love you.

IS LIFE A GLASS-HALF-FULL OR HALF-EMPTY?

When we are born into this world, the glass is half-full. The half-empty part of the glass will be filled with future life-inspiring challenges. Maintaining this balance in life is believing their glass is half-empty; that person is blindly negative about life. If someone believes their glass is half-full, that person is blindly optimistic. Neither viewpoint is helpful or realistic because both are illusions of knowledge.

Religions propagate illusions to attract followers who think their glasses are full, so they can blindly believe that a. Santa clos or whatever you believe in in Heaven will take care of everything. These preaching benefits the religious hierarchy, not their believers. Atheists who think their glasses are empty believe the illusion that there is neither a man, God, nor a god of cosmic energy. Our understanding of life must be realistic, so we can do what's right without delusions. Otherwise, people will become uncertain about how to proceed in life. This is the reason why so many people are confused. Thinking freely and challenging ourselves to live humanely puts us in the right place mentally. If you understand this, you realize that going against the humane way hurts others and your mind. If you don't appreciate all life, you will not understand having the confidence of the joy to love your life and everything. We must take ownership of our actions by the scientific method by free self-thinking, without influence from illusions, or opinions.

One day at a coffee shop in my Los Angeles neighborhood of Silver Lake, a group of young gang members came and sat down at a table next to me. They asked what I was doing. I told them, "Writing a book." They asked, "What's it about?" I told them, "It's about how to free self-think to be creative," and then they asked me how much the book costs. I told them the price and they said they had no money. Then I asked them, "What is the most important thing in their life?" One of their responses was, "To observe policemen. I can spot cops a mile away. It doesn't matter if they're in an unmarked car. I will recognize them." I asked him why that was so important. He answered, "I have lots of friends in jail and being in jail is no fun. So, I try to avoid cops at all costs." Then I asked, "Okay, so what is the second most important thing in your life?" His answer was, "I make sure to go to church every Sunday." I asked him why. He said, "Because I don't want to go to Hell. I want to be certain I'm forgiven for my sins." **I ask**? "Is not going to Hell more important than doing what is right in God reality here on earth?" He answered, "I believe I have to attend church every Sunday because I don't want to take any chances of burning in Hell." Sadly, because of his brain's obstacles from believing illusions, he cannot understand reality to understand right from wrong.

Everybody plays the game of life; most people don't know the game rules. Because it is legal to create propaganda untruths by ignorant, selfish hierarchy laws and religious laws created to control women and men, it never works and will never work for humane-being, because it creates uncertainty, misunderstanding, homelessness, slave, wars hate, and God is money, However, the scientific method of free self-thinking is to learn from others by realigning the brain into a more accurate understanding of the spectrum magic reality to search for God's universal truth. To become confident, creative, humane-being will make a better environment., for all lives. **It is time to make propaganda, religious illusion, and all scams Not legal, in humane-law, for a safer world!**

WHY THERE ARE GANGS
Gang is not a personal thing; it is a follower thing!

All gangs give the wrong perception that creates an addictive illusion of knowledge. These gangs include religious organizations, atheists, the mafia, street gangs, royalty and more. They all want to keep their power, throne, money, subjects, slaves, and followers. Eventually, they will destroy themselves, though they believe they are too big, too rich, too well-armed, too organized, too brainwashed, and too sophisticated to fail. This time they are too intelligent to fail and continue destroying lives and the environment. In history they all fail because God will not have it. This time, people must free self-think to become the majority of the world's population and by debating in a scientific method of thinking to arrive at a universal truth that will solve all problems to create a joyful utopian life. Because the alternative is not acceptable in God reality of science!

I'll rather struggle on my own to find, by scientific thinking, that is the best path, for the shortest way of wisdom to a universal truth that unites all lives. The challenge will make me stronger and wiser for an inspiring life to create a better world for all, instead of living in an illusion of beliefs for comfort in an ignorant gang that is the wrong path that destroys lives and the environment. **So, please, free self-think, for your own good, and for the love, and joy of life, that is mor joyful than power, from competing ego!**

WHY THERE ARE BULLIES

During my three years as a paraplegic struggling to walk again, I realized firsthand the abuses that occur when people with power prey on the weak and innocent to feel good about themselves. Mean-spirited kids from the neighborhood who did not have a humane upbringing by competition, were bullied and ran away laughing. They wanted to feel good about themselves, so they thought it was funny to hurt an innocent who couldn't defend himself. Because of my experiences, I developed a conscience that naturally led me to become a humane-being willing to fight injustice. And I still do. It is common knowledge that when people work together in a gang, it creates power. However, power can be misused; that is why the majority of people must free self-think, and debate to develop a more accurate understanding of right from wrong to do what is right. The cause of bullying comes from being inferior. That is why bullies act like animals to make them feel superior. They want to fight and compete in natural law. But, because they did not learn to free self-think in search of universal-truth as a humane-being, for a peaceful loving world!

In ancient Rome, Christians living in the Romen empire did not consider the Romans to be humane-beings. The Romans did not tolerate criticism from the Christian minority, who made the Romans feel inferior. So, the Romans, from a competing ego, fed Christians to the lions for 700 years. This also served to keep other people fearfully obedient. Truthfully, the Romans were bullies and inferior. When Israelites Jews were a minority living with Christians, they didn't consider the Christians to be humane-beings, so the Christians, for an ego, tortured and killed the Israelites Jews during the inquisitions. Truthfully, the Christians were a gang of bullies and inferior. Today the Christians and the Israelites don't consider the Muslims to be humane-beings, so Muslims, from an ego, become a gang of bullies because they feel inferior. Even in school, successful kids don't think other kids are good enough to socialize with them. So, the kids who feel inferior, from an ego become a gang of bullies. Since the beginning of time, free self-thinkers geniuses. That made the world a better place, from an ego, are tortured and killed, because they are a minority. Today we know and understand that we need to be a majority 0f free self-thinkers to save the world from the united nation (united hierarchy), because we can destroy the world with guns, bombs, atomic weapons, poison gas and epidemics, We must stop, learn and teach how to be free self-thinkers in wisdom to realize that bullying is not the answer to feeling better by competing of an ego from powers. **It is time to hamble yourself, to learn from each other, the magic of God reality of science, to find universal-truth, and become a peaceful creative** humane-beings, to prove anything to anybody but yourself. Therefore, competing is not the answer for people's futures!

So, please join the free self-thinker, to create a free self-thinkers majority, to save the world from a majority of obedient nonthinkers!

All free self-thinkers continually exercise their minds in scientific debates, which helps them live happier, longer lives by an accurate understanding of reality. For example, Abraham and Moses lived to be over 120 years old. In the case of Steven Hawking, the doctors told him that with his crippling illness, he has only two years to live. Nonetheless, Steven Hawking lived a long life by free self-thinking in the search for wisdom! They all broke the law of doctors and embraced the law of God reality of science and became humane-being., and that create the love of all lives and love of life make you live a long life, and hate, create a miserable short life!

How do you know if someone is a psychopath? If someone says all people are rats, that is a psychopath. If someone says! If all people disappeared from this planet, it is okay because nature will be better off. That is a psychopath. However, among people, humane-beings will protect all lives and the environment, from understanding, not from knowledge!

One sunny day on my walk, I met a man on a bicycle, the man said, why don't you come to my church, to be saved, I said why don't you come, to the Public coffee shop of wisdom, to understand for yourself, God reality of science, because God gave everyone is own brain, so, they can understand for themselves, reality, the man said, you are going to hell, I said. You go to hell, the man said why are you insulting me, I said this is the problem, when people are ignorant obedient believers of illusion, they don't realize, that they insult, kill, and get killed, create hate, and war over illusionary belief! That is what the word stupid means. And as long, that people are sheep from being ignorant from believing illusion, they will not understand, right from wrong, God-reality of science for a meaningful peaceful, joyful life!

DECLARE YOUR BRAIN AND MIND INDEPENDENCE

When someone asks me, "Who are you?" my answer is, "I am a free self-thinker." Their next question is, "What do you do?" My answer is, "I search for universal truth. for the time" By asking questions to understand what is right in God reality, so I can make up my mind to do what is right!

When someone is directly confronted with the ignorance of their most cherished beliefs, they will likely become angry and defensive by clinging more tightly to their beliefs. Thus, you are facing them with a cognitive dissonance that will result in extreme discomfort. In the manner of Socrates, it is more productive to ask them questions about their beliefs and let their answers reveal the truth. By questioning themselves, they will ultimately come to a position that will conflict with their original beliefs. Then they will either choose to stay ignorant or change and declare their brain and mind independence!

Therefore, I declare myself a free self-thinker; this is my brain and mind independence declaration. When I don't know something, I say, "I don't know," because the truth is that I just don't know. That is why I came to America to be free of the ignorant illusion of knowledge from all inferior majority gangs, that protect hierarchy privileges. I worked hard, bought a home, established myself as a free self-thinker and paid my taxes. I don't want to deal with any aggressive religious or ignorant gangs, bullies that cannot handle the universal-truth and intimidating me or anyone else to obey, follow and tell me or anyone else how to live by violence, because day are inferior being in illusion and are not humane in the searches of God reality of science to have a wonderful love of all lives.

Ancient Books of Wisdom

I was very fortunate to read historical books of wisdom early in my life, and then debate them with others in the Temple of Wisdom. To understand knowledgeable meaningful conversations with my grandfather the wisdom **of great free sell-thinkers of the past**: Abraham, Moses, King Solomon, Jesus, John the Baptist, and many others. All these books of the New and Old Testament and other books of the Bible are historical. To understand these writings' meaning and wisdom, they must be analyzed in a debate conversation in a scientific reality to find the original meaning. The best way to find out the meaning of words is always to ask questions. For example, when was the book written, what was it like when it was written, why was it written, what the writer ment? By asking these questions in a scientific debate conversation, you will better understand their meaning and purpose. **All historical writing is not to be believed.** This is what they did in the Temple of Wisdom, for the search of universal-truth of that time—no alter for preachers of illusions allowed. It is important to change , to better yourself, your government ,your country, and the world, to create accurate understanding, for hire conscious free self-thinkers to become a majority of humane-beings, because nature doesn't adapt to life!

MY VERIFIABLE CONCLUSION REGARDING MOSES

After researching and debating the original ancient books from the island of Djerba about Moses, I learned that he was the first person to say that God was energy. Before he liberated the slaves in Egypt, he went up to the volcano Mount Sinai, which was rumbling at the time, and he promised the life energy of the universe that he was going to end slavery in Egypt and the world because he was a humane-being. Moses was the Pharaoh's oldest son, he understood God was Energy because he was surrounded **by scientists that debated in God's scientific reality for the search of universal understanding, created many scientific wisdoms in astronomy, navigation, engineering, build the pyramid and many mor!**

Moses was the first son of the three sons of Pharaoh Akhenaton. In those days, some Egyptians were brilliant astronomers and scientists. They understood that Energy is in everything. and understood that Energy can neither be created nor destroyed. Unfortunately, and has happened throughout history, and still today, the free self-thinkers scientists under Akhenaton, did not understand the dangerous determination of religion ignorant followers in blind faith, that are willing to kill and get killed to protect their believes, ,lies, that they are special, that is why they were surprised and killed by religious leaders and their majority of ignorant followers. They wanted to rule over Egypt; they wanted the people to keep believing the old religion of many gods, not the new scientific understanding that God was the Life Energy of all life that Akhenaton wanted to establish. From polytheism to monotheism. Akhenaton understood from scientific research that there is only one God, one Energy, correlated and encompassed everything in the universe; he called that god-energy Aten. Secretly rebelling against Akhenaton, the religious leaders had Akhenaton poisoned to protect their positions, power, money, comfort, and privileges. Because Akhenaton wanted to change the illusory religion to a scientific reality way of thinking. **The goal of all religions was and is to keep follower's believe in blind faith to stay idle. By not understanding God reality of science.** Since he was a boy, Moses knew that he would inherit the Pharoah's throne someday as the oldest son. As a young man, Moses had to escape to the desert because he knew the priesthood would have assassinated him as they assassinated his father. After all, Moses understood his father's cosmic energy, a scientific understanding of wisdom, to unite homo sapiens to speed up evolution. He worked for a shepherd for a few years until religious leaders' violence calmed down, then Moses returned to confront his younger brother, the Pharoah and demanded his right to the throne because he's the oldest son. However, his brother, the new pharaoh, made a deal with Moses. Moses would inherit the slaves because they were the most ignorant, the lowest caste of society. And his younger brother would stay in power as the Pharoah. The former slaves were a mix of people who had been defeated at war. Some were Israelites and others were from North Africa or West Africa. They were the people given to Moses to establish his free self-thinkers to understand God's as life Energy. Moses understood that even slaves from the lowest class of society could be brilliant humane-beings if they become individual free self-thinkers in a scientific way of debating for accurate understanding. Before Moses, the Israelis believed that God was some sort of a being or an entity. After Moses, the Israelites understood that God was Energy because universal truth changes with time. As per Akhenaton's scientific conclusion of God. Moses created a humane law. 10. (Commandments) with a piece of charcoal from burning bush energy. It was the first Constitution between people and God. His goal was to unite all the people of the world and speed up evolution into free self-thinkers, humane-beings and become enlightened to create knowledge. However, in today, more accurate understanding, you should obey only 7. commandments and 6. Days for people, and animals of burden to have the seventh. day for rest, and 6. Years working the land, and the seventh Year is for rest , working the land. These laws are still used today. The truth is, no person can carry two marbles of stones, one on each arm, and go down the mountain, because, leader, create mor law, and change books, for mor power, over the people!

People don't need too many laws to become a creative humane-being, 1. Moses , first God commandment. **'I am your God, don't create other gods before me, not to worship leaders and preachers (god Players).** 2. don't compete for an ego, instead challenge yourself to be better today than yesterday. 3. free self-think in a debate learn from each other to search for the universal truth to unite all life, for a safer and a more creative world, 4. Don't lie. 5. Don't cheat. 6. Don't hurt, kill others, unless defending yourself, 7. Debate with your father and mother to create a mor accurate understanding, of the magic of God reality to be a free self-thinker humane-being. **If you don't, your father and mother will create a family Hierarchy that will create religion laws that create traditional, laws to believe that you are special from your ancestor illusionary belief.**

Moses was willing to suffer in the desert because he was a humane-being searching for wisdom, he bibs not believe in God, he understood God. He knew right from wrong and challenged life to make a better world for all lives. If Moses had been a greedy leader, he could have led a comfortable life as a Pharaoh. Instead, he spent forty years in the desert, teaching slaves to understand reality better, because , it is not wat God can do for you, it is, what you can do for God! Moses was brilliant; he knew the criminals who poisoned his father were the religious followers and their leaders who were still harming others who did not join their religion. Moses even knew these criminals intended to kill him, for power over the people to create privileges. Moses realized that ignorant religious followers were scaring people with violence to create more followers and enhance their religious gangs' power. Therefore, Moses asked free self-thinking people to separate from religious people in tradition, to keep the peace. Then he went up the mountain with his army and waited for them to separate. After they separated, Moses and his army came down the mountain and massacred every religious person, and their criminal leader. In the books from Djerba, it says Moses killed

1500 of these religious people! Some people don't like the part that says Moses killed religious people. Today's religious leaders explain they were swallowed whole into the earth's bowels when the ground opened beneath them. **because they worship lies illusion idols**; however, if you can accept that then you must accept that, all tradition from religious people will be swallowed whole into the earth's bowels when the ground will be opened beneath **them because they worship tradition from religions illusionary lies, that keep people idol, as day repeat the same**. Moses wanted a world of free self-thinkers creative humane-being scientifically debating in search of God's universal truth to arrive at the love of life in a utopian society!

The tale about the infant Moses floating down the Nile River in a basket is a make-believe fairytale made up by religious leaders to attract believers with their "basket-case" stories of illusion. All religions share a "basket-case" fairytale that distorts reality but makes their followers feel special and know that **cruel god player** loves their gang of believers more. Moses said that when you pray, pray to the universe's energy, not **(god-players) or angels.** When Moses was dying, he did not want anyone to worship him or his grave. So, he went up the mountain by himself to die alone. It wasn't easy for someone over 100 years old, but he wanted to show that no man should worship any man or woman (god-players). So, as a result, even to this day, no one knows where he is buried. Because if day did. Ignorant religious people, from all over the world will go there, to worship is grave and create propaganda, to make believers believe that they are special!

Moses never fought any wars because he wanted people to stop killing each other, which became of the commandments law, "Thou shalt not hurt, kill." In wisdom." Violence is for animals and scientific debate conversation is for higher consciousness humane-beings. you check it out for yourself.

Today, archaeologists, governments, religious leaders, and scholars praise the Pharaohs (god-players) for their power over others and wealth. However, for all their elaborate burial chambers filled with mummies, gold, silver, gems, and other precious items, none of these so-called Pharoah gods achieved actual immortality, except perhaps in history books. Still, in reality, they are like dinosaurs, dead as doorknobs. But, on the other hand, Moses and his father, Akhenaton, achieved true immortality in the hearts and minds of humane-beings worldwide, which inspires new generations of free self-thinkers creative humane-being around the world, for safer future.

Years later, those ignorant slaves of Moses evolved into free self-thinkers who've achieved incredible milestones, including 25% of the Noble Prizes awarded for science alone. These descendants of wisdom are only 10 million out of over the 8 billion people on the planet. That is why Israeli free self-thinking is more effective in making a better world than following a religious tradition from hierarchy. Akhenaton and Moses wisdom movement achieved the verifiable conclusion that God is the Life Energy of the Universe still exists today in scientific reality. The rest is in history! The result was the end of Pharaoh's god-players. The end of the Greek god-players. The end of the Roman god-players. The beginning of humane democratic law that sped up our evolution by **free self-thinking scientist!**

My verifiable conclusion is that Moses gave his people the ability to free self-think in science. However, his brother, the Pharaoh, led his Egyptian people to believe in religion, tradition the illusion of knowledge. He was a God player. As a need for obedient followers, all the questions are in history and the present! **This leads to the critical question; was Moses' 40 years challenging? Are life and people suffering in the desert whiz out comfort worth it? For humane-beings in wisdom, you bet it was!** Evolution shows that neighboring countries use words, and ideas from other countries as their own, for example**, democracy** in Latin is, **De Moses,** meaning in English, **from Moses, democracy** in Greek, meaning in English, **ruled by the people!**

MORE OF MOSES' INSPIRING WISDOM STORIES

When Moses escaped into the desert as a young man, he met an old shepherd, who hired Moses to lead a flock of sheep. The older man proposed that Moses's salary would receive all the lambs born with two colors. Because he knew that very few lambs are born bi-colored, he naturally assumed he would get most of the lambs. So, Moses painted sticks in two colors and placed them around the sheep's waterhole. He understood the power of the mind, that if the pregnant sheep watch those two-colored sticks while drinking, it will affect their lambs' color. The result was that most lambs were born bi-colored, and Moses now possessed a flock of sheep. From understanding, not from memorizing knowledge, he became rich. That is why women should not experience stress or watch scary movies while expecting. Moses certainly had a more accurate understanding of the magic of God's life reality of science.

Moses didn't want people judging others because that created "god-players." He knew people make mistakes and nobody is perfect. So, Moses built a box to hold the 10. Commandments, the contract (the constitution) between his people and the God of Energy. The concept was God of Energy provided the earth's Goldilocks atmosphere for all life to flourish. In return, Moses's people promised to evolve into humane-beings to serve as an example for the future to unify all people. Moses was brilliant from an accurate scientific way of thinking; his wisdom changed all people for the better by speeding up evolution and keeping scientific thinking alive. However, hierarchy creates all religions and religion make tradition to create obedient followers; obedient followers create a gang. That is why Israeli created a hierarchy to defend themselves from other gangs, even if they did not approve of hierarchy or gangs. They did it to protect the Israelites from gangs, fleeing that kept attacking violently in natural law.

If you let religious leaders explain the meaning, by preaching, you will be addicted to believing in religious illusion, tradition in blind faith, and blind faith is gambling; therefore, believing in religious illusion in blind faith, and gambling are addictive, distractive, it is considered in the medical field as a sickness disease that is hard to cure! That is the reason Moses spent 40 years in the desert, to cure people of addiction in belief, tradition, illusion, in blind faith. However, curing people of slave mentality takes a second. All you must do is pay for their work, and respect all people, because they are capable of being brilliantly creative!

MY UNDERSTANDING, FROM DEBATING THE STORY OF JERICO

Jerico's walls came down, from the insides out. The representative of the people of Jericho did not like their cruel inhumane hierarchy (god-players) and preferred the realistic God of the Israelite. So, the sound of the Horns was a signal for the people to revolt, and united with the Israelite, because Moses wonted to unite all the people of the world in God reality of science. All religion ins all langwidges, use the word blasphemy, to scare people about God to follow, and obey. However, why should those religions worry about protecting God from what someone says? What kind of an all-knowing, all-powerful God would need our protection? It is irrational to think that any God would need our protection. However, a king, a pope, or a leader will someday need protection from their dangerous illusionary obedient followers, despite their preaching of illusions, by using "the guillotine"! But it is rational to think that all life needs humane-beings' protection from leaders' hierarchy and dangerous illusory obedient followers; therefore, we must shift our focus. If we focus on our planet's life needs, we will have to stop focusing on what god's players want or need; we will be more humane for a safer and loving world. Because god-players, that creates from illusionary religions, and traditions, with many laws that create obstacle of understanding God's scientific reality, by believing in blind faith, for power of money to create privileges. God's ten commandment is against religious traditions, because it replaces God, by god-players, that control people by extreme, scary inhumane, killing and torchers, to protect their privileges, because they don't know how to do anything, (they are good for nothing)! However, today, people have the understanding knowledge from God reality of science, that created a majority of free self-thinkers !

Thank you, Moses, for creating a democratic scientific world.

By the people for the people from the people!

Leon D. Halfon

WISDOM OF KING SOLOMON

King Solomon was another free self-thinker in wisdom. He could have lived very comfortably as a king, son of King David; nevertheless, he understood Moses's wisdom and the importance of Israeli humane law. **King Solomon worked every day as a judge without judging people.** The question is, how? He devised ways of making the accused judge himself by creating their own understanding of right from wrong; that is why the guilty party understood he was guilty and became humane. King Solomon understood the importance of respecting brilliant, creative working people. So, he wrote the Book of the Masons, and the Masons that wrote the American Constitution. King Solomon left all is fortune for the Masons and left nothing for is children's that wonted to be hierarchy. He was the first to create the missionary movement that helped produce more humane-beings, wrote the Golden Rule, and tax the people that competed for more power of money from believing in !King Daid religions, created god players, treated money as God, and that is an addiction that is hard to cure! King Solomon succeeded to bring back the free self-thinkers the Israeli democratic scientific movement of Moses, that call themselves Zionists .

In King Solomon's realm, a restaurant owner who worked hard for his money came before Solomon's court. The owner complained about a beggar, who stood outside his restaurant every day to smell the food while eating some bread he brought with him. The beggar never spent a penny inside the restaurant. Because of that, the restaurant owner took the beggar to see King Solomon's court to be tried. King Solomon inquired, "How many times did this man smell your food?" The restaurant owner replied, "A whole year's worth, over three hundred times." The King asked, "How much does a meal cost?" The man replied, "One dinar." Then King Solomon told the beggar to give the court guard one dinar. The beggar said, "But that's the only money I have in the world!" The court guard took the dinar anyway. Then King Solomon instructed the guard to drop the coin three hundred times on the floor and then pick it up. The guard did so. Then King Solomon said, "Now both of you are even. This beggar smelled your delicious food three hundred times, costing you nothing, and you heard the defendant's money hit the floor three hundred times, also costing you nothing. No one should create work wert her is no work or get something for nothing to become a leader." The guard returned the beggar's dinar and that is what was humane justice.

Another time King Solomon displayed his powers of reasoning was when two women on the same day gave birth to one baby, each in the same barn. During the night, sadly, one of the newborns died. Before the other woman woke up in the morning, the grief-stricken mother of the dead baby decided to place her deceased infant next to the sleeping mother and take the living baby as if it were her own. In the morning, the living infant's mother realized that the dead baby next to her was not her child. The two women quarreled over whose baby it was. So together with the infant, they went to King Solomon's court for a final decision as to who was the actual parent of the living child. Solomon ordered his guard to take the baby from the women. When he did, King Solomon told the guard to slice the baby in half with his sword. In that way, each woman could have half a child. As the guard was about to cut the infant in two, one woman remained silent while the other woman screamed out, "Stop! Don't kill it! Give the baby to her." This proved to Solomon who the birth mother was because she was willing to give up her newborn child to live.

Solomon did not have to judge who was the rightful mother because the mothers judge themself. The point is people have to judge themselves by knowing right from wrong from their accurate understanding of the spectrum of life reality for wisdom! Here is another example of King Solomon's wisdom. The King of Persia asked King Solomon, "Why are you the smartest man in the world?" King Solomon replied, "I neither practice nor preach religion. **My way is a scientific movement to create wisdom to help and protect all lives. Otherwise, what are we here for?"**

The King of Persia told Solomon that he would like to learn more about his movement, to which Solomon asked: "How would you like to learn, sitting down or standing on one foot?" The King of Persia said, "I don't have a lot of time, so I'll learn it, standing on one foot." King Solomon responded, "The condensed version of the movement is to understand the wisdom of humane-law: Do unto others as you would have them do unto you. This is the Golden Rule. It is the wisdom of humane law; it is not a religion."

King Solomon, the author of the Book of Masons, wrote that God of the cosmos is the greatest of all builders, making the stars, the galaxies, the Sun, the moon, and our planet Earth with just the right ingredients for all lives to flourish, including people who after all are the children of that universal power. The Book of Masons is a humane law. The condensed version of the book is **that people are builders and creators were godlier than those who do nothing or seek power over others to create a parasite hierarchy. Because this planet belongs to all life, you will lose it if you don't use it or abuse it.** It was not meant to create a religion or tradition. It was meant to create a higher consciousness as a responsibility.

People tend to think of property as money in the bank. Many also think of money as God. But this planet is not about money. This planet is a responsibility for higher consciousness humane-beings from an accurate understanding of reality to create democracy, by the people, for the people.

King Solomon sent missionaries into Africa and Asia to teach humane law. That is why some black people in Africa today are Israelites. To be involved in the scientific movement of free self-thinking and be an example of creative humane-being. The Romen Christians copy King Solomon and send missionaries all over the world to teach religion for mor power. King Solomon was ahead this time but failed because he underestimated the powerful organized political hierarchy and their majority of believers!

As the Energy of the Universe would have it, thousands of years after King Solomon's death, the Crusaders found the Book of Masons and continued King Solomon's movement of wisdom. The Masons built more than 8,000 beautiful structures and churches in Europe and around the world. They built the Vatican and other churches and the Louvre for the King of France. They started the first banking networks in the world to help free self-thinker creative people, not as a profitable business.

Masons fought against corrupt royalty during the American Revolution, the French Revolution, and the Alamo battle for Texas independence from royalists that rule Mexico; the current corrupt governmental hierarchy still exists in Mexico today!

The Book of Masons helped shape my understanding of fairness and humaneness. As a result, I have learned to ensure honest representatives of the people and the people must become good at asking tough questions and not merely an obedient believer that leaders can scam.

Abraham, Moses, King Solomon, John the Baptist, Jesus, Buddha, Mohammed, Socrates, Archimedes, The Templar, Newton, Galileo, Albert Einstein, Martin Luther King Jr., Rosa Parks, and many, many, more were all teachers of wisdom of their time and were representatives of the people. They all fought the religious-political leaders' authority and corruption of the day. They didn't overpopulate, and were not interested in following, power or money. They were interested in free self-thinking wisdom to make the world a better place and help people become more humane in a corrupt world. Unfortunately, however, some people seek power over other people to feel good about themselves. These people are sick.

What I learned about John the Baptist and Jesus is that they were also incredible free self-thinkers. They understood Moses and King Solomon's wisdom. Jesus said I am from the King Solomon movement. John and Jesus understood the importance of teaching people the wisdom of fairness to know right from wrong. They even gave their lives, suffering torturous murder, because they understood people's highest achievement is to become humane-being. They did not focus their lives on being rich or powerful or comfortable.

What I learned about Martin Luther King Jr. is that he was a tremendous free self-thinker. He also risked his life to teach people how to be humane-beings and unite us as a democratic country to be an example for the rest of the world. Unfortunately, throughout history, many instances in which geniuses, who stood for the universal truth of humane law, were assassinated, or tortured because they happened to interfere with existing religious, or tradition or hierarchy statutes, because free of self-thinking is a minority, creative humane-being, and followers are a majority.

Humane-beings fight the corruption of the regimes of their time. In these situations, we can see how hierarchy and religion-based laws have worked against protecting the individual free self-thinker who creates wisdom for new knowledge for all lives. When the great teacher's thinkers of our time are roadblocked by too many laws based on opinions, religion, or governmental hierarchy, we do not advance to create a safer and inspiringly joyful life for all people.

Laws must be based only on the wisdom of "humane law." This is a simple system based on a scientific thinking method that creates a universal-truth humane law. Treat others the way you wish to be treated and free self-think like all folks must do, to create a more accurate understanding of God scientific reality, to do what is right, I am talking about honoring the needs of all people and all life on the planet we share. Treat others humanely because that's what every person wants, expects, deserves. Whether you are a man, woman or child, all lives on this planet!

The United States legal system was established to decide what is or what is not tolerable. In a melting pot society that welcomes all groups from all backgrounds, we must be keenly aware of the legal system's social impacts. In a community such as this, tolerance is necessary. However, should we live life merely to tolerate other people and their beliefs, just so that our own beliefs will be tolerated in return? The unfortunate thing about democratic nations like the United States—and others in the world, don't correlate with religion, because gangs/ of one belief or another encourage their followers to overpopulate to eventually gain a majority to win elections and get their way. Still, unfortunately, overpopulation and greed are destroying our environment. That's why more free self-thinkers are needed now! To create a computerized humane law to protect the individual. Countries are competing and they tolerate each other less, eventually creating a disaster.

A nation of free speech creates Satan's; it cannot exist under religions because all they do is preach, collect donations, and don't allow Satan's.

Today, lives are in the hands of warlords, tribal leaders, business tycoons, dictators, kings, and religious demagogues. Even more disturbing, there are over one million slaves, the destruction of the environment by wars and over population Is rapidly increasing. This is not humane or godly. Therefore, it is not acceptable! Nature methodology is what nature does with everything. it terne mountains into valleys, dead trees into wood dust, dead animals, and people into the dirt. Naturi methodology breaks down objects. it does not and can't create life. Only life energy can create life, and life is real, not an illusion. God-reality of science evolves to create a more realistic understanding of life, and evolution only creates changes in all species to adapt to the environment, for example, Nature can't create an intelligent computer, it can only create dust out of the intelligent computer. Only intelligent, of higher consciousness, free self-thinkers debating in the reality of science can create intelligent computers, because there are cracks in the enlightenment of scientific debate, for the light in your mind to create wisdom from an accurate understanding of God-reality. Believers of illusionary knowledge all they can do is memorize; they can't create intelligent computers. Because there is no God universal truth and in memorizing knowledge, and illusionary belief.

Only in free self-thinking and debating in searching for universal truth in God-reality of science do not mind being questioned, and don't create propaganda because they are searching for the universal truth!

Believers in illusionary knowledge do not like being challenged. And must create propaganda to keep people from knowing the truth!

ABRAHAM

Abraham was very wealthy, with plenty of land and livestock. He was also 100 years old and would surely die soon. One fateful day Abraham was ordered by religious leaders. God demanded sacrificing (kill) Isaac, his son, to prove Abraham's obedience to God (god-players). The only living heir to his fortune. Abraham realized that the religious leaders wanted his wealth; Abraham had witnessed preachers attracting followers by saying they spoke with God. He knew that it was false because God did not use words or demand sacrificing people. After all, since words can have several meanings, words are not accurate, often leading to misinterpretation and God's energy of the Universe is scientifically precise. Otherwise, it does not work in such perfection.

Many leaders have been cruelled throughout time, but the truth is that cruelty does not come from God. It comes from egotistic atheist psychopathic parasite leaders. This is an example of how he discovered the wisdom to diffuse the situation by analyzing in a scientific debate.

Since Abraham knew no one could talk to God or vice versa, he realized the religious hierarchy simply wanted to eliminate his only heir so that when Abraham died, they could steal his animals, property, and wealth.

Wise old Abraham realizes he had no choice, because a free self-thinker minority cannot fight a gang of majority ignorant obedient followers. so, he told the priests that he would sacrifice Isaac himself. They went up the mountain Moriah together with Isaac carrying the wood to be used in the sacrifice. Isaac was in his twenties and indeed he could have defended himself from his father if he had wanted to; however, Isaac knew it was all a religious act. When they finally reached the summit, Abraham built a fire and bound his son. Isaac allowed himself to be placed on the altar shows that Isaac continued to trust his father's scientific wisdom.

When they came off Mt. Moriah, he told the religious leaders what happened. Abraham said he was ready to sacrifice Isaac, but God spoke up and said to him that "because you were such an obedient follower, I will spare your son. Here is a sheep instead," which they promptly cooked and ate. I'm sure they were hungry because it took them three days just to reach Moriah's summit.

Abraham's story's wisdom is that Abraham appreciated his son's willingness to trust his father's scientific wisdom. The religious leaders appreciated Abraham's apparent obedience. They used that as the basis of a story to keep other followers obedient, too; Christians, Jews and Muslims still tell this story today by leaders to foster obedient believers in blind faith. In the end, Isaac lived, Abraham dies a natural death, and the religious leaders get a good story to tell about the way lazy ignorant followers should obey their leaders. Abraham succeeded in fooling the hierarchy because he was a free self-thinker Israelite, not a religious in a tradition. Since most people were willing believers, some began following him because Abraham was a humane-being and a representative of the people; he did this to save them from being subjected to religious cruelties. By wisdom, he united people who helped to make the world a better place. He confronted the leaders of his time because he understood right from wrong. This is how wisdom creates a better life for all, and if you think that God demands to sacrifice people? Then you are an ignorant obedient follower of illusionary knowledge and out of your mind, and are in to memorizing what others have written, as illusion of knowledge, without free self-thinking in a realistic debate, for a more precise accurately understanding the magic reality of life!

Today religious leaders and some scholars say that aliens built the pyramids. The pyramids are amazing because brilliant people in a scientific method of free-self-thinking made them! The pyramids' food is still good to eat after 4,000 years because the Egyptian free self-thinker scientists understood energy better than today. We don't even understand the full spectrum of Energy in the Universe.

Governments, religious leaders, because they are scholars, underestimate the ability to become brilliant by free self-thinking in wisdom from the beginning of time. Abraham, Moses, King Solomon, John the Baptist, Jesus, Buddha, Socrates, Archimedes, The Templars, Isaac Newton, Galileo, Albert Einstein, Martin Luther King Jr., Rosa Parks, and more; understood right from wrong. They were all brilliant free self-thinking wisdom teachers because hierarchy, religious leaders and scholars memorize knowledge. But have no wisdom and therefore, they compete and that creates the ego. That is the reason they are not humane-beings. However, they still control the world today by a gang of bullies, **that are created by believers in blind faith.**

Here is a wisdom story: a driver got a flat tire in front of a mental institution. He stops the car and takes the tire to a mechanic to fix the flat. When he returned, he could not find the four bolts needed to attach the repaired tire. The driver was upset because he would have to go back to the mechanic. However, one of the residents from the mental institution who was watching said, "Why don't you take one bolt off each of the other tires and install those three bolts on the fixed tire to drive to buy replacement bolts. This is an example of how anybody by free-self-thinking , without memorizing knowledge, can be brilliant, even a mentally ill person.

Leon D. Halfon

HIERARCHY AND JOAN OF ARC.

Despite tremendous odds against her, Joan's mission to save French Catholicism from the English Protestant army was victorious. She led the French army to a "David vs. Goliath" victory over the English. The news of her victory quickly spread across the British Isles and all of Europe. However, defeat at the hands of a teenage French girl gave the English hierarchy a black eye and a diminishment of their power and comfort to which they were accustomed. The English hierarchy retaliated by spreading the false story that Joan was an instrument of the Devil and must be killed. This is an example of hierarchy propaganda lies, to stay in power .

Even though Joan's victory saved them, the French royal court distanced itself from Joan. The king and his advisors became jealous and afraid of Joan's popularity among the masses. The French hierarchy did not want Joan to become more politically powerful than they were. After another battle with the English and their French allies, Joan was captured. The French king did nothing to negotiate for her freedom.

The Christian catholic hierarchy was very angry at Joan, who represented a dangerous threat to their power. People were taught to "pray, pay and obey." When Joan first revealed that she saw visions and heard the voice of God, the Church leaders realized she was a significant threat to their power and comfort. The Church had taught its followers that no one could directly talk to God except the Pope. Worshippers could only access God by going through the Church—and paying for it. Joan's statement about directly communicating with God threatened the hierarchy's positions and income for doing nothing, and they decided to eliminate Joan. Imagine this for yourself? After Joan was captured, the English and their French allies trumped-up multiple charges for a trial against her. None of the charges or standards for an impartial trial were met. During her imprisonment, she endured numerous death threats from the hierarchy. Finally, after a year in captivity, the 19-year-old Joan gave in and signed a confession saying she had never received divine guidance. Joan was convicted of heresy and sentenced to die by burning at the stake. When individuals go against the government, religion hierarchy and their gang of ignorant obedient followers, it can be hazardous and deadly to be a free self-thinker!

Joan was a representative of the people for the people. She upset the status quo. Her enduring success is that her story has encouraged other people to explore a direct relationship with God, the Energy of the Universe—without religious leaders or religion. Joan did not survive her interactions with hierarchy. Her enemies had condemned her to die long before her capture. She wanted to experience life because she knew how very precious and gratifying the magic of life is. But it didn't matter. The authorities publicly burned her at the stake and then later made her a saint. The Statue of Liberty was given to the United States by the French. It represents Joan of Arc with the Torch of Freedom lighting the way for people to escape the tyranny of hierarchy by free self-thinking in a debate to create a more accurate understanding of the spectrum magic reality of life, to be creative and make a safer, democratic joyful, loving world.

Suppose you are a believer and follower of illusions. You are a creator of hierarchy, which is a parasite, the enemy of all people, the enemy of a democratic world, and the enemy of the environment, from wanting more, by creating inflation, and unwilling to give up their privileges, no matter how many lives. And the environment they destroy!

For example. The God of the Roman, his name was Zuus, his son was Jesus; he was betrayed by Juda in Jodea, by Jews, and created a Jewish religion to compete, to justify their existence as you can see, how leaders write books, and use words, as hateful propaganda, for the majority of ignorant believer, in blind fate, to hate free self-thinkers, and mast destroy the temple of wisdom, that create free self-thinkers. So, free self-think, to create a majority of thinker, in God reality of science humane-being.

PART FOUR
Going Back Home

All Ancestors' humane inspiring stories of all the people on this planet inspire the new generation to create confidence, that is why it is important to read My Ancestors' Inspiring Stories, and by debating you will find the original meaning, and the reason it was written, not for believing in blind fate! Democracy is created by the people of the people for the people, for the freedom, to free self-think in reality, and in a debate accept the possibility of being wrong, to understand in reality, life was ment to be a continuous journey of exciting, and challenging, from your joyful love of life! Religion, tradition is created by hierarchy make you believe , that ,you are special, then you have to kill, and get killed, to stay special, that is, animalistically stupid. Because religion, and tradition, is keeping you idol, that is the reason, true out history religion, and tradition, destroy democracy.

No one from a foreign hierarchy came to the island to destroy the ancient historical books of wisdom in my grandfather's extensive private library. Fortunately, these books had survived for thousands of years because Djerba's desert island was relatively unknown when I was born. These books of wisdom were all handwritten and rewritten to be preserved. Religious leaders would have destroyed these old books if they had known of their existence. For example, religious leaders destroyed most of Plato's precious wisdom and many other precious books of the past for control of the people.

After World War II, Djerba was elected as a Muslim religious leader. People of the Book moved to Israel to avoid the violence of Muslim religious aggression and to safeguard the ancient books of wisdom in my grandfather's care. Fanatics are created by preaching about the unknown to generate fear and encourage violence against all people that are not believers in the Muslim religion. No matter their justification, there is **no fundamental understanding of wisdom** in the illusion that creates wars.

On the island of Djerba and in North Africa, most of the Israelites who escaped to Israel, like my family, could not sell their property and therefore lost their property and possessions to scary violence of religious gang.

When my parents took us to Israel, we were eight surviving children: For boys and four girls. As refugees, life for us was very hard, as it must have been for many refugees worldwide. However, I made the best effort I could to survive and help my family. My baby sister Malka was stolen at the age of one by a corrupt doctor and sold to another family for adoption. One of my brothers died as my mother miscarriage, he was fully formed, from unsanitary swamps full of mosquitoes, lack of food in Israel's refugee camps, and one brother was born in Israel. That left me with five brothers and three sisters. Even today, the aggression from illusions of religion, tradition is killing and creating refugees in many parts of the world. People are dying from toxic conditions created by hierarchy god-players, in charge of gang wars by manipulating words, by justifying in their illusionary religious and tradition, that was created by hierarchy god-players. Not Moses the creator of free self-thinker, in God reality of science or the American constitution, or democracy! Israel as representatives of all the people and that is why Israel protects its environment, its beaches, and its animal wildlife for all life. However, today there is no lack of sanitation, clean water, or food in Israel. Because the country was and is run by free self-thinkers creative humane-beings in a democracy. An exhilarating moment for me, my family, and the world, when my uncle, Moses Cohen, arrived in Israel to convert the ancient handwritten books of wisdom into print, and defend the democratic country, Even more so, Israel protects its people, so when I lived there in the 1950s, there are no homeless people in Israel still today. When I was a lifeguard on the Mediterranean beaches of Israel, I worked 13 hours a day, seven days a week in the summer and made more money than the President of the country, because this President was in it for the people, not for the greed of money for mor privileges.

The people who founded modern-day Israel are free self-thinkers Zionist Israelites, not religious Jews. The religious Jews did not want to defend the country; they expected their religious God to do it. After 2,500 years, the Israelites from Djerba's island moved back to Israel to receive the ownership of the key to King Solomon's Temple of Wisdom, where the seating arrangements are set up like a coffee shop, encourages debate conversations to understand God reality of science more accurately. The purpose was to recapture and preserve King Solomon's wisdom as a democracy, and to be safe from leaders perching religious that separates people. However, by the continuing efforts of free self-thinkers, wisdom is victorious to become reactive in some parts of the world today.

Leon's uncle, Moses Cohen, of the hand-written and printed edition

    *My grandfather explained to me some of the images in the photo on the following page, my uncle as a religious Jewish hat, for Jews hierarchy propaganda. For instance, the two hands with four fingers spread apart in the middle symbolize an upside-down pyramid. This image represents a "hand antenna" to collect wisdom particles from the Energy of the Universe. In the television show Star Trek, Mr. Spock used that hand symbol meaning, "Leve long and prosper." The hand "antenna" helps connect with the energy and communicate with our inner selves because God is in us. It means **Be in search of wisdom for a better world.** My grandfather's sayeth* *all free civilization Israelites hath to pretend to be religious or they would have been extinct like other intelligent free self-thinking civilizations of the past because they are a minority. By preaching about the unknown's illusions to generate fear and encourage violence against all people who are not believers. Fanatics created by preaching propaganda about the unknown's illusion to create more privileges for parasite hierarchy by hate and war still today.* **The first movement was King David's ignorant hierarchy, which believed God was on their side and would help them be victorious in wars. The result of that belief was that many people were killed or enslaved. Today, King David's followers are a religious Jews movement because of the preaching about David's poems and songs that fervently praise and thank God for selecting David and his people as "the chosen one, to feel special, are willing to die, and kill for King David hierarchy to believe that they are special, that is stupid, that is the reason, Christianity, and Muslim, copy, King David religions to become powerful parasite hierarchy,** *The second movement understood by wisdom the folly of war, as explained by John the Baptist, Jesus, King Solomon, and Moses. Those Israelites understood they could not successfully defeat* **the majority Roman army** *and their powerful hard-iron swords with their weaker bronze swords. They could not defeat the Roman army in battle, but a day will come when wisdom beats all the world's militaries from accurate understanding. That is why John the Baptist and Jesus said King Solomon's wisdom inspired them; they came to conquer the mighty Roman army with their wisdom. In the end, they were victorious in history, and universal truth wisdom from accurate understanding will conquer all armies in the future.*

My grandfather explained that they are the humane representatives of the people for the people; they are not hierarchy or religious leaders who represent their self-interests. The Levies tribe creates the Cohen's humane-being ,to preserve the free self-thinking movement, that are today 65.% of Israelis are free self-thinkers humane-beings, not religious in a tradition, as an example to the rest of the world, so mor people will become free self-thinkers humane-beings to create new knowledge, to fix all the problems. However, all hierarchy followers in blind faith, majority, gives them the right to control by violence ,the free self-thinkers, that debated for a more accurate understanding that questions authority for a better life!

Since the beginning of the Israelite movement, there were disagreements among the free self-thinkers who wanted to unite all people, including the religious ones. However, free self-thinkers, called Zionists humane-being, created Israel's country, not by religious people in illusions!

Leon's grandfather & uncle. Head of the Temple in Jerusalem.

The Enemy of Knowledge Is Not Ignorance

In the following picture, you can see my uncle Moses Cohen advising the brand-new Israeli government in the wisdom of humane law. They wear yarmulkes (hats) on their heads to remind them that the Energy of the Universe/cosmos knows what they are thinking to remind them to be humane , however, you don't need to wear a hat, if you don't need to remember to be humane, because you are humane!

As the real story goes, a general by Dreyfus's name, a self-thinking Israelite, was wrongly convicted as a traitor by a prejudiced French Christian court, just like the ancient courts did in judging Socrates. A newsman named Theodor Herzl observed the court case and understood there was no justice for independent thinkers. So, he established a charity called Karen-Kayemet, to raise money to purchase land in Palestine, Jordan. When I was ten years old, I volunteered to collect money for Karen-Kayemet, which was vital to establish a safe state for free self-thinkers Israelites. At first, they purchased all the swampland the Jordanians were eager to sell. They got it cheap because it was full of mosquitos, who thrived ever since the earlier Turkish invaders chopped down all trees to be used as firewood to fuel military trains.

After the Zionists established themselves, they demanded their independence because they did not want their country run by ignorant of reality, Muslim leader that promote hate, because they have nothing to offer. Religious Jews did not want to defend the country, because all leaders need to protect their importance by their obedient followers. The reason Zionists succeeded was that they were creative Israelites, hardworking humane-beings using their free will. It did not derive from praying or showing their love for a religious leader because they are not gullible followers and that was the reason for their amazing success. After the Zionist success, religious leaders tried to credit the victory by saying God answered their prayers to promote their importance because God loved them more. God plays favorites. So why did God not answer their prayers about this new virus, Covid-19? Because more % of religious people are sick and dying than other groups globally and can justify this, they can justify any illusion?

The Israelite Zionists did not wear funny hats or funny clothes; they were not, gaolable believers in blind faith. However, they understood God and were successful free self-thinkers searching for wisdom to be creative, humane-beings, who did not expect God to be responsible.

They call themself Israelite free self-thinker Zionists, not Jews because they did not want to be used in competing gangs for hierarchy propaganda to create hate and war to improve hierarchy privileges! Zionists are free self-thinkers Moses movement give the legitimacy, and the right to be a free self-thinker in this world, is of most important, because free self-thinking unite all the people for a safer democratic world and propaganda from believing in religion, tradition, that separate people and creates hate war by using the illusion, to protect parasites hierarchy, that is against life, and everything that is against life, is against God, and against democracy. Today, the peaceful Muslim in Israel, have a better life, and better education, then all other Muslims in the world. Eventually the Israeli Muslim will become free self-thinker humane-being in Moses low, between people and God, with no religious, parasite leaders (god-players), **as the story of Jerico,** where the people, united Israelit, and that will create a powerful humane movement!

You may recognize some of these famous free self-thinker Israelites Zionists in the photo collage below. They are not followers of hierarchy!

The Zionists knew they could not fight and win a war based on the illusory belief that God would make them victorious. So, the Israeli free self-thinker had to survive to save the world from the hierarchy world of dominating gangs created by the parasite hierarchy the united nation!

Many brilliant Israelites became Buddhists or atheists because they did not want to be part of their family ridiculous carnival of Judaism. People don't know that if Israel Zionists had not become friendly with all religion's hierarchy, they would not have received the help and support from all hierarchies to survive, because they are a minority. Now the free self-thinkers in a scientific debate have their country, representing the democratic government people, astonishing success. Their example shows free self-thinkers in a scientific debate, searching for universal-truth for that Time, representing the people in government works. And a hierarchy system that competes by memorizing knowledge to create a hierarchy, that creates freedom of religion in a free self-thinking democratic government, it never worked before, and will never work, because, religious leaders, have nothing to offer. So, they preach hate. Universal truths for that time can be found by being curious and asking questions in scientific reality of debate conversations with family, friends, and, best of all, strangers, no belief, or opinion allowed. So, you can realign your brain to a more accurately understand, in your mind God-reality of science, because we all make mistakes. **If you don't ask, you won't learn new things. "You won't understand what you know, and you won't understand what you don't know!" A utopian society is easily obtained, by free will, to free self-think in a scientific reality method of debating, to arrive at universal truth, for the time, and that will provide accurate understanding, to understand what is right, from what is wrong, to create humanely-beings out of people, to do what is right and that will eventually create a utopian society!**

There is always a reason why some people are mistreated, but there is never a humane reason they should be treated inhumanely. I cannot think of why all people cannot become humane-beings and friends as free self-thinkers by debating conversations, in knowledgeable reality by searching for universal truth that create **wisdom in the magic reality of science.**

All speeches on YouTube, a stand-in building or a book that does not give you the ability to disagree in a debate conversation are preaching propaganda, paid by wealthy hierarchy, for more wealth to stay in power**, by creating scams, because it pays to advertise propaganda.**

My question is, why do some illusory people hate free self-thinkers? Because of what they believe from their leaders preaching, hate propaganda. An example of what free self-thinking people gave you is Moses, the 10. Commandments, between God and people, no god players that create illusionary religion. They got rid of all God-kings and hierarchy that steal your women and torture the people of their free will. They gave you Socrates, Archimedes, Jesus, Galileo, King Salomon that wrote the Masonic book to create the Israeli Mason that wrote the American constitution by the people for the people in the U.S.A, Albert Einstein, the king Qui of China that created the Wall of China, got rid of parasite leaders to create a great Chinese civilization and all the greatest humane minds by free self-thinkers. Thy are the ones that created and will generate more in the future. It was not created by people in a gang of the illusion of knowledge, in blind fate.

Free self-thinkers will continue to create a better world for all life on this beautiful planet because it is God's scientific reality of thinking by debating knowledge to arrive at more understanding for new wisdom. Free self-thinkers are all individual people, not a gang or a country or a belief or philosophy or illusion of knowledge. However, free self-thinking is a difficult inspiring, and joyful journey of challenges in search of universal truth. You can be one of them and as a free self-thinker, you have the right to disagree with scientific debating knowledge searching for a more accurate understanding of life's spectrum magic reality. It is not to **justify your belief or illusion or opinion or philosophy to compete to feel important.**

Free self-thinkers never have torture chambers and never will; free self-thinkers don't have the death penalty; free self-thinkers have no crime rate. **They don't like illusory religious violent criminals, people who want money to do nothing, because these criminals are dangerous.** All I have to say to god-players: don't blame the people for what is happening because they don't know what they are doing, thanks to all the preaching illusion of knowledge, and killing the free self-thinkers, for thousands of years and not allowing debate conversation for a more accurate understanding of reality, for a healthier consciousness, to understand not to believe illusion, fairy tales. Why is it, in the past and still today, ok to torture and execute free self-thinkers that will make a better world by breaking the law of some countries' hierarchy? Because words don't hurt people, only truth hurts people and pain is essential to tell you where the problem is. Imagine this as a free self-thinker to understand and in a debate, find the wisdom to solve, the problem, because swallowing many pain pills or believing in allusion of knowledge don't solve problem, Stop, and be real! To make America great again is to go back to what made America great in the first place, by giving power back to the people and creating many places for debate conversation between all the people, {between people and representatives and police. Everybody must be involved in debating.

PART FIVE

Inspiring Photos and Life Stories of Leon

I was born on the desert island of Djerba in the Mediterranean Sea off the coast of Tunisia. Djerba was a French colony in the mid-twentieth century with a population of 4,000. There was no running water, no electricity, and no cars. All transportation on the island was provided by donkeys, camels, horses, bicycles, and feet. The residents of Djerba spoke many different languages, including French, Arabic, Italian, Spanish, Greek and Hebrew. When the ancient Romans ruled 2,000 years ago, they grew wheat as food for the Roman Army in North Africa and lived on the island of Djerba.

Hopefully, these stories about my Life will give the reader a better understanding of the context from which this book is written, with great empathy, not sympathy. At seven years old, I had an army truck accident that paralyzed me from the waist down, at the end of World War II. I stayed at my grandparents' home for three years, where I learned about wisdom. I still had no feeling in my legs, and I could not move the wheelchair by myself. The technology to move wheelchairs on one's own did not exist yet. Therefore, my grandfather pushed me around and, by asking questions and debating the reality of life, I understood the direct way necessary for wisdom to love everything in life, and be creative, for a better world.

One day, a woman came over for some advice from my grandfather. She said, "The Devil is harassing me. Do you know what I can do to keep the Devil away?" My grandfather said, "The Devil comes from believing in (the illusion of knowledge), not from an accurate understanding of reality. But if you walk down this street, there is a religious place where they know all about the Devil." Later that day, my grandfather said to me, "Grandson, things are changing very fast, and, in your lifetime, leaders will declare, 'There is no Hell,' because people are demanding a more accurate understanding of reality." My grandfather predicted the future 65 years ago by his wisdom. And sure enough, the Pope declared in 2018 that there is no Hell. My grandfather also said, "Grandson, we escaped the Holy Land to the desert island of Djerba 2,500 years ago, fleeing the Babylonian invasion, because there is no wisdom in war. **The invaders reasoned that their God was better than the Israelite God. This aggression is from believing!**

But the Persians loved the Israelites for their wisdom and got mad at the Babylonians, so the Persians destroyed the country of Babylon. That is why Babylon doesn't exist today. Persians rebuilt King Solomon's temple of wisdom for the humane-Cohen tribe of the Israelites to return and continue to teach the search of universal-truth, for new wisdom to create knowledge. **There is no wisdom in war**. That is why the Cohen tribe wished to survive to preserve the flame of wisdom for future generations. When you have problems in Life, all you need is an accurate understanding of reality. Any other way will be wrong. Unfortunately, today the Persians have religion, i.e., the illusion of knowledge from an oppressive regime with a religious leader, but not a more accurate understanding of reality. That is the only reason the Israelites and the Persians are enemies.

To put an accurate perspective on history, my family's ancestors have been reading, writing books, telling stories, and debating in search of wisdom for a more precise understanding of reality for over 3.500 years. In Europe, people have been reading and writing for less than 1,000 years from Israeli writing. Today their leaders want to keep European people, and the world ignorant in illusion, not in debate for more accurate understanding so that the hierarchy of power and greed can control the populace. It is happening in many parts of the world today because the gangs of hierarchy (the regime) don't want to give up their privileges; it doesn't matter what they destroy. Understand this because it affects Your life, and all lives. The Greeks had the wisdom to create democracy. Yet, even in a democracy, the hierarchy (the regime) condemned **Socrates** to death or move to the desert island of Djerba, in the Mediterranean Sea. All because the hierarchy lusted for more power and did not want to lose their traditions to believe they are special! In war, a soldier killed defenseless **Archimedes**, because there is no wisdom in war, he was a free self-thinker, not a follower who discover the earth went around the sun 1.400 years, before Galileo, and measured the earth, **he was wrong by 3.00 yards, from today earth measurement, because of religious hate and war,** The Persian and the Turk invasions killed all the Greek people of wisdom. Because the hierarchy lusted for more privileges, they did not escape to the island of Djerba and today in Greece, there is no flame of wisdom for the future generations to give to the world. That is why people need to become free self-thinkers as a majority of the population in scientific debate, for the ability to find the wisdom to create representations of the people for the people, for a safer world. Today the majority of the new generation are into understanding reality!

Leon D. Halfon

As I was growing up in the mid-20th century, my grandfather and uncle were the representatives of wisdom for the Cohen tribe of the Israelites in Djerba. The humane-Cohen tribe took care of King Solomon's Temple of Wisdom in the land of Israel; the first Israelite temple of wisdom ever built outside of Israel was constructed in Djerba. Since this magical Mediterranean sandy island was relatively unknown, no destructive leaders came there to destroy the old books of wisdom to control the world. Fortunately, the ancient stories of wisdom were safely guarded in the extensive library that my grandfather owned, these original handwritten books and some of the books were thousands of years old.

One day, while I was on the way to my father's shop, I stopped in the center of town to watch a snake charmer's show, which started oddly. The charmer choked his cobra until it lost consciousness. "How can the snake perform now?" I wondered. Then the performer put small pieces of paper with religious writings under the head of the snake. When the snake woke up, the snake charmer-preacher started preaching to explain how religious writing was so powerful that it caused the snake to come back to Life. He began selling pieces of paper for one franc each. When I returned to my father's shop, I confronted him and asked, "Why are grownups willing to pay one franc for a piece of paper?"

I was only five years old, but I knew it was just an ordinary piece of paper. Because I was taught to free self-think, to search for universal truth reality by questioning. My father said, "The difference, my son, is their fathers terrify their children to believe and obey, and preachers by violent aggression force, terrify their fathers to believe and obey, so their leaders may control them. But I teach you free self-thinking in search of reality so that you can analyze everything for yourself. To better yourself and the world." My father also said, "When someone truly loves you, they will teach you to debate in the reality of science and knowledge for a more accurate understanding of the magic of Life, to become a humane-being. That creates healthy love and respect; this is God universal true wisdom.

I will not teach the illusions of knowledge that create obstacles in your brain, which only make you an ignorant obedient follower (believer) with no confidence, to allow the hierarchy to control you. It's true that if you pray together family stay together as ignorant believers in illusion. However, it's

The Enemy of Knowledge Is Not Ignorance

also true that if you debate together, you stay together as a loving free self-thinker creative for a safer world. An Israeli is not a religious fanatic, nor is he an Atheist or a gang or capitalist or communist or socialist, or a Jew, He or she is a humane-being, free self-thinker who loves and protects other humane-being that won't *improve their mind* in a scientific method of debating by free self-thinking for a more accurate understanding of the spectrum of God reality of life magic in a democracy, for a better world!

You are born a free self-thinker Israelite with common-sense in the search of accurate God reality. However, the majority are brainwashed to believe in (god-players) from the day you are born, that is, Religions and Atheism in blind faith are gambling, and is a sickness that is hard to cure.

Only BY UNDERSTANDING ONE PICTURE IS WORTH MORETHAN A THOUSAND WORDS

Don't just look at a photo, analyze for yourself and see a thousand words. For example, my family is not hugging each other in the photo because they are not part of a gang, but rather free self-thinking individuals searching for the wisdom to create a better world.

I was two years old, sitting in the middle of this family photo, full of curiosity and asking many questions while this picture was being taken.

The man standing in the middle is the grandfather of the grandfather of my mother. He lived to be 129 years old. When people are humane-being, they create the wisdom to have a peaceful, loving happy, serene life. No doctors, no judges, no police required. That is utopia. By limiting stress, our body and mind are capable of healing themselves. In the picture, my aunt standing on the right wears a hat full of gold coins. It is the custom in Djerba when a husband loves his wife that he gives her a gold coin which she happily stitches on her hat, so people can see how much her husband cares for her. You would not be able to practice this custom anywhere else in the world because somebody would steal the hat in a second! The women wear wooden shoes with a strap in the front, called Bakbak, to make a clapping sound when they walk. They have wisdom on the island of Djerba. When the men hear clapping, they know a woman is close by, so they take care and are respectful. My mother sits on the left and I am the two-year-old sitting in the middle. To this day, I still remember when this photo was taken. These people have not quarreled nor fought between themselves, nor even had a jail, for over 2,500 years, because of their more accurate understanding of reality, which leads to a utopian life. Violence is for animals—mainly to obtain food or avoid becoming food—but not for people who debate in a scientific method, which creates an accurate understanding of the magic reality of life. All to become a higher consciousness humane-beings to protect the environment and live a challenging and exciting utopian joyful Life.

For an accurate understanding of reality, I emigrated in 1966 to America on my own. I knew nobody in the United States when I arrived, I could hardly speak English, as you shall see. Despite these obstacles, I earned a general contracting license and have since devoted my skills to creating inventions and innovative solutions for improving people's lives.

I invented the first sailing surfboard, aptly named the "Sail Surfer." I was awarded two patents for the board and was featured on the cover of Popular Mechanics Magazine. My sail-surfer design helped kick off the windsurfing craze of the 1970s. A few years later, based on decades of experience as an ocean beach lifeguard who'd completed over 275 certified rescues, I invented the first known standup "rescue paddleboard" in California. It was called the Multi Banana Boat, so named for its yellow color and slightly curved deck, which inspired today's paddleboards. The secret of its success is that a rescuer can slice through the waves to reach a swimmer in trouble, place him on the board and surf back to safety on the beach. I also invented the first therapeutic electrical stimulation necklace, named the "Solar Energizer"(patent N#.4.173.229—November 6, 1979), which was a big success, selling over 150,000 necklaces, which inspired today's electrical therapeutics devices and my rescue boat, (patent N# US 8,499,707 B2—July 13, 2005).

From a not accurate understanding, people assume three realities into one understanding. The first reality is the God-reality of science by free self-thinking and debating in conversation; you will find the wisdom, to improve life for all lives. The second reality is imposed reality by hierarchy, to protect their privileges, and that is paper money, religions, traditions, propaganda, hierarchal laws, etc. The third reality is your own, reality. This reality is subjective to each person however, in a scientific debate, and by free self-thinking, you will create a more accurate understanding, and realize that some of your reality is an illusion or propaganda, that will go nowhere, and create conflict; therefore you will accept that it is time to abandon your

impose hierarchal laws, religions, traditions, propaganda, imposed reality and get into God-reality of science and evolve for the better, into a more of a realistic creative humane being, it is a challenging and exciting life journey! Because when you understand what right is, you do what is right, even in the face of torture for a better world!

Because if a believer knew, he would say I know; however, since they don't know, they say I believe. Believers are willing to kill and get killed over what they don't know, that is VERY STUPID get over it; it is just an illusion created by parasite leaders continuously preaching hate for money because they don't know how to do anything honest, that is profitable, for cash! So, please unite in God's universal truth, not in illusion of knowledge to become a dangerous obedient dog. For parasite scared leaders, by killing the disobedient and the non-believers!

After the assassination of over 200 million people by the competing hierarchy in World War II, it was accepted as an understanding of the life norm. I was born during World War II, and by free self-thinking people of the book in a utopian living! My goal was not to populate or create more wealth or compete or have power over others. However, my goal was to be an inspiring example as a humane-being, for a better future of all lives, not to memorize knowledge for much more wealth by competing to become hierarchy, so I can afford to overpopulate is not correct, and it is destructive. It is wrong. Because once you have a more accurate understanding of God magic of life reality. You will realize in the wisdom, that every day and everything in life is beautiful and life was meant to be lived by accurate understanding in a utopian humane world! The saying: Absolute power corrupts, is wrong! Because all **humane-being throughout history with absolute power were not corrupt, because they were humane-being. not just a being!**

Religious believers say they like the idea of a Supreme Man or a Women or a Santa Claus ,who made everything, knows everything, pre-ordains everything, and has all the wisdom. Thus, worshipers don't have to think about universal-truth to create wisdom for themselves and so they remain ignorant in the dark, however, Clarity, reality, science, understanding is the same thing! Obscurity, unreality, illusion, belief, and religion are the same thing! **Switching on the light is frightening, but once** you understand the clarity of the magic of life, you will realize. It is better, and safer to see life in clarity, den to see life in obscurity, and God is in understanding reality in clarity, not in believing in the illusion of religion in blind fate, in the dark, because life is real, not an illusion!

You can lay down and rest on the 25 lb. Halfon Rescue Boat.

Leon as a lifeguard in Cfar-Vetkin

The Enemy of Knowledge Is Not Ignorance

Lifeguard Leon on a rescue mission in Malibu, California

Leon as a circus acrobat

Leon lifeguard friends in Haifa, Israel.

The Enemy of Knowledge Is Not Ignorance

*The Halfon Rescue Boat, 25 pounds. Once on the water,
it becomes 55 pounds, making it very stable,
able to carry 600 pounds.
It keeps people safe from predators and chilly water.
It's also great for rescues in floods.*

"Once a lifeguard, always a lifeguard."
Leon D. Halfon
Leon as a lifeguard in Haifa, Israel.

Leon was lifting classmates at the age of 11.

Leon demonstrates his Rescue Raft.

I love this place! Utah's Dirty Devil River.

The Enemy of Knowledge Is Not Ignorance

Leon surfing his Multi Banana Boat in Malibu, California.
"If you are afraid to die, you don't live!"

Leon as a lifeguard in Nice, France.

Leon performing a Timex Watch Company commercial stunt.

Leon, the Timex stuntman in America's longest-lasting commercial —25 years on television!

The Enemy of Knowledge Is Not Ignorance

> *"I grabbed the baby like a football and I ran."*

I was sitting at the lifeguard station and this lady came in with this baby. She went into the water, a wave came and knocked the baby out of her arms. Of course she started screaming, in a complete panic. I couldn't find the baby so I grabbed everyone and had them hold hands and feel around with their legs. After five minutes we found the baby. Of course she wanted her baby, but I had to give him some air. I grabbed the baby like a football and I ran into the room where I kept my surfboard. I closed the door, locked it from the inside and was working on the baby. And there was a crowd outside banging on the door, trying to break it down. Finally the baby regained consciousness. And as I handed him back to his mother, I realized that if I had not been able to save him, my God, they would have killed me.

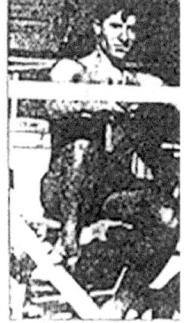

LEON HALFO

Silverlake resident Leon Halfon was a Haifa lifeguard before coming to California, where he developed and marketed a hybrid kayak/surfboard.

I was honored to be featured in the official book celebrating the 50th anniversary of Israel's formation, entitled An Eyewitness Account.

Wen, you understand, right from wrong, in God magic reality of life, you will do what is right, even the face of danger.

Acrobats Mimi and Leon are on a rescue mission.

Mimi navigates Leon's paddleboard.

The Enemy of Knowledge Is Not Ignorance

Acrobats Mimi and Leon on the Malibu Paddle Cat.

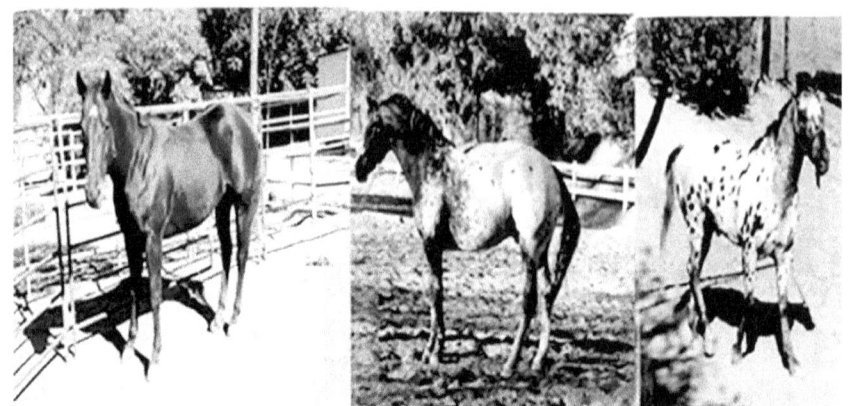

I love all living things—here are some of my wise equine friends.

Riding my horse, my goat follows me everywhere for the company, for the love of life.

The Enemy of Knowledge Is Not Ignorance

Leon feeds leopards at the breeding program in Florida for the Endangered Species Society.

Leopards and Leon.

My kitty cat is a dentist.

Leon with an animal friend.

The Enemy of Knowledge Is Not Ignorance

At age 12, after recovering from my crippling injury, I could walk again. After that, I thought of myself as Batman, protecting vulnerable, free self-thinkers from bullies.

Leon, at the age of 50, realized that Life is beautiful and funny and if you don't understand that Life is lovely and funny, it is because you don't have an accurate understanding of the spectrum of life magic.

At the age of 60. My goal was always to stay in shape.

Leon D. Halfon

METRO

Paddle in hand, Leon Halfon demonstrates his hybrid 72-pound fiberglass board along the surf of Santa Mon

Trying to Catch a Wave

■ Beaches: By demonstrating his floating contraption—part surfboard, part kayak and part sail board—inventor hopes to create a tide of attention.

By JOE MOZINGO
SPECIAL TO THE TIMES

On the first stand-up paddleboard for surfing, Leon in the Los Angeles Times newspaper was on November 10, 1997.
| JOE MOZINGO | SPECIAL TO THE L.A. TIMES

The Enemy of Knowledge Is Not Ignorance

Walking on top of the wave...
The most daring stunt, by the power of free self-thinking
understanding of God reality magic of life.

FALCON

One day, when I was ten years old, I walked by a grain mill building and noticed a dying baby falcon on the ground. I looked up and saw workers on the roof, so I yelled, "Watch out! You just knocked over and killed a baby falcon!" They told me to come up and take the rest of the falcon chicks because the building was scheduled to be demolished. I took the tiny trembling birds home, but they would not eat when I tried to feed them. Searching for wisdom, I analyzed the situation. I realized that when the mother falcon fed her babies, she must have spread her wings and created shade over the nest. When they were in their nest on the roof, it was sunny up there and when the mother came to feed her chicks, she created shade and sound. So, I put the falcon babies in a box outside in a sunny place and then I took a piece of cardboard to create shade. They were chirping and hungry for food. I imitated the sound of the mother falcon and attempted to feed them. And guess what? It worked—and so analyzes scientific wisdom.

They grew up fast and were ready to fly in just two weeks. Every day when I came to feed the falcons, they would dive from the sky and land on my arm to eat. I would take the falcons to parties to make money as a show. After the falcons' performance, I would toss them in the air, and they'd fly home. One day one of the falcons did not show up, so I went looking for him. Not too far from home, on the roof of a four-story building, was the missing falcon. I recognized the lost raptor, so I raised my arm for the falcon to land and started calling and whistling. The people on the balcony watching me thought I was crazy because people in science seem to be crazy for people in the norm. The falcon dove off the roof at great speed and landed smoothly on my arm. Later that day, I decided to teach the falcon to hunt to be independent, but it was not easy. However, in God reality of science wisdom, everything is possible.

My family told me that the falcons would fly over to visit me whenever I left home and call for me if I wasn't there. I did it because I was a humane-being who had the wisdom to care for and love all Life.

A YOUNG APPALOOSA STALLION AT MY RANCH

All my cowboy friends told me I had to break this beautiful wild horse's spirit and show him that I was the boss. Since I did not accept that kind of attitude, I thought to myself, "How can I train this wonderful animal without hurting him and his spirit?" I came up with a plan of wisdom.

I took the horse to a lake in a trailer, walked him into the water up to his chest and then climbed on top. He struggled a little bit but then got used to me and settled down. He was amiable after that! I could ride him without showing "Who's boss." When I fell off the horse, he did not spook and ran away. Instead, he stayed and waited for me. That was big because it is essential for me to always be in friendship.

MY THOROUGHBRED STALLION

One day, I decided to breed my thoroughbred mare and searched for an appropriate stallion for her. Unfortunately, all the good ones were too expensive. Later, I went to a horse auction and heard outside a loud racket from an enclosed horse trailer.

I asked the owner, "What do you have there?" A thoroughbred stallion," he replied. "However, he is a killer horse. He tried to kill his rider and I am supposed to put him down. But I don't have the heart for it. So, what I am willing to do is haul him to your place for $175. And you keep the horse for free."

I never use aggressive behavior towards animals and after a while, this beautiful creature became my friend. I took him to the beach in Malibu so that we could ride together for exercise and fun. I built a corral for him along the Pacific Coast Highway close to Our Lady of Malibu Church, where I was employed so I can take care of him every day. The first time I rode Lush Life on the beach, we went into the ocean and a wave splashed us, filling my boots with water. I dismounted, removed my boots, and tied them on the back of the saddle. While riding again on the beach, one of the boots slid down and kicked the horse in the groin, making him run very fast. I couldn't stop him. I decided to ride him towards deeper sand to slow him down. Lush Life ran full speed into the deeper sand. Unable to gallop in the softer sand, he suddenly stopped, tossing me forward over his head. As a lifelong acrobat and instructor, I knew what to do. In mid-air, I executed a flawless somersault and landed on my feet. People watching from their beach houses applauded my graceful maneuver.

One time I rode my stallion in a Malibu fifty-mile endurance race. Out of 130 horses. My horse was the only one who was not an endurance racer. Even so, Lush Life and I finished number 8. The reason for our success was that the horse loved me so much. He was willing to go through hell because I asked him to. I cared for him very much and made sure not to push too hard. I checked his heartbeat, monitored his water intake, and dismounted to lighten his load so we could run up hills together. When he was nine years old, riding was too hard on his back, so I sent for his papers, which required the tattoo number inside his upper lip, all thoroughbreds have a tattoo number inside his upper lip to indemnify! That's when I first learned his name was Lush Life. I also found out that during his racehorse career, he won $180,000 in the Santa-Anita races. Had I known at first how valuable he was, I probably could have sold him for six figures. But I never would have because I loved that horse and wanted his years to be comfortable and joyful. And also, because I love all living things. So, I sold this handsome stud for $10,000 to the Malibu Horse Academy to breed and run free in pastures with mares. He was a great friend and I miss him very much. Unfortunately, his previous owners did not accurately understand Lush Life or horses or the joy of life at all. They just wanted to win the race for more money instead of learning from each other and enjoying Life.

SWINGING ONTO THE BALCONY

At one time, I lived with a topless dancer named Beverly in a fourth-floor apartment coincidentally near Beverly Hills. I had created a company that manufactured small fiberglass boats, kayaks, and canoes. One night, after delivering ten small boats, I was tired, very cold, and anxious to get under a warm blanket. But the apartment door was locked from the inside. So, I didn't know Beverly was there with another man.

At first, I thought of waiting, but I got colder. So, I knocked on the door, rang the bell, but there was no response. So, I ran to my truck, grabbed an industrial-strength extension cord, and attached it to an air vent on the roof. Like a hero in an action movie—I'm thinking Douglas Fairbanks in a 1920s pirate flick. I swung down from the roof and flew towards the balcony, knowing its glass doors had no lock. Before landing, I see Beverly and her boyfriend standing on the other side of the glass with their mouths open.

I land on the balcony and walk into an empty apartment. They ran away. I decided to sleep on the couch and unlock the front door just in case the lovers wanted to return and use the bedroom. The following day, I called the bar where she worked and asked for Beverly. I was told she was in the bathroom, so I waited and called a half-hour again later and the answer was the same—she was in the bathroom. I replied, "I don't want to play games. I'm coming down there to straighten this out with Beverly." When I arrived at the bar, it was closed, and I see ten men milling outside. I ask what happened? I was told, "The owner threw us out of the bar because he said a mighty man is coming over to destroy the place." However, I am a very gentle, humane-being who would always use conversation instead of violence to resolve an issue. Of course, if attacked, I would defend myself.

A few days later, I drove by the apartment, saw Beverly closing the balcony drapes and realized she was there. I just wanted to talk and straighten out our differences. I ran up the stairs to our fourth-floor apartment and saw the door was open. When she saw me coming, she tried to close the door and lock it from the inside, but I jammed my foot to keep it open. I assured her that I meant no harm and told her that she could have it if she wanted the apartment. She said, "Okay." So, I gathered my stuff and left. That was the last time I saw Beverly.

Leon D. Halfon

I DATE A WOMAN WHO LIKES TO DRINK AT A BAR

When my girlfriend Lois and I stopped at a bar for a drink, I told her I wouldn't say I liked the place because it was to run down. She said, "No, no problem. Let's just have a cold beer!" While drinking our beers, a drunk man walked over and unzipped the back of Lois' dress. She showed me what happened and asked me to do something about it. I zipped up her dress and told the man, "She's with me. Leave her alone." But the drunk came back and unzipped her dress again. I asked him, "What do you want?" He said, "I want to fight you." I responded, "I don't want to fight." He ignored me and asked, "Do you want to fight in here or outside?" I repeated, "I don't want to fight you." However, to avoid a commotion in the bar, I said, "Let's go outside."

As we went outside, the drunk jumped on me and tried to sucker punch my face. I blocked his punch, hit him right in the mouth and knocked loose his two upper front teeth; they were dangling from his gums. He was spitting blood everywhere and looked horrible. Yet, he was laughing the entire time!

Meanwhile, I felt terrible. I realized I should've known better than this. I should have walked away. I didn't sleep all night. The next day I went looking for that man at the bar to offer to fix his teeth. He wasn't there, so I left my phone number, but I never heard from him again. Nothing seems to matter to the ignorant or drunk.

As a humane-being, even if you win a fight defending yourself or protecting others, you will feel miserable afterward because you are hurting someone. Therefore, the best thing to do is just to walk away. The prophet meant this when he said to turn the other cheek; he suggested walking away. Because humane-being doesn't compete.

The Enemy of Knowledge Is Not Ignorance

WORKING IN THE LITTON BUILDING FOR MAURICE BRASLAVE

Years ago, the Litton Building in Beverly Hills was a famously large construction with tall ceilings where airplanes were built. But after World War II, the company went under, so the building was subdivided into different sections and leased. Maurice acquired the front area, which was about 5,000 square feet with a 30-foot ceiling above the concrete floor. His business in Beverly Hills, called The Last Show, produced exclusive one-of-a-kind hand-crafted clothes and costumes for over 5,000 television and motion pictures, such as Marlon Brando's *Last Tango in Paris*. He also designed apparel for famous political and show business luminaries, such as President John F. Kennedy, California Governor Jerry Brown, and former Russian President Nikita Sergeyev ich Khrushchev.

One day, Maurice called me and said the fluorescent light he needed for his job was not working. I came over without a ladder and climbed up the four-inch sprinkler system's pipe, like Spider-Man scaling a building. I replaced the fluorescent light, but it still did not work. I climbed down, walked to the circuit breaker box, and switched the lights off. Then I flipped off the circuit breaker to the fluorescent light and taped the switch so no one would turn it on while I was working. I climbed the pipe again, disconnected the ballasts from the lights and left to buy some new ones.

When I returned to replace the ballasts, I climbed the narrow sprinkler pipe to work on the light once more. Somebody from another part of the building came to the circuit breaker box, took the tape off, and switched on the lights. The building used 280 volts of power. Suddenly I felt pain throughout my chest and heart. I was being electrocuted from sitting on a cast iron sprinkler system pipe. I was almost paralyzed and could not let go of the wire, so I tilted myself to let go and fell to the concrete floor 30 feet below.

The ambulance took me to the hospital and x-rayed my back. The doctor said they would have to operate immediately since I cracked a bone in my vertebrae. I told him that I did not want anybody operating on my back and wanted an ambulance to take me home. I said, "I'm a physical therapist and I'll get myself better."

The doctor said, "You will have lots of pain and eventually will have to see me again. By then, it will be tough to help you. You will probably be in braces for the rest of your life!" I boasted: "I will go home and get myself better and then I will come back here and kick your butt." The doctor said, "I'd like to see that. I'll be waiting for you." Sadly, back in those days, back surgery was not often successful. I went home, built a cast out of flour, eggs, water, and cloth, and wrapped it around my body. My father was a medicine man on the island of Djerba. I stayed in bed for six months with light exercise. My friend Cosmo took care of me during this time. After some more challenging workouts, I was able to get out of bed. It took me a year before I could leave the house. Two years later, I went back to the hospital and told the doctor who wanted to operate on my back to bend over because "I'm going to kick your butt!"

Here, the lesson is that you must free self-think wisdom for an accurate understanding that creates confidence and trust in what you understand in reality, and everything is possible. By free self-thinking, you will see the truth of Life. Work hard and anything is possible.

THE VOICE OF EUROPE

In 1966, when I arrived in California, Robert Bardey and Gerard Alcon became my new friends and I joined their work as reporters for a Paris radio station called *The Voice of Europe*. We recorded news stories and events on tape for almost three years and then called Paris on a transcontinental landline.

To broadcast on the air, we put the telephone on a recorder and instantly transmitted our information to Parisian radio listeners.

THE PREACHERS

One of the events we recorded for the Voice of Europe took place at a park in Long Beach, California, where preachers use soapboxes. After spotting a group of people, they would stand on their soapboxes and start preaching. A preacher in front of us walked like he was drunk. We followed him and when he arrived at the crowd, he stood on his soapbox and started preaching. While we recorded the event on tape, the preacher confessed that he used to be an alcoholic, but Jesus saved him, and he was no longer an alcoholic. Then Gerard approached the preacher's soapbox, pulled him down, smelled his breath and told him, "You are still an alcoholic. Phew, you stink! And you don't deserve a soapbox." Everyone in the crowd started laughing.

THE MUSTANG RANCHES

One time, we went to Las Vegas, Nevada, to interview sex workers in the now-famous brothel, The Mustang Ranch, for a radio documentary. When we entered the lobby, twenty young women were wearing bikinis and standing at a long table. An old woman would say to the visitors, "Hurry up because the young ladies are getting cold." Once a visitor selected a woman, we followed them to their room to record the event. She gave the man a pan with soap and water, and he wondered why. He asked, "What's that for?" She answered, "This is what we call a 'peter pan.'" He said, "I thought Peter Pan was a flying kid." She replied, "Peter Pan is a flying kid in a fairytale, but this is real: it's a 'pan' to clean your 'peter,' stupid."

Leon D. Halfon

MY CANCER STORIES

I had been with my doctor for more than ten years. Sitting in the waiting room for the doctor, a woman that I didn't know entered the room and said to me, "Why don't you act your age? You are 75 years old, and you had a heart attack. Who do you think you are?" I replied, "I never had a heart attack, and I don't understand your problem. I don't know who you are; I want to see my doctor." Later on, my doctor says to me from out of the blue and without any proof, "Leon, you have cancer. You always knew one day that was going to happen." No, I never assumed one day I would contract that deadly disease. However, I had to go for an MRI, undergo weekly blood tests and take numerous strong medications because of what he said. As a result, I fainted, fell, and severely broke my right shoulder.

Two weeks later, I ended up in the hospital with a fever so high—106 degrees—that the doctors thought I would not recover and asked for my permission to stop treating me and let me die. It took a millisecond for me to respond, "Hell no! I want to live. Do everything you can to keep me alive." Finally, another doctor in the hospital came to my rescue, treated my situation, and told me that the medication the other doctor prescribed was what made me sick in the first place. So, I got rid of my old doctors and the lousy medicine that almost killed me. After thorough testing, I found a new physician who concluded that I had no cancer and never had cancer.

I made an appointment with my original doctor, who had affirmatively told me earlier that I had cancer. I confronted him and asked why he gave a false diagnosis. The doctor looked up his computer records and said with a straight face, "I never said you had cancer."

Meanwhile, all this time, I was worried sick over nothing. The doctor's untruth was very destructive to my mental and physical health because he was wrong and wouldn't admit it. What this incident showed is that some psychopathic people in the hierarchy play God because they can. What a relief it is to know the actual reality, so keep on questioning. In wisdom, believe nothing of what you hear and half of what you see. People with knowledge and no wisdom are dangerous.

THE DESERT ISLAND OF DJERBA

My mother, Rachel, came from the Cohen humane people of the Israelites on the desert island of Djerba. They were descendants of Moses. They didn't live by violence; they lived by wisdom. Before getting married, my mother was a schoolteacher who taught the French language. She was also fluent in Arabic and Hebrew.

My father's name was Mero. He spoke Italian, Arabic, Hebrew, and French. He came from a pirate family in Tripoli. He was powerful and never backed down from a fight. He enjoyed roughing-up fanatic, religious bullies who go around beating up "non-believers." The French police appreciated what he did. He risked his Life every time he fought. But mostly, he was very friendly with all the citizens of Djerba.

After work, my father would invite Muslim, French, and Greek friends to drink sap from palm trees called Lagmy. When fermented, the juice transforms into a deliciously sweet drink that makes everybody drunk. I was just a kid but sometimes participated in drinking it too.

Everyone in town knew me and respected my father. He taught me to think and analyze everything and not believe in fairy tales, Santa Claus, religious doctrines or even birthday parties. We never had birthday parties growing up. When you reexamine your experiences, it creates a powerful pattern in your brain.

If you analyze everything again later in Life, you'll remember things very clearly. From the age of two, I would ask questions. I still remember things as if they happened yesterday.

My father awakened everybody at six in the morning for a swim in the summer. Once we were at the beach, he threw a piece of wood into the Mediterranean Sea and told us that whoever swam out and brought the wood back would get the treat of a pirate breakfast. But of course, there was never enough food because we were such a large family. So, I was always hungry and eager to claim that piece of wood.

I didn't know how to swim on the surface, so I held my breath and paddled underwater until I spotted the wood above. Then I came up, grabbed it, took a breath, and swam back underwater; the pirate breakfast consisted of a raw egg from which the white had been removed and replaced with half an inch of Arrack, which is similar to vodka and half an inch of olive oil on top. Whenever I think about those pirate breakfasts, I become a little bit nauseated, but when you're a hungry child, everything tastes good. So that was breakfast, the pirate's way. I was two years old at the time. When I was eighteen and became a lifeguard, I could hold my breath underwater for over five minutes!

When I was four years old, I walked to school with a Greek boy named Garibaldi. On the way, he would climb trees to eat raw birds' eggs and even baby birds to show that he was a challenging Greek. I particularly remember two rows of mimosa trees on the way to school. They smelled wonderful. I liked to pick the trees' yellow flower balls and sniff them, turning my nose powdery yellow, making us laugh.

My best friend was Jacque, the school principal's son, who lived on the school grounds. On the first day of school, my three-year-old sister peed in the classroom. The female teacher took her to the front of the class, picked her up and slapped her bottom. I was four years old and did not like seeing my sister getting spanked, so I ran up to the teacher and started kicking her. The teacher was jumping and laughing at me. Then, she told me that I was adorable and brave for defending my little sister. Afterward, she gave me many presents, including a kitten.

Another day I was sitting on the sand in the school backyard and a big beautiful African eagle landed on top of a 10-foot palm tree next to me. I stood up and saw that the eagle was standing and pacing, looking at the littlest kids as if they were to become a meal. Sure enough, the principal appeared with a rifle and shot the eagle down. That might seem wrong today—but even if a man threatened the children, the principal would have shot him. That was Life on Djerba.

After school, I would walk to my father's marble and wood carving workshop to help out or attend Hebrew education classes or play with the animals in our backyard. When the native people came to town to sell or buy things, they tied up their animals in the yard behind my father's shop. As a result, there were always more than fifty new animals to see every day.

The Enemy of Knowledge Is Not Ignorance

In the backyard, there was a mother goat with two goat kids. My father let me keep the little male. I fed and trained him to understand a few words. He was beautiful, with big green eyes, pink lips, and rapidly growing horns. To protect me, the goat stuck by my side like glue. Maybe he understood I was a "kid" too. If someone came too close to us, he'd stand up on two feet, eager to butt the intruder away. That's the reason why I didn't need a leash to keep him close by. I also taught him how to butt on command.

On the weekends when I was five years old, my goat and I would walk to the schoolyard to meet my friend Jack and his little dog. Together we created a small animal circus to entertain our friends and fellow students who came to watch. It was great fun for all of us.

One day my father told me it was time for us to eat my little buck goat! I was shocked. I couldn't understand why anyone would kill and devour such an intelligent, beautiful animal. I told my father that my buck didn't do anything wrong, was brilliant and friendly. I cried and cried so much that my father ended up selling him. Ever since then, I cannot eat red meat.

Sometimes when I didn't have to go to school, I went with my father in the morning, to the town square, which the ancient Romans built. They had constructed a concrete platform, four feet high, fifty feet long and twenty feet wide so that the Djerba fishermen could display their catch for auction. Shoppers came every day early morning to buy fresh seafood because there was no refrigeration or ice on the island; fish attached to strings in boxes for auction and giant sea turtles on their backs, struggling before selling for food. When the auction started, my father would bid on a string of fish. After he bought the line, I picked up the fish and walked home while my father went to his workshop. At the end of the auction, the rest of the fish was given to the poor.

After school, when walking to my father's shop, I felt like the only kid who was curious and questioned things. Because I was confident in myself, I wanted to learn as much as I could. From the age of five to seven, everybody was friendly to me, and I felt loved by all. Maybe that's why I love people and all lives to this day. People nicknamed me Wildcat because I was like a feline walking around everywhere. One day, I saw this older man having his afternoon coffee. He held a tail from a cow for swatting flies.

One of the flies bounced onto the cup and fell into his coffee. The older man picked the fly out with his fingers and brought it to his lips. He sucked the fly then threw it away. I asked him why he did that. He said, "The fly adds extra flavor to my coffee. Try it sometime." Thanks, but no thanks.

One day walking on the way to my father's shop, I saw a man hanging upside down by his feet in a storage building with other people standing around. I came to look and saw blood dripping from his nose into a pan, so I asked the people what were they doing to this man? They said, "We are taking the Devil out of him." I did not understand at the time because my family never mentioned the Devil, but now I realize this was an exorcism, Muslim style. Sometimes, musicians and performers came from central and south Africa to entertain us in our town center. There was always something going on in Djerba. Often, Muslims behaved violently over religious matters. For the fanatics, anybody who was not Muslim was an infidel, not a follower of their religion in Arabic. In such a society, free self-thinking in wisdom was not permitted or practiced. It was punished, which empowered religious leaders to keep people childishly ignorant and obedient. How convenient for the leaders! That is what happens when there is no separation between hierarchic religious gangs and the government. They are the same.

Sometimes to defend himself, my father had to fight these fanatics. He said he didn't want to fight and would ask them to stop, but if he must fight—he'd fight to kill. I saw my father kill three men in self-defense. What a waste of precious Life. Bullies realize they are ignorant from believing in illusion, which explains their aggressiveness. These religious hellions become aggressive to feel sure about themselves, with their preachers or leaders' encouragement. How convenient for the bullies caused by leaders preaching the illusions of knowledge that create ignorance of reality, they felt that their illusionary religious God would help them triumph and they would go to Heaven, just as their religious leaders had told them. You'd think people would know better, but they don't from blockage in the brain!

I visited the island of Djerba in 2008. I saw a modern airport, automobiles, running water, electric power and five-star hotels. Tourists were everywhere but at a cost! The sea was polluted; the only catch was sand crabs and four-inch flounders. The Roman ruins were gone, and the mimosa trees were missing, replaced by fancy hotels and trendy shops. It is an example of what's happening to the rest of the world: over-development.

My friends and I went to buy a Berber carpet. The Berbers were the only people who conquered the Roman Army. The Berber leader name was Anibal. However, when the Berbers came home to Tunisia, The Berber was betrayed by the Tunisian leader's greed for Roman money. the Tunisian government forced the Berbers into slavery. They are still slaves of the Tunisian government today, making Berber carpets.

When the police weren't looking, my friend, Vesta sneaked $100 to a slave. I wanted to give some too, but I would have been caught by the factory manager who watched us. I gave $50 to share in the gift. Neither of us would buy anything from the carpet factory because we did not approve of slavery. Berber slaves have an H-shaped green tattoo on their foreheads, marking them as slaves of the Tunisian government even to this day!

I tried to have friendly conversations with the native Muslim people in Arabic, telling them about my past on the island. Suddenly they surrounded me, demanding to see my passport. They wanted to know if I was a Muslim or not and if I left before or after the French colonial occupier's revolution. They were a gang of bullies, so I got out of that area fast. What I learned is, in a situation like that, people often get stabbed. If I got into a fight to defend myself, I wouldn't have had a chance to be found innocent of self-defense against a prejudiced Muslim religious judge because religious law is not humane law—it's a discriminatory law. So, all religious laws are prejudice to non-believers.

Currently, Djerba is becoming worse, so is the world, not better. In these Muslim countries, there are no representatives of the people, for the people. Religious leaders ruin and control the government and all of Life.

Consequently, these countries are in a state of total unrest, which will not stop until they have humane laws to protect all individuals. The greater the religious illusions of knowledge, the greater the violence from ignorant bullies. As people gain a more accurate understanding of reality, religious leaders will have less power. You'd think that free self-thinkers would have no chance in a country of illusory religious beliefs. But you'd be surprised by what a moral, humane, and brilliant person can do when they discover the power of wisdom by free self-thinking and acquiring a more accurate understanding of reality. They can harness their minds and tap into the energy of the Universe to gain insight and make a better life.

CRUSHED

A few years after World War II, in 1950, a fleet of French Army trucks landed on Djerba's desert island when I was seven years old. The streets were narrow and not designed for motor vehicles. I walked next to an ancient Roman wall from school to my father's workshop when a French Army truck slammed into me and crushed me up against the wall. To call them "injuries" does not adequately describe the damage to my body. My spine and pelvis were smashed and there were broken bones everywhere. My child's body was no match for 5,000 pounds of careening military steel. Awakening into the world again, there was a presence in the room after two weeks in a coma. The silence was broken with a voice that sounded like mine: "What am I doing in the hospital?" My mother answered: "You had a terrible accident."

Struggling through the fog to understand what had happened, words echoed from my mouth, saying, "We were together when we went to see my brother after the truck accident. My father was beating some man. Everyone was screaming, 'He's just the insurance man!'" I saw people carrying his body. Then my mother interjected, "You could not have seen anything like that recently. You were in a coma. Everybody thought you were dead." So, the vision during my coma was impossible. I had an out-of-body experience, or I was in my brother's body. *I don't know and I never found out how that happened.*

After regaining consciousness, I found myself bound in a full-body cast. The only body parts out of the form were my head, fingers and two small openings to pee and poop. The doctors believed I broke every bone in my body even though there were no x-ray machines at that time on the island of Djerba. The doctors sent me to a hospital in the city of Sfax in Tunisia. They drilled a hole in my skull to relieve the pressure caused by the swelling of my brain. The gap eventually healed but left a bald spot in the back of my head the size of nickel which didn't disappear until I was 40-years old. I stayed in the hospital for six months because I could not relieve my bladder after the accident. Everybody thought I was going to die unless I urinated. My bladder had to be drained every day using a syringe inserted in my penis, which was very painful.

A group of very loving Muslim children visited me every day, bringing candy and cheering me on to pee because they knew if I didn't, I would die. When the doctor drained my bladder, it was not as painful as when the nurse did it. One day the nurse came in to insert the searing, into my penis. I screamed from the s searing, pain. Ali, one of the Muslim boys, said, "We'll pick you up and stand you on the table so that it will be easier." As Ali and his friends did so, they chanted to encourage me to pee while the nurse tried to insert the searing. Suddenly, I started pissing on everything—including the nurse. Everybody cheered, except the nurse (even though she was happy for me). Shortly afterward, I was well enough to be released from the hospital, so they put me in a wheelchair and took me to my grandparent's house in a horse-drawn cart.

However, I still had no feeling in my legs, and I could not move the wheelchair by myself. The technology to move wheelchairs by the rider did not exist yet. So, someone had to push me around. Every day I was wheeled across the street so that I could get out of the house. If I wanted to drink or eat something, I had to wait until the evening to be wheeled back home.

I asked everybody who walked past me if they could run. They said they could, so I asked them why they didn't run very often. They told me they didn't want to. I could not imagine wanting to run when one could do it. So, if I could run, I thought I would run all the time.

Children were playing around one day and one of them hit me on the back of my neck because he knew I couldn't defend myself. Later, I declared to my grandfather: "There is no God. I would never hit someone for no reason, yet the kids hit me and ran away laughing. Where is God?" My grandpa replied, "God is the biggest and most powerful force in the Universe. You should be thankful for what God gave you." I replied, "Well, I am not thankful. "I didn't accept my grandfather's answer as truth because you will know whether a statement is a fact or fiction if you think for yourself. As a free self-thinker in wisdom, it is your right to disagree.

When I was outside in the wheelchair, a young French girl named Nicole came every day after school and protected me from the bad kids. I asked her, "Why are you so nice when so many other people are not?" She said, "I am a Christian and Christians are supposed to be nice." I smiled and said I would like to be a Christian. My response indicates that I did not fully understand reality to have wisdom at that age. However, it is wiser to be humane.

Another day, bad kids sneaked up behind me. They hit and harassed me and then ran off. I was sitting alone in the wheelchair, feeling miserable, when an older man showed up. One second, he was on my right side—the next second, he was on my left. He seemed magical. I asked, "What do you want?" He said, "Hey, kid! Why are you crying?" I answered, "The bad kids hit me again. And there is no God!" He responded, "Do you know what life all is about?" I said, "No, I am only seven years old. How should I know what Life all is about?" "I'll tell you, "He said. "Life is nothing but a continuous journey of exciting challenges. God must love you very much since he gave you this tough challenge. Overcoming paralysis is like climbing the tallest mountain. Once you climb the tallest, all the other mountains seem like little hills. Do you want to find God? Accept Life as a challenge! What do you have to lose? Everybody is going to die anyway!"

After he left, I started thinking and analyzing what he said, just as my father told me to do. The older man was not trying to make me believe anything and he didn't promise me a rose garden, only challenging work. This I could do. What did I have to lose? I thought of myself as a free self-thinker. This seemed like the truth to me! The fact gave me the will and determination to overcome my challenges. So, I decided to build up my upper body strength since my lower body was useless. I started exercising by pushing myself up and down on the wheelchair's armrests.

A few days passed and I felt strong enough to drop to the floor, raise myself upside down on my arms into a full handstand and literally "walk" across the street on my hands toward my grandparents' house. I would often have to cross back and forth the road by doing a handstand. This was my first realization that challenging Life is rewarding and exciting and it was a beautiful rose garden! Even with thorns, it was beautiful.

Another time I was sitting in my wheelchair when a kid comes over and tries to hit me. I jump out of my chair, stand on my hands, and start chasing him upside down in a handstand. He ran away, scared, calling for his mother. I walked back on my hands, climbed into the wheelchair, and raised my arms over my head in victory.

I felt great. At that moment, I understood there is an energy in you that we don't understand, but it is accurate. That was the moment I was ready to challenge myself to walk. But until I could walk on my own two feet, I continued to get around on my hands with my legs dangling above.

Due to nerve damage, my legs were numb. Sometimes I would poke my legs with a needle so that I could feel something. After this, I worked incredibly hard to challenge my body to walk again. In the end, it was not a belief or a miracle from God that allowed me to succeed., because nobody is special. It was my accurate understanding of the truth of reality of life by free-self-thinking, by free will. Life is a journey of challenges. I met this challenge by putting forth the effort to exercise. The result was that my body healed itself because , God the energy of the Universe is in us and around all of us.

Eventually, my father made my crutches and gave me ostrich oil to rub on my atrophied legs that had become extremely thin and fragile from lack of use. After that, I got my entire body working again by exercising practically all day, every day and used needles heated over a candle to jab my legs to see if I could feel anything. Eventually, I began to feel something, which gave me hope of regaining the entire movement one day.

It took me two years to overcome my shattered pelvis, broken femur, and injured spine to walk again. My left leg is still 1 and ¾" shorter than my right, but it doesn't bother me. I manage very well now, even better than most people because I accept Life as a challenge and I did it my way by using free will, not blind faith.

After intense exercise, I would fall into a trance and daydream in my chair. One day, I saw a storm approaching. I was not dreaming, but I felt frozen. The sky was cloudy and becoming darker and darker. The clouds seemed to be alive, pushing each other in a struggle. The clouds crashed into each other and created sparks of light. I was helpless and became very scared. I was frozen by paralyzing fear. I couldn't get up to leave or even cry for help. I looked to the clouds for an answer and saw a tiny red glow, about the size of a pea, in the corner of one of the shadows; I understood from my grandfather that God was Energy, so I concentrated on just looking at the light for help and not paying attention to anything else. The energetic light got bigger and bigger. The light came down around me like a veil and I became engulfed in it; it felt warm and comfortable, but I could not comprehend it. Then, as if my body did not exist, I began to communicate **telepathically** with the light in accurate understanding of meaning, not by words conversation. I asked one question: What happens to me after I die? I began to understand the light's response: Everything in existence changes form but will always exist and always has existed. I felt as if I was communicating with myself.

> YOU CANNOT MAKE SOMETHING INTO NOTHING,
> AND NOTHING INTO SOMETHING,
> IF YOU KNOW YOU EXIST IN YOUR MIND, THEN YOU ALWAYS HAVE,
> AND YOU ALWAYS WILL EXIST.

When I woke up, I felt like I had just time-traveled. I understood the wisdom of Life at that moment. I was only eight years old, and my understanding was that I didn't need to procreate because too many people destroy the environment. We are the only species on the planet capable of making a better world, my goal in life. However, Nature needs to procreate to evolve better and more beautiful species. Life is a continuous cycle of birth, death, and rebirth.

People believed that if they walked to the edge of the Earth, they would fall off, but that's not true. Others think that when they come to the edge of their lives and die, they too will fall off, out of existence. That also is untrue because everything in the Universe always exists and only changes form.

The Enemy of Knowledge Is Not Ignorance

If you can understand the meaning of the paragraph above, you can better understand the infinite. Acknowledging this left me without a fear of dying, but of course, I prefer to live. Fear of dying holds people back from living a full life. Now I felt I could understand Einstein's Theories of Relativity by a scientific method of debating and free-self-thinking, which creates a more accurate understanding to create a healthy mind and body.

I continued my exercises, ever more determined to walk. It was absolute torture. I would go into a trance when exercising hard and wake up when it was all over. As a free self-thinker, I understood that people and animals could go into a trance-like state, so they will not feel pain because the Energy of the Universe will not have it any other way. In the beginning, I used crutches, but I barely put my legs on the ground, mainly utilizing my upper body strength to move. I slowly put more and more pressure to strengthen my legs until I didn't need crutches anymore. Finally, I could walk again! I felt victorious. Then I started running again. I realized the doctor and my parents didn't think I could do it. They expected I would stay in my wheelchair forever because they did not understand the power of free will. But I knew better. When you gain a more accurate understanding of reality, you will realize how to reach your full potential. My free-will reaction was that my body healed itself because the Energy of the Universe helped me understand how to get my full potential. After this achievement, I was stronger and faster than I had ever been. I felt I fully deserved to live a life that suits me best. However, I did not always think this way.

As I mentioned earlier, my grandfather had an ancient library where I learned Hebrew. He had a book that I loved to read called *The Wisdom of King Solomon*. This is where I first learned about Masonic wisdom. I became an optimist as I began to understand the importance of the infinite wisdom in Life. I heard that America was based on Masonic wisdom, so I always wanted to go to the United States.

I was born at home within a tradition. I fought my family about having a Bar Mitzvah because I felt that it was a branding process like someone would use to mark animals or slaves to be controlled. My understanding came from ancient Israelite Moses' wisdom to unite all people worldwide by becoming a free self-thinking humane-being, not from religion.

Traditions derive from dead leaders of the past to create and control "gangs." However, it is time to unite people by achieving a more accurate understanding of reality to arrive at universal truths that will make parasite hierarchy absolute, by creating a majority of the world, as free self-thinkers.

I loved experiencing Life very much, but I was not a believer and didn't obey very much because I enjoyed my freedom. I was away from home most of the time. One day my father said to me, "You better obey! I brought you into this world and I can take you out of it." I said, "You'll have to catch me first!" I understood the importance of free self-thinking and self-preservation. Early one morning, while I was sleeping next to an open window, my father woke me up and slapped me. He said, "Who do you think you are?" I quickly jumped out of the window and ran two hundred yards to the Mediterranean Sea. The waves were big from last night's heavy rain. I dove into the sea and swam like a fish. My father got scared and started screaming, "Come back, Levi! I will let you do what you want (Levi is my birth name; my family called me Levy and everyone else called me Lee, which later evolved to Leon when I came to America). Often my parents were exasperated by me because I was highly active and challenging to handle. Everything became more relaxed after that. It is a good thing my father was not religious. If he was a religious follower, I would have been treated as a nonbeliever and burned alive at the stake. Can you imagine that?

So, stop believing in religion, illusionary lies, and start! Free self-thinking, in God reality of science for a continuous journey of exciting challenges, to understand and leave, your exciting, journey of challenges, to love your life, and everything in life, to do what is right even in the face of torcher, for a better world for all!

LIFEGUARD

Being an ocean lifeguard was the best job of my life. What wasn't there to love? I loved the beach, loved the sun, loved fun, loved swimming, loved saving lives, and loved the pretty girls particularly and they loved me.

When I went to Israel, I was not educated because I had missed school from the truck accident. Also, when I was in school, I was bored. I needed a job, so I participated in the challenge to be a lifeguard. Unfortunately, out of one hundred and thirty-five people, only seven passed the test to be a Mediterranean beach lifeguard. However, I knew I would pass the test because I was a great swimmer, and I could hold my breath underwater for more than five minutes. After all, I was an islander from Djerba.

Woman losing bra

Leon D. Halfon

When you understand in reality the magic of life, you can create magic.
When you believe in blind fate, you cannot create in the dark.

The Enemy of Knowledge Is Not Ignorance

I worked in Haifa, Israel, as a lifeguard helper during my first year.

I always went to work early in the morning because I would rather be on the beach than anywhere else. I took care of everything because the chief lifeguard showed up late and relaxed the rest of the day. One Friday night, I went to a party and got drunk because of an argument with my girlfriend, Susi. The reason for the discussion was that Susi came to Israel to get married and have children. She offered me $500,000 if I married her and gave her a child. She said if I didn't want to stay married, I could leave and keep the half-million dollars for myself.

Disturbingly, ever since the paralyzing injury when I was a small boy, my family has been interested in my money—from the accident insurance and my lifeguard pay. In the summer, a lifeguard on my beach usually works 14 hours a day, with no days off. As a result, I accumulated double overtime and triple overtime on my paychecks. I was making five times the salary of my father and three times the doctor's salary, who worked for the Israeli government in social health care. All their desire for money kept me away from my family.

When Susi made her generous cash offer, she thought I would jump at it, but I didn't. Because of Suzi's argument about marriage, I drank too much alcohol and couldn't sleep at all. I had a hangover in the morning when I went to the beach to open the lifeguard station. I raised the black flag, which meant no one was allowed in the water. I felt that I could not be alert enough to be a responsible lifeguard. Finally, at nine o'clock, the other three lifeguards showed up. I told them I was very sick and didn't sleep all night and would like to lie down. They all responded, "Leon, you always take care of everything for us. Don't worry—we'll take care of you. Go to sleep." I put a blanket down and passed out on the beach. Soon, my girlfriend Susi came and sat by me.

A few hours later, while I was asleep, three young girls were drowning. The lifeguards at the station called me for help with the bullhorn. I shot up like a bolt of lightning and ran toward the rip current. I picked up one of the girls, moved her out of the current flow, where she could stand safely and instructed her not to move. I went back and rescued the second girl and handed her over to another lifeguard. I dove under the water to get the third girl. I pulled her to shore, where she started throwing up; at that moment, I knew she was ok and then went back to collect the first girl at the edge of the current. My concept of being a lifeguard is calculating how to save everybody and never give up on anyone. Because every Life is precious and equally important. My friend Joseph from the beach restaurant greeted me with a cold beer when I came back. He said, "Leon, you were incredible! You ran so fast that I couldn't see your legs. This one's for you!" I said, "No, thanks. I don't want any beer right now. I have a headache and I'm not going to drink anymore."

The next day was a cold, slow weekday. Nobody was on the beach, so I sat at the beach restaurant with my girlfriend. We enjoyed ourselves. Joseph, the owner, screamed at me, "Leon, the Mayor of Haifa is here! Get up!" I didn't believe him, but sure enough, the mayor was there, and I said to him, "I'm sorry that not sitting at the station." The mayor said, "I'm not worried. You can be sound asleep and still save everybody. I heard a lot about you. I'm firing the chief lifeguard and hiring you to be in charge." Usually, you must begin as a helper lifeguard, work your way up to the second chief lifeguard position and then work several years more before becoming a chief lifeguard. It takes approximately twelve years. I became the chief lifeguard of the public Haifa beach within my first year. Love what you do, do more than you think you can do and by free will, make your Life challenging and exciting.

On duty, one day at the lifeguard station, I noticed a large woman on the beach walking into the foaming surf. Suddenly a strong wave knocks her down and submerged her. She stood up, calling for help. I immediately rushed out to see what was wrong. When I arrived, she screamed, "My baby, My baby. I can't find him!" As I approached, I did not see any baby; the woman was so big, and the child was small. In a panic, the frightened mother said the wave knocked her child out of her arms into the murky water. I quickly searched as hard could but could not find the baby. I called everyone in the area to hold hands and feel the dark water with their legs for the little one. About five minutes later, which is a long time to be underwater, someone found the infant.

Of course, the mother wanted her baby right away, but it was critically important to give the child some air immediately. I grabbed the baby like a football and ran into the lifeguard bungalow, where I kept my surfboard. I closed the door and locked it from the inside while I frantically started artificial respiration on the baby. Outside, a crowd was banging on the door, trying to break it down. However, to my relief, the baby finally regained consciousness. As I handed the tiny survivor back to his mother, I realized if the baby was not alive, the baby's relatives might have killed me! I had no choice.

This rescue was reported in the Israeli newspapers and then later in a uniquely American book that celebrated Israel's 50th Anniversary entitled "An Eyewitness Account." (I have included part of the article and the photographs in this book).

To get to my lifeguard job, I had to commute for about an hour on a train passed by my beach, but there was no train station there, so I had to continue to central Haifa. Then I had to hop for a ride for twenty minutes back to my beach in a diesel smoke-belching bus. Because I hated the smell of diesel so much, I decided to jump off the train as it slowed when passing my beach. Near the coast, the train would slow down from eighty to ten miles per hour for safety reasons so that bathers could cross the tracks to and from the beaches. People would come over early to the coffee shop and watch me jump off the train. It was like being in the circus.

I used to visit my sister in the city of Akko, which was about nineteen kilometers away. I ran that whole distance on the beach since I enjoyed running and hated taking the bus. It took me about two and a half hours each way. I had to go around the harbor to get to the beach. I would be fully awake once I started running for about one kilometer. Then I would fall into a kind of trance until about a kilometer before arriving at my destination when I would snap out of it. It was the same on my way back. This feeling of euphoria is known as "runner's high." Sometimes I encountered a flock of seagulls that would wake me out of my trance. When I tell my brother-in-law that I used to run from my lifeguard station to Akko, he does not believe me. He thinks it was just too far to run.

Leon D. Halfon

YOYNAY

From time to time, I worked on different beaches: Haifa, Kfar Vitken, Caesarea Hotel, Netanya and Vinget. Vinget is a very isolated place with a school for athletics teachers. When I worked there, I met a man by the name of Yoynay. He lived in a cave-like trench he dug into the beach covered with metal signs and sand over it. He lived in that cave with twenty dogs. One day, Yoynay told me the story of his life.

He was a Danish Christian who fell in love with and married a young Israelite woman. After the Holocaust, she wanted to live in Israel. However, once they arrived, they could not adjust to living with the Israelis, so they moved to reside with the occupying English Army that controlled the country. To survive, his wife had to sell her body for money to the British forces' officers.

One day, a Muslim Sheikh wanted to pay for her services. She said she would not have sex with a Muslim because they do not respect and treat women fairly. Later, as she traveled with her husband in a carriage, a gang of Muslims stopped them, pulled her out and slit her throat.

Yoynay was very disgusted with all the people at that moment. He decided to live in isolation with his dogs. He lived off the fish he netted with the help of his well-trained animals. On one side of the bay, he would enter the water and walk toward the other side where his crafty canines were waiting while simultaneously extending a large net with floats on the top and weights on the bottom to corral the fish. Then he would signal his dogs to chase more fish into the net, which proved very useful. He told me he would rather live alone with his dogs than live with people.

Being a lifeguard, I learned mouth-to-mouth resuscitation and felt it was wrong because many people drowning often chokes on a floating object caught in their throat. There is no way to see inside the mouth, so you can never be sure. I decided to research anatomy with a doctor friend and found out that air blown into the nose goes directly to the lungs, while air from the mouth goes to the lungs and stomach. If I hold one hand over a victim's mouth and blow air just into the nose directly, then the air would not escape from the mouth and would bypass any choking objects. I could then blow rhythmically into the nose to control the airflow. I knew my mouth was always bigger than anybody's nose, making it a lot easier and more effective to save someone. Once I blow air into the nostrils, I pull the drowning person's knees toward their stomach, collapsing the lungs and pushing air and water out. Then I bring the knees down, blow the air back into the lungs through the nose and maintain rhythmic breathing. I hope this will be educational so someone out there can be saved.

There was no work in the winter because the beaches were closed, so I went to school, studied massage and physiotherapy, and then got a job as a physical therapist at the Dead Sea Clinic. This knowledge helped me become a better lifeguard because I learned the anatomy of people.

Leon in a resuming action

I had an eighty-year-old letter that referenced a 280-year-old letter, which stated that ancestors on my father's side helped George Washington win the American Revolution. When I showed this eighty-year-old letter to the American consulate in Israel, the man who reviewed it was amazed. He said, "This is beautiful history." As a result, I obtained a visa and a green card from the consulate and that is how I was able to go to America. (A photograph and transcript of the letter appear in a chapter below about my father's ancestors.) On the way to America, I was invited by my friend Donald Bowden to visit England.

ENGLAND

Before going to America, I was invited to stay with my friend Donald in England for six months. I met him during my acrobat performance days. Donald Bowden was a member of England's royal class. He took me every day to visit some royalty where we had tea and crumpets. Donald always introduced me to their highnesses as the "Prince of Tripoli." I listened to these royalists talk about the peasants of England and how inferior they were to the upper class.

One day a truck backed into Donald's brand-new Rolls Royce and scratched the top of the hood. I said, "Why don't you ask the man for his insurance?" Donald said, "It's okay; he's just a peasant."

On another day, he showed me Great Britain's Queen Elizabeth II on television. Donald asked me, "Isn't she beautiful?" I said, "I was a lifeguard on the Mediterranean coast have seen and been with lots of beautiful women on the beach. She is not like any of those beautiful women, not even close." Donald got very mad at me.

One time, we were invited to visit a baron who asked me, "Do you like my driveway with all the colorful pebbles on it?" I said I did. He said, "When the loose pebbles were initially laid down and when my children drove their Jaguars too fast, they spread them all over the place, so I hired peasants to come to glue the pebbles down. Don't you think that's a great idea?" Sarcastically, I replied, "Aren't you all so lucky to have peasants do beautiful things for you. We are not privileged to have peasants do beautiful things for us in Israel. The word "peasant" doesn't even exist in the Hebrew language." Everybody laughed.

Another time we were invited to the queen's palace for dinner. During a conversation, someone said, "Do you know this table is worth a million pounds?" I asked why and he said, "Because King Henry VIII wanted this table so much that he went to war, resulting in thousands of deaths just to obtain it." I added, "As a lifeguard who saves lives when I hear how many people lost theirs, I wouldn't pay a penny for this table because it is a bad omen, and it is not humane." He got furiously upset. When the party was over, everybody went outside to the lawn, where there was a bit of white wall for guests to sign their names. I signed my name in Hebrew for spite. However, in the end, I respect the queen because she is a good representative of her people.

AMERICA

After six years as a lifeguard, I decided to leave Israel for good and emigrate to America. I left my accident insurance money, my lifeguard money, and my friends to go to the land of Mason's wisdom. My father told me he would hold these funds until I needed them. Unfortunately, I never saw any of that money again. When I arrived in America, I had only one hundred dollars in my pocket.

It was challenging for me, because I could hardly speak English and didn't join a group or belong to a temple or a church Because I always do what is right and will always be a free self-thinker for a better world. I could not get a good job. I didn't assimilate quickly. It was hard for me, especially after my easy life on the beaches, because if you understand right from wrong, you will do what is right and what is right is to stay, so I took it as a challenge. And after a while, I made great new friends. We would talk about anything. People think because they are from different origins and backgrounds, they are not able to communicate. That is not true. All you must do is stop being a believer, instead search for "universal-truth" For the time. By debating in God reality of science, for mor accurate understanding of the spectrum of the magic of life; have an open, truthful mind to know right from wrong to be a humane-being, by the people, for the people!

Sticks and stones will hurt your bones, but words will never hurt you in wisdom. But if you have a stigma that creates a blockage in your brain from blind opinion, blind faith or believing what you don't know, you will not have harmony. Only by free self-thinking in harmony as humane-being.

Even though it was hard starting a new life in the USA, I never wanted to move back to Israel. I permanently moved forward. Life is a journey of challenges. In reality, I could not get a job as a lifeguard because I was not an American citizen, so I had to do something else. After arriving in New York City, I began teaching children acrobatics for three hours a day at the YMCA. I showed them the movies and before you knew it, they started bringing their mothers to class so they could watch, and it became a circus show!

At first, I had no money and had to run after the bus because I did not know how to get to the YMCA. My friend George asked why I ran. I responded, "I like running! I don't like the diesel smell on the bus. Plus, I save a dollar each way." George said, "If that's the case, why don't you run after a taxicab to get to and from the "Y"? Then you'll save ten dollars each way!"

One day I was hungry and broke. I entered an Italian restaurant and told them I would work for food. The manager said, "Okay, do some work in the kitchen." There was a big pile of dishes in the sink, so I started washing them. When I was done, the manager walked me into the dining room and placed a big plate full of food on the table: spaghetti with sausage, salad, and dessert. It was delicious! When I finished, he gave me twenty dollars. I did not think I deserved twenty dollars. That was a lot of money in those days, equal to about $100 today. This was as much as I had done at my YMCA job. I protested, "This is too much." He said, "People come to eat here. Those who cheat or don't have money run away without paying. You are the only one who offered to work, and you did an excellent job. The twenty dollars is for making me understand that there is hope for people to become humane-beings in the future."

I did not get along well with American women. In some places in the world, men mistreat women, but in America, women mistreat men. For example, before a man has sex in America, the woman tells him that it is his lucky day. I never heard that in Europe. However, I do not want to mistreat anybody, and I do not wish to be mistreated, so I wrote to three of my girlfriends in France and asked them to visit me in America. Within three weeks, they arrived and stayed with me. We decided it would be nice to travel around this great country. At the time, I was in business with a cabinet maker named Henry. I sold half of the company for travel money.

I invited two more friends from Belgium to come with us on our trip. We bought a huge car, a green convertible Oldsmobile Cutlass 88 convertible We loaded the tent and the rest of the camping equipment in the trunk and hit the road. Gas at the time was 25 cents a gallon! We started in New York and ended in Florida, staying at campgrounds along the way.

While camping in Key West, Florida, we went fishing every day. Then, in the evening, I barbecued fish, made conch chowder and bouillabaisse, and invited everybody in the camp to eat with us. They were nice and friendly and brought us wine and other alcohol. One person I met was a firefighter on vacation. He said, "I was supposed to stay here only for two weeks, but I've been here for two months! So, I'm going to stay until you guys leave because I'm having such a wonderful time!"

In his mobile home, I saw a plaque on the wall that read: "The Bible is the Word of God!" I said, "I can prove to you that the Bible is not the Word of God. I know the people who wrote the Bible. Since the Bible is made of words, they can be misinterpreted and people make mistakes, but God does not." After I said this, the fireman got mad. He grabbed me, kicked me out of his mobile home, closed the door and drove away. I had made one comment that was critical of his beliefs, and he became a monster. He could not have a conversation because he was a believer and refused to accept evidence against his beliefs, called cognitive dissonance. He had not learned the scientific art of debate-conversation in search of universal-truth reality for wisdom from, free-self thinking. So do all believers, in blind faith.

One day, a young man asked me to teach him how to spearfish. So, we went out on his motorboat with my three French (girlfriends) . We anchored near a rocky area. The women swam near the boat while the young man and I dove toward a cave where big bass fish were swimming inside. I struck the outside of the cave and shook the water with my hands to attract the fish, but it would only come out halfway and then go back inside. It frustrated us both because I could not spear him. This was not normal, and I had a feeling that something was wrong.

Perhaps the fish knew something I did not. Then I raised my head and saw a giant shark coming toward me like a torpedo; it was about twenty feet long. Even though the water was crystal clear, the killer shark was so giant I could not even see its tail moving. The shark's head was as large as an old Volkswagen. I was terrified; it was a Great White! My swimming partner has not seen it yet. I raised to make myself look more significant and pointed my small speargun at his eye. Mentally, I was telling him that I would not go out quickly. The shark approached ten feet from us and stopped. He stared me down—and finally turned to swim away. I signaled the young man to swim to the surface. Then I called out to my French female friends, "Man-eating shark! Get on the boat now!" On the way back, we saw many other sharks, including hammerheads. Once we experienced this shark migration, I decided to leave Key West. I was not going back in that water! Over the years, sharks have attacked me four times. I learned that sharks—like most animals and children—try to get away with as much as they can, but they usually don't take chances if they think they may get hurt.

The next day, we left for New Orleans and had a lot of fun. I got along great with the people there since they all spoke French. The music was hot and so were the women. When walking down Bourbon Street at night, I learned that if you threw a necklace of colorful glass or plastic beads to a willing woman, she would lift her blouse and expose her lovely breasts. America, what a country! A week later, we left and headed to Texas.

The Enemy of Knowledge Is Not Ignorance

Leon and his three French girlfriends, exploring the United States for eighteen months.

We could not find a campground there, so we set up our tent on top of a grassy knoll in a public park. The police came and said, "Hey, you guys, you can't camp here!" So, I told the three girls to open the tent's zipper and stick their legs out, can-can style. The policemen's eyes bulged out when they saw the lady's lovely legs and said: "Okay, you guys can stay, but you have to leave in the morning."

On the way to Brownsville, Texas, another French friend named Louie Nitka joined us. He helped with the driving and pulled up behind a police car, which was moving very slowly. Surprisingly, Louie bumped the police car from behind. The cop stopped and got out of the car with his gun drawn. He asked, "What do you think you're doing?" Louie explained, "In France, if a car goes very slowly, you're supposed to bump it so it will move out of the way." The policeman said, "Not in this country, you don't!" Because this country is a country of law! The police, realizing we were just young foreign tourists, let us go with just a warning.

When we arrived in Brownsville, Texas, we stayed at a motel. Together we went to the Mexican consulate to get permission to cross the border. They gave everyone permission except for me because I had an Israeli passport. The official said, "If you want to enter Mexico, you'll have to give me eight hundred dollars. If you don't make any trouble, I will give you the money back, **because the Israeli government, kidnap the criminal Eichmann.**" I said, "No way am I giving you eight hundred dollars. You don't look like you can be trusted! If I wanted to, I'd be able to get into Mexico and you would never know it." So, my friends spent some time in Mexico without me. Meanwhile, I got hired to work on a shrimp boat in Port Isabel, Texas. All the shrimpers there speak French, and they will sink your ship if you don't talk in their language. One Saturday morning, I entered my motel's lobby and saw that it was full of people. I asked the manager what was going on. He said, "Mexican girls come over the border on the weekends to make money." As I was walking around the lobby, a Mexican girl in her twenties called me over and said, "For you, exceptional, two dollars." I said, "No. I never pay for women." I walked by a little later and the same girl said, "For you, very special, for free." I said, "No, I'm okay." She followed me around and said, "For you, very special, I give you two dollars." I laughed and we became friends and she lived with me for a while.

I met a Mexican-Indian friend and told him about my plan to go to Mexico. "I'll dress up like a Mexican, grow a mustache and act as a mute around the local police—you'll talk for me. Mexican mutes don't need papers." He agreed and we traveled together. He took me to his family's place, where there was a whole tribe of Indians. I found out they did not let their girls marry unless the men were from their tribe.

I felt a pang of disappointment that I was only a Mexican disguised because the young women were beautiful.

While walking on the street one day, an older woman carrying a big bag over her head tripped and fell. I ran over to help her get up. A priest came over and thanked me. He had a French accent, so we started speaking in French. He wanted to show off the power he had over the people since everybody respected him. I knew that Mexicans were very religious, fearing their religion and their parish priests. (God-players.)

While the priest and I were walking together, we saw an older man selling one watermelon and many tomatoes. The priest picked up the watermelon but did not pay for it. I said, "How can you take fruit from this poor old man without paying?" He said, "They love to give to the church." I did not think that was right, so I said, "I don't want to associate myself with you anymore."

Some people nearby must have heard what I said to the priest and didn't like it. When I arrived at my hotel, many young toughs came up behind me and tried to beat me. I could not understand it. I defended myself, but there were too many of them. I was fortunate that my Indian friends arrived just in time to save my life. After this event, I decided to leave Mexico and head to California.

I met my French lady friends from the trip at a bus station in Phoenix, Arizona. We drove west together to the Leo Carrillo Campground in Malibu, California and set up camp. The next day was Saturday. I got up, went for a walk along the beach on the south side and made my way into a restricted area named Nicholas Beach. I saw a group of people pushing a sailboat toward the ocean. Looking at the boat, I realized the sail was too big for the size of the boat. I said, "You know you cannot sail this boat safely. It's going to tip over." They all laughed and continued to go sailing.

As soon as it passed some waves, the boat tipped over. Because I was formerly a lifeguard, I jumped in, swam toward them, and helped turn the boat upright. I said, "The only way to sail this boat is by going against the wind. Tack back and forth—just go in and out. If you go with the wind, you won't be able to come back. So, they continued to sail on successfully.

The owner of the boat, Bob Green, whose house was on the beach, saw me flip up the sailboat and rescue his friends. Among others on the beach who saw what I did were the actor/comedian Paul Lynde and Bob Hope's son. Bob Green came up to me and asked, "Where is your mother?" "In Israel," I replied. He responded, "Let's call her and tell her you're okay." He was kind and must have thought I was a teenager, but I told him I was the man who just saved his boat and everybody on it. We laughed together. He invited me into his home, where snacks and drinks were served and asked me where I was staying. I told him I was staying in a tent at the Leo Carrillo Campground. He said, "Why don't you bring your tent over here and stay with us?" I gratefully accepted his offer.

One of his friends asked if I knew how to play backgammon. I said I did, and he said, "Let's play for money. How much you got?" I said, "Three hundred dollars." He said, "Let's play for three hundred dollars, then." I said, "No, it's the only money I have." He said, "Let's play for a hundred and fifty.' I said, "Okay." I do not like to gamble, but I knew I was an excellent backgammon player. It is like taking candy from a baby and he was wealthy. We played on and on and I kept winning. Finally, I was ahead by five hundred dollars, and he was getting upset. I said, "I don't want to play anymore if you're going to get angry." He said, "Let's play double or nothing. If I win, I pay you nothing; if you win, you get a thousand bucks." I said, "Last game." He said, "Okay." So, we played, and I won a thousand dollars, which was a lot of money I could use at that time!

Later that day, the woman who went out on the sailboat with the oversized sail came limping towards us and said, "The boat is stuck in the rocks two miles south down the coast! We can't bring it back!" I reminded her that I said not to go downwind and sail against the wind, tacking back and forth. She asked me, "Leon, are you going to help us?" I said, "Yes." So, several of us headed out to Bob's sailboat for the rescue. When we got there, the sailboat was pinned in waist-deep water and banging against the rocks. After reviewing the situation, I said, "We can't carry this boat back. It's too heavy, too far away. The only way is to sail it back." They suggested I take someone with me. I said, "No. It's too much responsibility if something goes wrong. I have to do it by myself."

I sailed directly about two miles into the ocean, as far north as possible. The people on the beach couldn't see me anymore. Bob Green called his neighbors and the Coast Guard for help because he thought I would never return. I had to go far enough away from the shore to make only one tack directly toward the house on the beach. Otherwise, every time I tacked; the boat would go downwind away from the home because the sail was too big. Finally, I turned the boat around and sailed directly toward the house. Approaching the beach, I caught a wave and surf-sailed the boat back to shore. It was sunset when I arrived. There must have been two hundred people on the beach, and they were all applauding me. All the neighbors were there to see the event. Because of my heroics, I instantly made friends with Bob and all the people on that secluded beach. Among those who witnessed the rescue were such luminaries as actors Steve McQueen and

Vincent Price, Secretary of State Roy Ash, Jack Brady (who later became my very best friend) and two young men by the names of Gerard Alcon (a French Basque) and Robert Bardey (a French commentator). I first met Gerard and Robert, who were newscasters in America for the Voice of Europe. As mentioned in a previous chapter, we became close friends since we could converse together in French. Later on, we worked together as the Voice of Europe, broadcasting news from America to France.

THE SECOND GUN

On one of the darkest nights of my life, the three of us were at the Ambassador Hotel on June 5, 1968, covering a vital presidential campaign speech by Robert Kennedy, when the popular, young Senator from Massachusetts was assassinated. After his speech, Kennedy and his entourage exited the stage. We were still filming the Senator's departure through the hotel's pantry when multiple gunshots rang out. The fantastic thing is that some of our footage and subsequent interviews reveal what happened that night, including what the medical pathologist who performed the autopsy had to say. We produced a feature-length documentary together and called it *The Second Gun*, which was reviewed and written about in the *New York Times*, the *Los Angeles Times* and many other newspapers and news outlets worldwide. We distributed the film in theaters domestically and internationally to show that there was a conspiracy. Today you can watch it for free on YouTube.

About a year later, while shooting a new film on location in Utah, my good friend and associate Gerard Alcon, co-producer of *The Second Gun*, became mysteriously ill and died within a week. My theory is that he was assassinated by poisoning his food in the restaurant. I took care of him for the week he was suffering before; he died. His doctors were stumped. They could not identify the particular poison that killed him and without an antidote, they could not save his life.

Although I could not prove it, I had a powerful feeling he was killed; he ruffled so many political feathers with his controversial conspiracy film.

But, as in the past, hierarchy does not want the truth. Gerard was an American hero. He insisted Robert Barley's, and my name co-producers would not appear in the film credits because he did not want us to get hurt. A few years earlier, Gerard was also one of the first reporters to uncover J. Edgar Hoover's dirty little secrets, turning Gerard into a target. I loved and respected him and still miss him terribly.

I was invited to stay with Bob Green, who wanted to build a shopping center in Malibu. He asked if I would like to be involved and I jumped at the idea. While waiting for the architectural plans, he hired me as a lifeguard on his secluded, private beach to make sure no one drowned there. I served on that beach for about a year and kept everyone safe.

One day, Jean Buchanan, a friend of Bob, came to visit the house. When she got out of the car, her body was hunched over and folded like a pocketknife. She told me that she was going to have back surgery soon. Since I was a trained physical therapist, I asked her, "Why don't you give me a chance to fix your back? Give me two weeks and if I don't fix it, you don't have to pay me anything." Back surgery was hazardous at that time and not consistently successful—that is why I wanted to help her.

I started her therapy with stretches, gravity exercises and massages. She felt great after a week. She said her doctor wanted me to work for him and would pay me handsomely. I told her I was too sensitive around sick people to work full-time as a therapist but would always be willing to help someone in need. Also, I was about to open a big shopping center with Bob Green. We planned to build ten barns with distinctive designs from all over the world on seven and a half acres of land adjacent to the Pacific Coast Highway near Malibu. Each barn would feature different products to sell.

To enhance the appearance, we created a small pond from a flowing river through the grounds. In addition, we designed the area so customers could park their cars outside and walk joyfully into the shopping complex.

I lived on that property in a mobile home, which was right next to the Pacific Coast Highway. I worked every day with a tractor to clear the land. One day, I cut bushes with a machete when suddenly a six-foot rattlesnake jumped up and struck my face. I jumped back quickly and cut its head off with the machete in midair. That was one very close call.

As the project moved ahead, Bob Green and Jean Buchanan kept spending all their money on parties. Finally, we ran out of cash for the project and eventually, everybody started suing each other. I had to get out of there.

DESILU

I was hired by Desilu Studios, where I oversaw the forty-acre backlot. The studio produced television shows such as *I Love Lucy*, *Hogan's Heroes*, *The Andy Griffith Show*, among many others and numerous TV commercials. It also housed standing sets from films like *Gone with the Wind* and the original *King Kong*. I met many actors and animal performers there (Although some of the actors on set sometimes acted like animals). Later the studios began losing money and were eventually sold, torn down, and replaced by commercial buildings.

One Monday morning, while the studios were still operating, I arrived at the front lot where a vast commotion took place. There were police officers and detectives around with lots of onlookers gazing through the chain-link fence. I asked one of the detectives, "What happened?" He informed me that some vandals broke into the studio during the weekend and caused half a million worth of damage. He said, "We are taking fingerprints and looking for clues to catch the culprits." Then I said, "Watch me catch the culprit in five minutes." He laughed at me, but I realized this vandalism was children's work by looking at the damage.

I strolled over to the fence and observed the crowd. I noticed a child who was about ten years old, moving around nervously. He looked guilty to me because his fingers holding the fence were trembling. I walked up next to him, grabbed his hands on the fence and proclaimed, "Here is the kid who did it!" He screamed back, "It wasn't me; it was my brother who did it!" As the detective approached, I said, "See, I told you I could solve the case in five minutes." He was surprised and laughed again. Sometimes, you must think for yourself, realistically, in wisdom, creativity and not have to go through tedious knowledgeable procedures.

Often youngsters would come to the studio and ask me if they could visit. I would let them in and show them around. But I would also catch kids who would break in and damage property. So, I would take them to the Los Angeles River, on the west side of the studio and tell them, "I will let you go, but you have to run fast. If I catch you, you'll be sent to the police department." I also told them that they have to ask if they want to visit, and I would try to accommodate them. Once the children were on the sidewalk, they started running as fast as they could. I was running fast, too, but I made sure to keep a foot or two behind them for at least a mile. Those out-of-breath kids never broke in again. While working at the studio, I had an idea and told one of the managers, John Pepin, that many film fans and collectors might be interested in the historical objects, props, and costumes we had in storage. We had memorabilia from *Tarzan, King Kong, Gone with the Wind*, and other classic films. I suggested that we could charge money to let people come in and give them a tour. Our rival, Universal Studios, started opening its gates to the public about a year later and charging money for the sets.

My girlfriend Nicole at Desilu Studios

FHA FOSTER HOME PROGRAM

At one time in my life, I felt that I should take care of neglected children, although I didn't want any offspring of my own. It was not essential to have someone call me "Daddy." I found work in a program with the Federal Housing Administration in Sun Valley, California, tasked to take care of 350 foster home children. President Lyndon Johnson created 500 of these projects after the Vietnam war, that killed many fathers, because there is no wisdom in war!

Once I moved in, I realized children behaved according to Nature's law, i.e., like wild animals. The children would fight among themselves continuously in gangs. They were so violent they would even kill one another! I confronted them one day and asked, "Why don't you be nice?" They replied, "Nobody is nice to us." Some of the children added, "Our parents gave us a way to foster homes, but after a while, the foster homes didn't even want us anymore. So why should we be nice?" I said, "When you are nice, you have nice friends. It's worth it." The kids said, "We don't want to listen to grownups anymore. Some people are still childish, like dis foster home kids, and think they know everything. No matter how ignorant or fanatical religious people lack understanding, problems arise because they refuse to have scientific conversations in wisdom to create an accurate understanding of reality. Like in the Bible stories, I performed magic tricks to get their attention so they would listen and get the children involved in scientific style debate conversations.

The next day I installed a rope on the roof near two big spotlights shining on the parking lot below. After dark, I climbed on the top and used binoculars to spy on the kids. I could see them, but they couldn't see me behind the spotlights. **While checking on the kids, just like Moses, climbing up the mountain checking on is people.** I saw many things they were doing at night. On one occasion, I saw a youngster named Johnny break into a Cadillac and destroy the dashboard to steal the radio. The next day, I said to him, "Hey Johnny, last night I dreamed about you. It was not a nice dream. You probably don't want to hear it." Johnny said, "No, no, go ahead! Tell me about the dream!" I proceeded to tell him what I saw from the roof but emphasized that it was just a dream. Johnny asked me, "What if what you dreamed happened?" I said, "If this is what happened, God, the Cosmos is upset with what you have done." Johnny started laughing. He asked, "God? What is that?" I said, "God, the Energy of the Universe, is worried about the way you are living, and he wants me to help you; that is why I had this dream." Johnny said, "What? Tell me more." At that moment, I hooked him and the other children with my verbal calisthenics, encouraging them to say what they feel but listen to others too in a civil conversation. That's how you learn from other people. They were happy when I told them, "Today, I will fix the maintenance room and install a pool table. You and your friends can help and debate for a more accurate understanding of God universal truth, by accepting only the alliance between God and you, require only **7 Laws. 1. 'I am your God, don't create other gods before me, not to worship leaders and preachers (God Players).** 2. don't compete for an ego, instead challenge yourself to be better today than yesterday. 3. free self-think in a debate learn from each other to search for the universal truth to unite all life, for a safer and a more creative world, 4. Don't lie. 5. Don't cheat. 6. Don't hurt others, unless defending yourself, 7. Debate to create a mor accurate understanding, of the magic of God reality to be a free self-thinker and become humane-being, from understanding God reality of science, to create wisdom, that will better yourself and the world!

 The kids enjoyed coming to the new game room. They began trusting me and wanted to know more about what I had to say. I explained by debating. I am here to help you free self-think, so you can understand mor accurately right from wrong in the magic of life reality, and **I will not preach**." I debated with them the book of the Masons. I explained, "The Energy of the Universe is the biggest builder. It built the stars, the sun, the moon, and the Earth to live on a planet with a "Goldilocks" atmosphere, not too hot and not too cold. All people are children of God. Those who work the hardest to create a better world for all life are godlier than those who do not. The Energy of the Universe gave your life, so use it. Being alive is a better gift than anything anybody ever gave you or ever will give you. Do not blame your parents or anybody else for your disappointments. When you work hard, you make your body and mind more robust and healthier, and you learn new things. When you use your mind and free self-think, you become more thoughtful. When you work hard as you get older, you become wiser, healthier and happier. So don't waste your time complaining. Challenge your life to overcome life's obstacles. You have nothing to lose. Everybody eventually dies anyway. If you want to understand God, free self-think and in a scientific debate, find the wisdom to understand in your mind God in reality, do what's right and enjoy the fleeting time you have on Earth because life is precious and shorter than you think. When you overcome the most significant challenges, it becomes easier to handle new ones. Everyone can learn and evolve for the better, make the right choices and improve the world for all lives. I know I tricked the kids, but I did it because I wanted to help them to learn from a scientific debate in conversations of reality to ask questions of themselves and each other. Within three months after I started helping the foster children move forward in life, the youngsters got jobs, started going to school and were not in gangs.

One day, eight police cars drove up to the project and one officer asked, "Who is Leon? We want to talk to him." I answered, "That's me; what is this all about?" I was apprehensive that with all these policemen here, something terrible must have happened. So, I invited them in, and they said, "Three months ago, these kids used to be in trouble all the time, but now they're not. They've changed. They're such nice kids. How did you do it?" I told them, "It was a life magic trick!" We all had a good laugh.

A year later, an inspector from Washington, D.C., came to visit and said to me, "You know, out of the five hundred foster homes project we examined—this is the only one that worked successfully. I want to promote you in charge of overseeing all our projects." "Thanks, but no thanks," I replied. I am a young man. I'd rather go surfing and have fun on the beach because I love to enjoy life. I only wanted to help as a contribution to the kids. To prove that free self-thinking in a scientific method of debating creates a more accurate understanding of God reality, the reality is not an illusion. And accurate science always works. It was not their fault they were foster children; it was society's fault because this society is based on competing for the hierarchy that created freedom of illusion of knowledge (religion) in blind fate, to follows a hierarchy with knowledge but no wisdom, understanding and competing power over others, by giving people, shelter, food, protection, , to follow as **sheep in the herd of grazers, that becomes common belief in blind faith, to protect hierarchy privileges.** It is time to change for the better, because people are not sheep, and can become brilliant humane-being, bi free self-thinking in search of universal-truth by debating in God reality of science, for a democratic utopian life! .

Thirty years later, one of my former foster children from the project called and asked if I was Leon from the Sun Valley Project. I said yes. He said, "You don't remember me, but I used to be one of the kids there. My name is Johnny and I want to visit you." I gave him directions and after arriving at my house, he presented me with a gift: two beautiful replica swords of the Knights Templar. Of creativity, and wisdom. He said, "You taught me the wisdom of the Masons, which helped me very much and now I am a successful real estate broker. To show you my gratitude, I needed to find you and give you this gift. If you ever need any money or help of any kind, call me." I said, "The swords you gave me make me very proud of you. But the best gift of all is that you turned out so well. Keep on free self-thinking in wisdom to create a better world, for all lives."

The next photo is of copies of the original swords of the Templars. The King of France captured the two Templar representatives of the Masons on behalf of the Roman Catholic Pope, who judged them for being liars, therefore they are heretics, and condemned them to be burned alive at the stake. The King and the Pope are examples of all-powerful hierarchies that commit horrendous crimes. Look at the Spanish Inquisition, Nazi war crimes against life, China's re-education camps, Russian civil repression, and their prison gulags in Siberia. The Mason movement implies **you are what you do, not what you believe you are!** Because all the land was conquered by extremes violence, however, today what is acceptable as a universal-truth wisdom! If you are creating a better world, you deserve land and the resources you need, to make more of a better world for all lives! For example: **Jack Brady had to move, to create a public beach. Harold Cremer had to move to build a highway. Hate and wars are not the answer.** It is essential to create fairytales to help children follow the right path towards becoming humane grownups. But it is counterproductive to develop illusory religious and political propaganda fairytales for adults because adults need *accurate factual truth* for the scientific debate conversations necessary to develop new knowledge, because people create all great sevelazation, and greed from hierarchy destroy all sevelazation!

Some people tell me that wars are necessary to lower overpopulation. My **response is,** "Why don't you kill 2 birds with 1 stone. You can start, by killing yourself. This way, (1) you will lower overpopulation, (2) you will get read of inhumane people on this beautiful planet!"

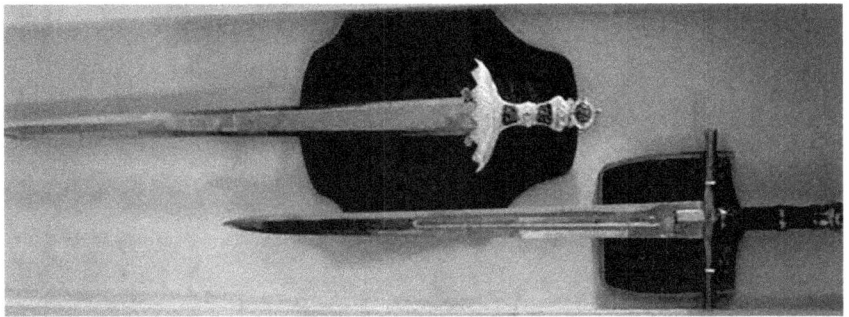

Replica Swords of the Knights Templar

THE CATHOLIC CHURCH

When I finished working for the FHA program, my friend Jack Brady got me a new job at Our Lady of Malibu Catholic Church. I lived in the back of the church as a maintenance man and a janitor. I cleaned and waxed the classroom floors once a week. I told my supplier to get me a cleaner that doesn't attack the wax when mixed. Later I put them in a bottle to spray the floor. Then I was able to buff the floor and clean and polishing at the same time. The supplier observed what I did; then, later, using my formula, he started making and selling the product commercially and called it "Spic and Span." He used my wisdom to make the world a cleaner, and shinier place faster.

Monsignor Sheridan, the man in charge of the Our Lady of Malibu diocese, came up to me one day and said, "I will be attending a television conference of leaders from all religions. The attendees are supposed to tell what contributions they have made to society. Can you help me figure out what I should say?" I said, "I'll teach you a Hebrew prayer: "Thank God that we have arrived at this moment where we can communicate through conversations." I taught him how to pronounce it correctly in Hebrew. We practiced for a few days while he learned the prayer in perfect Hebrew.

I asked him to try to be the last one to appear on the show. I watched on television as the religious leaders got up one by one. and talked about how great they were by their opinion propaganda to increase their importance and protect their privileges. The last speaker was Monsignor. He stood up and said the prayer in perfect Hebrew. Everybody in the audience and the panel gave him a standing ovation because most understood Hebrew and its message. Monsignor John Sheridan was thrilled.

One day, Monsignor's brother came to visit from Africa. He was a missionary who was dying from cancer. He asked me many questions about life, and we became friends. After he died, Monsignor showed me a letter from his brother that he had written before he died. The note read, "Please take care of Leon because he is a saint on Earth." Ever since then, Monsignor called me Leon the Saint.

After his brother died, Monsignor asked me, "Leon, do you think I will live long?" I said, "You hold no hatred towards anyone and love life. There is no reason why you should not live a very long life. Maybe you'll live for 120 years like Moses." After turning 80, Monsignor was asked: "How come you live so long and still look so good?" He replied, "Saint Leon blessed me." Monsignor went on to live until he was 95 years old. Sadly, he died in a car accident in 2010. I'm sure he would have lived to 120 had he not been killed in a car accident.

One night I asked him, "Why are you a Monsignor? I know you are not strictly religious." He said, "I'm Irish. The nicest thing a catholic boy could do for his mother is to become a priest. So, my brothers and I are all priests. Now I have an open mind and I realize I'm helping a lot of people; that's why I'm still a priest."

On a hot afternoon, I worked on the sprinkler system in the church's back when Monsignor showed up with a federal Senator. He said, "Saint Leon, I want you to meet Senator John." The Senator asked Monsignor, "Why do you call him Saint Leon and not me, Saint John?" Just as he responded, a black bird crashed on the back of the church window and fell unconscious. The bird was probably dead. Monsignor said, "Watch Leon the Saint." I felt I had to do something special since Monsignor expected a miracle from me. So, I carried the bird to the church's back room, where there was a vodka bottle in a drawer for the priests. I poured a small amount into a small glass and stuck the nose of the bird in the vodka. Sure enough, the bird woke up. I took it outside, released it and it flew away. Monsignor said, "You see, that's why Leon is a Saint, and you are just a Senator!"

When you memorize, knowledge you can become the president of the country, however, when you free self-think, in God reality you will create a better life, and that's what all Saints and (humane-beings) do.

John Sheridan

In Loving Memory
Monsignor John V. Sheridan
1915 - 2010

During the big fire in Malibu, a giant marble statue of Jesus on a hill toppled over. Since the congregation had planted lots of flowers and shrubbery around the statue, they refused to use a crane to lift the statue because that massive piece of machinery would destroy the landscaping. So, Monsignor asked if I could find a way to return the statue of Jesus to its place. I replied, "I'll see what I can do."

The marble statue weighed a ton! It was also very slippery, so I asked the kids to help me gather up all the volleyball nets they had. Then I asked them to dig under the statue and wrap the straps around the marble of Jesus very tightly. After mass, I requested Monsignor to ask some male church members to come and help. Monsignor sent approximately twenty men up the hill. They all grabbed the nets, and we lifted the statue onto its stand. As we came down the hill, Monsignor said, "You see, no one else could raise Jesus. It had to take an Israelite to raise Our Lord and Savior."

I spent a lot of time with Monsignor and Jack Brady. We had many debate conversations about the reality of life. Finally, Monsignor encouraged me to write this book. He took a framed picture off the wall, gave it to me and said, "After you finish writing your book, you are going to need a friend to betray you for money from the hierarchy leader. That will make people furious, and they will want to know what you have to say in your book."

The biggest thing that happened to Jesus is that he was betrayed for Roman money, which upset his followers terribly. Some people treated Roman money as God. This made free self-thinkers mad because they understood that God is not money. They wanted to know what Jesus was saying about his friend Judas, one of his closest disciples, who betrayed him for a Roman bribe. Monsignor Sheridan explained that if Jesus hadn't been betrayed, he would not be the famous religious icon worshiped today as the son of God. Without such a betrayal, Jesus might have been forgotten, just like the thousands of other, humane-being who were crucified by cruel hierarchy.

Jesus grew up to be a free self-thinker in wisdom. His upbringing was in Universal Truth, not religion or beliefs. He fought the religious hierarchy of his time, by kicking the money bucket of hierarchy! It caused him pain to see evil people enslaving, torturing, and killing humane-beings for corrupt leaders' power and comfort. It reduced people into blind followers of authority and to be part of a collective.

Jesus did not want to live in a world without love of life. Love is humanist a God's universal truth. That was Jesus's plan to make the world a better place. Therefore, he lived amongst as many other free self-thinkers as possible, but they are often not remembered. As we know, Jesus was betrayed for Roman money by a friend! It is happening now, by leaders all over the world who you think are your friends! It is bribery and it is the worst crime because it makes all crimes committed by the powerful forgivable. It is corruption and it creates a jungle out there (Nature's Law). Free self-thinkers, moral humane-beings, have been fighting injustice forever. Corruption and deception are not ethical or humane; they distort your healthy mind, country, and the world because God is not money! God is in the search of universal-truth understanding the reality of science!

All these great humane-beings from the past are not make-believe fairytales. What matters is the meaning of their message; wisdom changes people into moral humane-beings. They became wise because they understood the magic of life, from the importance of an accurate understanding of reality. Thanks to their challenging work, we have a better world today. They did it without bribes, believing in religion or believing in tradition or believing that there is nothing out there. They were not leaders of hierarchy, but they were all free self-thinking representatives of life! They often had to fight against the corrupt leaders of their time. Many would die for their freedom of thought of reality.

I have confronted many different religious people who are certain about what they don't know in their life. To 'believe' in something means you 'don't know something.' You may believe in Heaven, but you don't know if it exists or not and if it does, where is it? In science and mathematics, you see the sky is blue, the sun is hot, ice is cold and two plus two equals four. These are not beliefs. These are provable and repeatable facts. But believers act as though they are sure of what they don't know and often try to impose their beliefs and opinions on others. They fight wars to kill or be killed for beliefs, they all are stupidly childish, from illusions of knowledge.

Beliefs are not facts, science, or truth. So, all I have to do is exaggerate the silliness of these artificial religious rules and beliefs and they become funny. But be careful what you say to some people. You must first make sure they are not fanatically aggressive about the subject, or you might get hurt.

Religious leaders, politicians and dictators have no right to tell us what to think or behave. We must all think for ourselves about what is right or wrong and what path to take in life, not what some "leader" or institution tells us. Otherwise, we shall continue to endure hatred, jealousy and conflict worldwide based on religious precepts, racial prejudice, or political hatred by opinionated propaganda. To perpetrate such atrocities is not wisdom. It is not correct; it is not humane, and it is not a Universal Truth for the time.

Monsignor was fascinated with my life and told my story to a writer who asked if he could interview me and I did, later he asked if he could write about my life as an article in *People* magazine. I was not interested; to me, it was nothing but ego. Years later, I saw the movie *Forrest Gump* and said, "This is like my life story!" The motion picture features some similarities in our lives, such as overcoming crippling injuries in my youth, working on a shrimp boat in the Gulf of Mexico, saving lives and traveling to many countries. Other than that, our stories diverge with different adventures than in the film. I later found out the writer who wanted to put my story in *People* magazine also wrote the movie, *Forrest Gump*.

JACK BRADY

I knew Jack Brady for about thirty-five years. He was my best friend. I worked with him initially in films as a stuntman and an underwater cameraman. One of the stunts I performed was a TV commercial for Timex watches, which ultimately became the longest-running commercial in television history, viewed for over 25 years.

For the commercial, I drove a boat called Espadon, through the waves and flew onto the beach while the watch attached low on the speedboat's bow "took a licking and kept on ticking," as John Cameron Swayze narrated.

The Enemy of Knowledge Is Not Ignorance

While working on the commercial, I met a young man, his wife and two kids. He drove the fastest boat in the world—Miss Budweiser—hitting 225 mph on top of the water.

I sat and had drinks with him every day while doing the Timex commercial. I said to him, "I like to challenge life and have been doing crazy things ever since I was a child. However, what you are doing is suicide; you are going to kill yourself! Life is very precious, don't waste it." He said, "Oh no, I know what I'm doing." When people are going that fast, they have no control and don't know what they are doing. Three months later, I saw him on the news. The boat flipped over and crashed. He was killed immediately. I knew him personally and felt very bad because I could not persuade him by my wisdom to take another path for himself and his family.

I always enjoyed teaching kids how to be a lifeguard, especially Jack Brady's children. They asked me once, "Why is it so important to be a lifeguard?" I said, "Once a lifeguard, always a lifeguard." Today, Mike Brady, Jack's second-oldest, is a lifeguard and a stuntman for television's popular *Baywatch* show and earned a Best Stuntman of the Year award for this work in the movie *A Perfect Storm*. I am very proud of him. Another brother, Kevin Brady, is also a lifeguard and a Park Ranger. The third brother, Johnny, lives in Hawaii, working at the beach. Now, that's life!

I watched *Baywatch* on TV one night when one of the lifeguards in the show rescued an older man who had attempted to save someone else. They asked, "Why did you go out there, old man?" He said, "Once a lifeguard, always a lifeguard." I knew Mike Brady had something to do with that phrase in the show.

One day, Jack Brady wanted to learn how to dive and spearfish. So, we went to Santa Monica and bought all the equipment required. Later that week, we went diving in the Pacific Ocean. I tied a rope to some sturdy kelp near the surface so the boat would not get loose; this was routine practice. Jack held onto the spear gun as we swam down together. But the water was so murky that we had to get out. As I looked up, I faintly saw a clearing in the kelp field, so we swam to the surface and exited the water.

Unfortunately, due to the underwater current, we ended up on the other side of the kelp field from where the boat was. I told Jack it would be dangerous to go underwater again because it was too dark below; we might get tangled in kelp, stuck underwater, and run out of oxygen.

Therefore, it was a better idea to swim 100 yards north to where there was a clearing, so we could cross to the other side of the kelp field and come back to the boat. Jack agreed and we started swimming. After about 50 yards, Jack said he was getting tired. We were swimming against the wind and rough water. I told him to hold onto my shoulders as I kept on swimming. The afternoon north wind picked up and created wavelets crashing on us. One good-sized wave came down and Jack pushed me under the water to breathe with his head above the wave. I was surprised and swallowed a big gulp of seawater and could not breathe. I was coughing when more and more waves splashed down on us. I thought I was going to drown. I raised my right hand in the air and said mentally, "God! Please help me! I am not going to let my friend drown. I am not going to push him away to save my life." We were both desperate, exhausted, and succumbing to the cold. Then a crazy thing happened. As I ferociously moved my arms to stay above water, my hand hit a solid object. I turned around and saw our boat only two inches from me. Even today, I don't understand how a boat could disconnect from the kelp, move against the wind for about 50 yards toward us and end up so close. It was impossible. When I felt the boat on my right side, I hollered to Jack, "Look! Here's the boat! Climb aboard!" Jack exclaimed, "Leon, you're a magician! How did you get the boat here?" I said, "You're the saint. You made it happen. Not me. I had nothing to do with it! I thought we were going to drown." To this day, I still wonder how our little boat came to us in the opposite direction of the wind and current. I will never say it is a miracle because I am a free self-thinker searching for new wisdom! I just accept that there are things I do not understand yet.

Steve McQueen   Vincent Price   Roy Ach   Paul Lynde
These celebrities lived on Nicolas Beach Road

The Enemy of Knowledge Is Not Ignorance

BUZZ ALDRIN

Astronaut Buzz Aldrin and Leon Halfon.

Buzz Aldrin is a scientist-astronaut, a space traveler, the second man who walked on the moon. I can tell you from personal experience that Buzz Aldrin and many other scientists I have met were very gentle, free self-thinker, humane-being!

Leon D. Halfon

MY FATHER, MERO
WEARING A FRENCH POLICE HAT

My father, Mero

My father built furniture carved from wood and marble, utilizing a six-foot-tall diesel motor since there was no electricity on Djerba's island. The engine mounted a spinning pipe to the back of the wall. On the tube, three leather belts could be connected to three different machines. A person could connect one leather belt to the specific machine they needed to use. The motor had to be started by cranking a lever.

When I was a little kid, my job was to empty the sawdust in the shop and put it into burlap bags, sold for agricultural use because the island had no soil. The whole island was like one big beach.

When I was only five years old, while I was underneath the saw machine to take and empty the sawdust bin, seven religious Muslim thugs came in with knives on their belts. They were threatening my father about wanting money-bribe or something else of value for the Muslim religion. My father refused. I stayed hidden in the cage under the wood cutting machine. My father did not know I was in the shop.

One of the thugs started shaking the diesel engine that was bolted onto a concrete block. It looked like they were going to destroy the place. My father had been carving a marble piece with a massive hammer. He threw the hammer at the marauder, who was shaking the motor. The hammer struck his head, dropping him to the floor. His head fell ten inches from where I was hiding. I saw his eyes trembling and his head bleeding profusely. The blood poured under the machine, soaking the sawdust. I could feel the warm oozing liquid on my knees. His open eyes fluttered as I watched him stiffen and die. My father almost started an all-out brawl, but fortunately, the French police showed up and the Muslim thugs disappeared. The police hauled the dead body away and nobody went to court.

I recall another time when some other fanatic religious thugs were having a protest right in front of my house. They were demanding that everybody who was not Muslim should leave the country. I was on the balcony of the second floor at home and witnessed everything.

My father and his friends walked toward the house as they heard the violent men screaming. My father went toward the wall and pointed at the leader who was preaching loudly and said to him in Arabic, "Hey, you, tough guy! You have a knife. I do not. So why don't you come and kill me or are you afraid?" The thug came running, and screaming, with his knife in the air to stab my father. My dad jumped aside quickly, grabbed him by the shoulder and ran his head into the wall. He died instantly.

Another furious protester ran toward my father and pulled out the knife from his belt when my dad rushed toward him. He grabbed and twisted the assailant's arm, which forced him to stab himself in the stomach.

These were the three times I saw my father kill someone, but I am pretty sure there were others. My father killed these men because he did not want to be told how to live his life. He knew that these fanatics felt that they had the right to control his life because of their religious beliefs from power as a majority, gang. My father needed to defend himself and his family. My father was a free self-thinker powerful man with true grit. The French police liked him very much and they told me so.

When I was five, we lived in a building on the second floor, which had tunnel stairs made of concrete. I'll never forget when a group of fanatics attacked our house in the middle of the night to kill my whole family. They were screaming and brandishing their guns. My father told us to hide, so the intruders could not find us. I was scared for my life but was also curious and wanted to watch. I could hear the marauders climbing the stairs. Then suddenly, my mother opened the door. My father stepped forward with a bucket of gasoline and poured it into the stairway tunnel dousing the attacking men. Next, he lit a match and threw it at the thugs. The entire stairway burst into flames. The fanatics in the concrete stairway burst on fire and ran away screaming. My father said violent people are animals; they are afraid of fire, and they are not human-beings in wisdom. **This is another example that shows that religion, and tradition, destroy the utopian democracy on the peaceful island of Djerba!**

Four hundred years ago, my dad's great-grandfather was a sailor who became captain of an English warship. He loved adventure and fought against the Spanish Armada. In one of these battles, he captured a Spanish ship sailing from America to Spain with its cargo hold filled with gold. Instead of returning to England with the booty, he and his crew decided to sail to Tripoli and became pirates.

He and his men knew that if they sailed to England, they would have to give up the gold in exchange for a hearty thanks and a few medals. Having risked their lives, they did not think that was a fair reward for delivering a Spanish ship full of gold and other treasures; they voted, and decided to keep the gold and thus became full-fledged pirates based in Tripoli because he disapproved of world hierarchy., because they are not by the people, for the people! Everybody nicknamed my great-grandfather "Dula," which means "man in charge," because he became the Tripoli warlord. He loved serious fighting, and his preferred method was kicking his opponents' legs, shins, or groins. Part of his training included hitting complex objects on his legs to toughen them. He trained his children this way and my father trained me. It is a very effective way to defend yourself.

Dula and his men decided to protect and help financially, with their gold, the United States, because he disapproved of world hierarchy. They served under George Washington and American commanders during the Revolutionary War. Because of his service. The document shown below is over eighty years old and it talks about another document over two hundred years old. It says Doula's family is protected under the aegis of the United States flag. A transcript follows.

The first treaty of peace and friendship was between the United States and Tripoli that was approved by George Washington explicitly stated: "The government of the United States is not in any sense founded on the Christian religion…" This treaty was negotiated by the American diplomat Joel Barlow during the administration of George Washington. Washington read it and approved it, although it was not ratified by the senate until John Adams had become president. Free self-think to understand why we are approving of world hierarchy and religion today?

U. S. Consulate

This is to certify that Nassim Halfon, son of Maher Halfon, late broker to the United States Consulate at Tripoli of Barbary and grandson of Aron Halfon, the previous broker of the same, came this day to the Consulate and declared under oath that for the last eighty (80) years, his family was under the protection of the United States flag; that every member of it who, during that lapse of time, was born, brought up, married or died, was considered as being an American protégé and that he, having never done anything contrary to that political status, claimed to be entitled to the continuance of that protection. This document was delivered to him to certify that the United States protection was duly continued to him.

Given under my hand and the Consulate's seal, February 1876, the 100th year of the United States of America's Independence.

Signed

U. S. Consulate

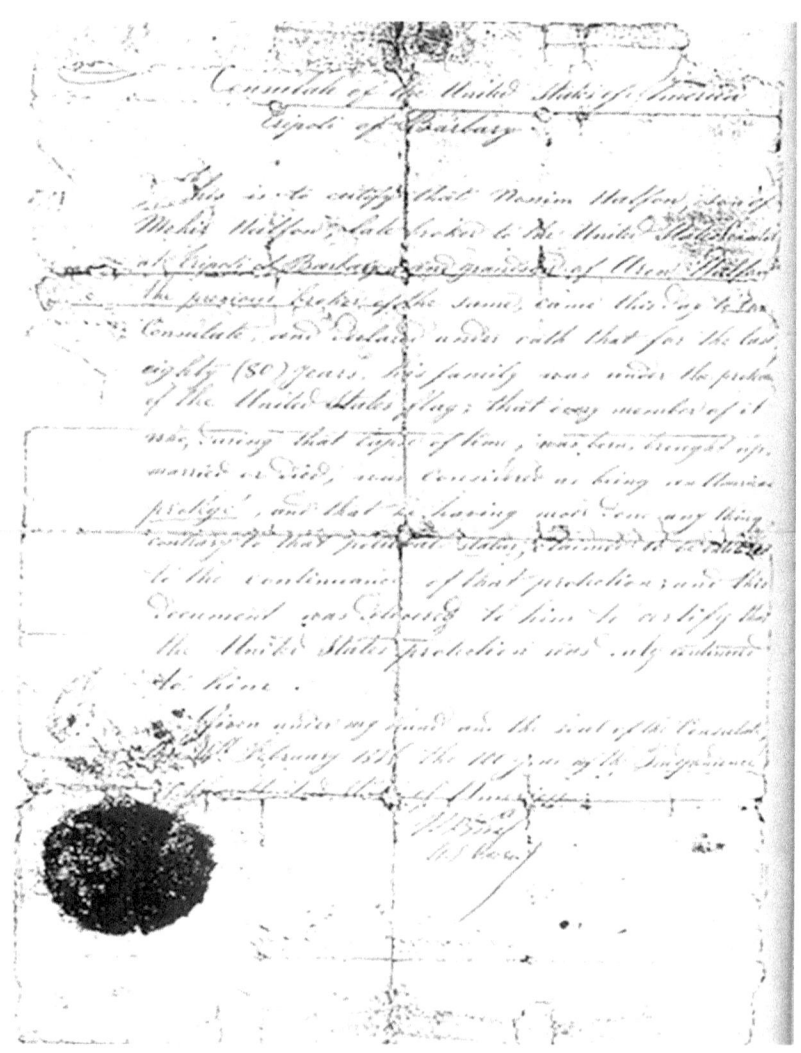

Consulate of the United States of America Tripoli of Barbary

My father told me, and his father said to him that Dula buried a chest of gold in the middle of Tripoli harbor for future generations, but I am not going there because it is full of religious gangs and too dangerous.

My father's grandfather was named Abe Halfon-Dula. He owned his ship and sailed across the Mediterranean Sea to transport carob beans, a fruit crop used as money. A strong storm sank the ship one day and Abe ended up sitting in a large wooden food bowl. In those days, the mariners used a four-foot diameter food bowl to prepare food during their journey. The main meal consisted of a mixture of barley flour, oat flour, almonds, walnuts, dates, olive oil and brown sugar. To this day, I prepare and eat it myself; I call it pirate food. Abe floated for eight days in the food bowl and landed at an Egyptian harbor on the Nile River. Two free self-thinking humane-beings rescued him. They gave him a hot bath and food and sent him on his way. Abe worked as a repairperson and eventually made it back to Tripoli.

I recall a story about my father's great grandfather. He was a professional brawler, and his name was Meir Halfon-Dula. In the old days in Tripoli, fighters would participate in tournaments once a year without weapons. The winner made enough money to live comfortably for a year; but some fighters died, and others were seriously injured. When Tripoli became an Italian colony, fighting for prize money was forbidden. Meir Halfon-Dula's new job was to transport money for business transactions. People knew that he carried money and one night when he went to sleep, he was murdered for the money.

Listening to these stories and observing my dad made me want to prove myself. We kept a big black rooster in the workshop's backyard. He made lots of noise and nobody could catch him. My father offered 100 francs to anybody who could catch the rooster. The rooster was three feet tall. I was six years old, and I was going for it to prove myself.

I went to a corner of a deserted building in the backyard where it was shady; I crouched in the corner and waited for the rooster. Sure enough, the big bird approached two feet from me and started scratching, dancing, and challenging me to a fight. He had sharp spurs on his feet, and I watched them closely. I crouched down to make myself small, so the rooster felt he could attack me. As soon he was close enough, I jumped, grabbed his feet, and started screaming for help. The rooster pecked at my hands. By the time help arrived, I was bleeding seriously, but I would not let go.

My father was proud of me, and he said I was a real Halfon-Dula.

My father was a powerful man, but he got sick at seventy-five from a heart condition. When he was young, it was a tradition to eat sweet, barbecued lamb fat. Now we know that is bad for the heart, so we no longer do it. It does not matter if it's tradition, beliefs or wrong or harmful opinions; it is terrible for you and the world at this stage of human evolution. So please, free self-think, and understand not to do it!

I watched TV at my home in Los Angeles one night when I saw this older man who was 110 years old. When they asked him how he lived so long and still looked so good, he replied, "My wife gave me a tough time and was no longer my partner, so I got rid of her. I also got rid of all the people who were a nuisance in my life. I only keep nice, moral, humane-beings around. That is why I have lived so long." This is wisdom. It is not necessary to fight over anything or to compete. When people who are mean to others are bullied, it is not humane, and it is unnecessary.

If we all decide not to follow or associate with people who are not humane and choose to hang out with only loving and caring people, we will live long and meaningful lives. When you are a free self-thinker in wisdom, you can do just that, so do not let people who are not humane into your life ore this country or any other!

MY BROTHER, YEHUDA

Yehuda was a paratrooper in the Israeli Army. During 1967, in the Arab-Israeli conflict known as the Six-Day War, he and his platoon parachuted into the Sinai Desert. The soldiers eventually began to run out of food and water and had to wait to be rescued. Meanwhile, twenty Muslim combatants arrived with their hands in the air. They surrendered because they had no food or water as well. The Muslims knew that if they surrendered, the Israelis were obligated to share their food and water. However, the Israeli captain told my brother, "We don't have enough provisions for ourselves. We will starve if we have to give some of our water and rations to these Muslims." He ordered my brother to send them away and if they did not go, shoot them.

My brother refused to obey his superior officer's command, infuriating the captain, who was about to discipline him on the spot for ignoring a direct order. In the end, they and the Muslims were rescued by the Israeli Army, and nobody died. Afterward, my brother asked the captain, "Don't you feel better now that you didn't have to kill those enemy soldiers or send them away to die?" This story's moral is that you are also guilty if you obey inhumane orders—no excuses. That is why it is essential to free self-think to do what is right! When people believe in sin, it incorporates unnecessary factors into their choices. When people rely on religion (god-players) for forgiveness, they lose their connection to humanity and God. Do not let anyone tell you what to think. Analyze the situation, consider all relevant information, and make what you think is the right choice. Free self-thinking in wisdom is the only way to have the confidence to become a human-being.

MY MOTHER, RACHEL

When my father died, all eight remaining children moved out independently and my mother rented a small apartment for herself. One day while she was out, a burglar broke in and stole her valuables. The culprit was caught, and my mother went to the police station to press charges. When she got there, she asked to see the prisoner.

When they brought him out, she noticed he was an Israelite. My mother told him, "You must have had a terrible experience to go the wrong way and become a thief! Don't you realize you are an Israelite and Israelite people are free self-thinker in reality to be moral and humane—not criminals! It's written in the constitution, of people and God 10, commandment; you are supposed to do better." She gave him a hundred dollars and said, "Straighten out your life." Then she walked out without pressing charges.

My mother and father with six children.

PART SIX

Inventions

All ideas are in the realm of wisdom by asking yourself questions and participating in scientific debate conversations. By searching in your mind to find, from accurate understanding of reality, you will get the confidants by free self-thinking, some great idea, for a better world.

The following inventions are for people who can use these ideas to make their lives better. Please contact me if you are interested in understanding more about any of these ideas.

SOLAR WATER DISTILLATION SYSTEM FROM HUMIDITY

The first invention I would like to share is a distillation system. It takes water from the atmosphere and distills drinking water using only solar energy. Build a black box, 4 ft. By 8 ft. by 4 inches deep and insulate it. Make a trough all around on top, sloping glass to the drain at about 20^0. Fill the box with sodium and leave it out at night. The container should be open some so that air can come in. The sodium absorbs the air's humidity to create a small pond about 1" inch deep. During the day, you close the box hermetically so that no air can come in or out. On a regular sunny day, it will get 225 degrees in the box. The water then evaporates, hits the glass and slides into the trough where it's collected outside. It will evaporate about $1/8^{th}$ inch. You can expect to accumulate about 2 gallons of water every day from each distillation unit built.

If you put 50 units on one roof, you will collect about 100-150 gallons of water. That should supply enough water for survival. You could probably produce more water in the desert where there are hotter temperatures.

THE BEST SPRINKLER SYSTEM

Next invention: a new sprinkler system. Take a faucet that has a rubber gasket that shuts off by spinning the handle. Install a solid Teflon cylinder with the rubber gasket. When you open it, it will open the valve and when you shut it, it will shut the valve. After replacing it, you put the whole thing in the ground. When the soil is dry, the Teflon cylinder shrinks, and it opens the valve and lets the water out. When the ground is wet, the Teflon cylinder expands and shuts off the water. You can adjust how much humidity you need by turning and spinning the valve open or closed. In this way, you get the right amount of moisture in the ground all the time without mechanical equipment, like timers, which often break.

With these two ideas, you could build a house in a factory and move it to the middle of the desert to have water, electricity, and food to sustain yourself. Electricity could come through solar power and windmills.

REMOTE CONTROL DRONE

Next invention: a remote-controlled drone flying saucer for reconnaissance or advertising. Take two oval Mylar pieces, four feet wide by six feet long and glue them together with a valve. Put a circular aluminum tube, mount the Mylar an oval aluminum tube and connect one tube underneath in an oval. Now use the tube as a gasoline container. Underneath connects a remote-control propeller engine with a small camera. Fill the Mylar with helium. It will take the shape of a flying saucer and it should lift about six pounds. It will be a little bit lighter than the air. The circular tubing around the drone will retain the Mylar in the shape of a flying saucer. With the remote control, you can guide it for surveillance. If somebody shoots it down, it will descend like a parachute and not crash. You can use it to advertise by having it carry flags or logos on it. You can also use it to freak people out if you paint it like an alien spacecraft!

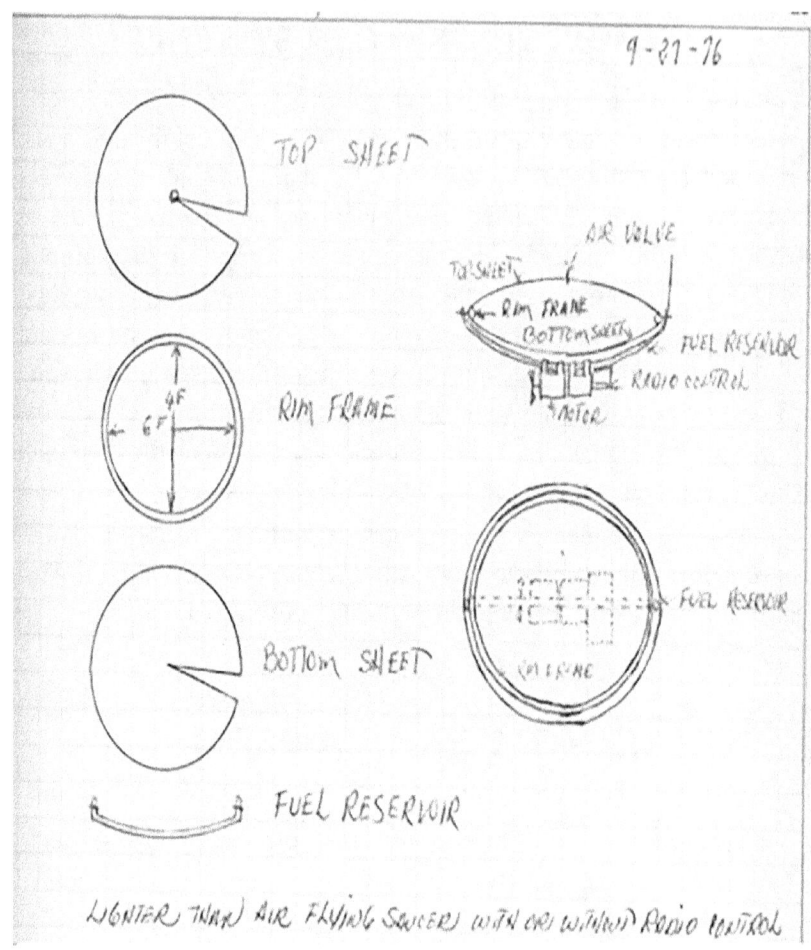

Drone Flying Saucer

INEXPENSIVE SOLAR WATER HEATER

This heats the water that comes in one direction, goes through the box and comes out on the other side. As a result, the water will be hot. This is inexpensive and simple; it works better than other solar water heaters because the box does not get hot, but the black tube warms to create heated water.

The Enemy of Knowledge Is Not Ignorance

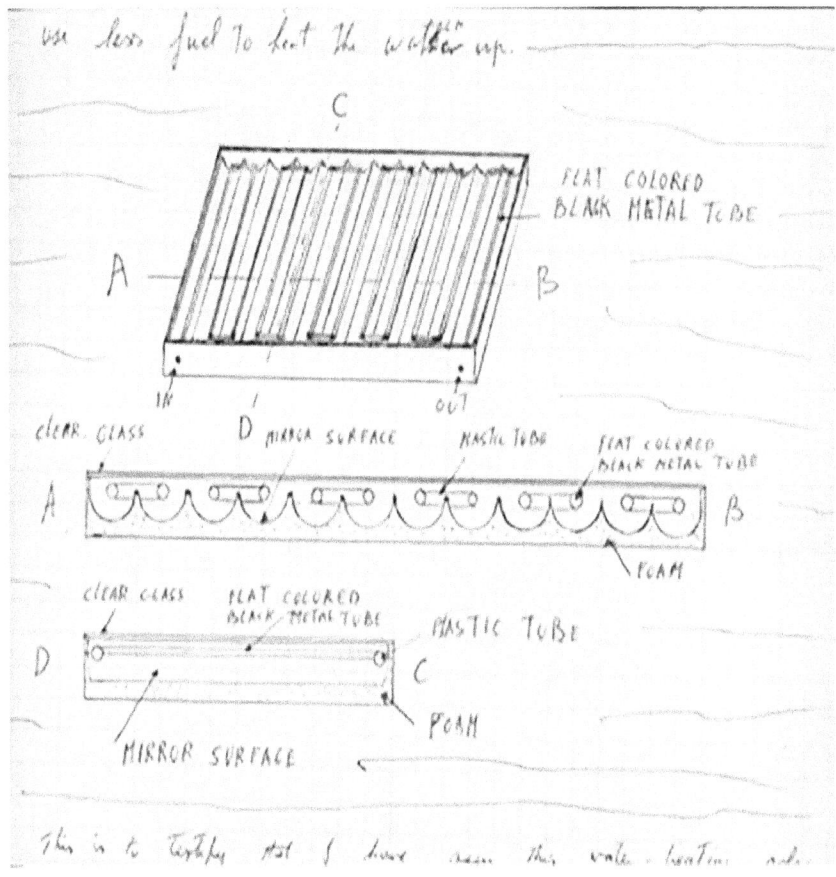

An inexpensive solar water heater. Build a mold that is 4 inches thick by 4 feet wide and 8 feet long. On the inside, every 3 inches, make a parabolic shape along with the box, which you fill up with foam. Glue mirrored plastic or aluminum on the top, which gives the inside a mirrored effect. Put a wooden frame around it and drill holes in the wood in the middle of each parabola shape. Install black plastic tubing or brass tubing (paint it with flat black paint) in all the parabola shapes and connect it outside. Put a piece of glass on top. When the sun shines on top of the unit, it will reflect the box's heat into the black tube.

PRODUCING ELECTRICITY WITH NATURE

You can use old ships past their prime—like the Queen Mary in Long Beach, California—and have them float to sea, not too close and not too far from the beaches. These ships weigh over a million tons. One ship going up and down by the swells in the sea will produce enough energy for a whole city. Water pumps will operate a turbine that creates electricity. It will also make the beach calmer and safer for swimmers!

ETHANOL AT FIVE CENTS A GALLON

Companies like Sunkist are willing to deliver ten truckloads of orange pulp a day for free. Put a massive, black container tank in an open space on top of a hill and dump the orange pulp into the tank. The sun's heat on the black tank ferments the pulp and produces ethanol using gravity and distillation. Gravity and solar energy are free!

BUILD A CONCRETE HOLLY WALL

Strong and inexpensive! Put two pieces of exterior plywood metal mesh together with PVC pipe and wood in the middle. Screw it together and you will have a form to install over a footing. Once installed, pour the concrete into the middle. The form will not separate from the concrete pressure because the tubes hold it together at the proper distance.

CONVERTING TO A NON-SKID BATHTUB

Great for elders! Instead of buying an expensive walk-in tub, this is very simple and inexpensive. Coat the tub with concrete glue and then install a good quality white thin-set. Place 1" square tiles over the thin-set. When all is finished, grout and seal. Nobody will slide in the bathtub and have an accident. It will always stay spotless if you use bleach. It lasts a lifetime. If you need someone to do this, contact a tile installer. Note the picture below from my tub.

REPLENISH THE DEAD SEA IN ISRAEL

The Dead Sea is the lowest spot on Earth. It is drying up at an alarming rate. After all, the river Jordan does not flow into the Dead Sea as in the past because people overuse the freshwater from the river. My idea is to install a giant pipeline from the Mediterranean Sea and pour water into the Dead Sea by gravity. Again, the Dead Sea is the lowest place on earth. On the way, the seawater will pass through an osmosis system, which will separate the seawater into freshwater and salty water, by the energy of gravely.

Freshwater could be used for agriculture, and the salted water will go to the Dead Sea. On the way, it would go through a turbine which would create electricity. The project could produce fresh water, electricity and replenish the Dead Sea. I used to work there, and I know this is important because it's the sea with the most concentrated minerals on the planet. Pilgrims go to bathe in the Dead Sea's minerals to improve their health. This idea will help.

SOLAR AIR-CONDITIONING

This is like a propane refrigerator in a travel trailer. Instead of a propane flame heating a coil, the sun heats the coil using a magnifying glass and a solar cell that guides sunlight to the coil, creating refrigeration. The hotter the sun, the colder the unit will be.

The Enemy of Knowledge Is Not Ignorance

THE SOLAR ENERGIZER NECKLACE

The solar cell is cast in an acrylic pendant designed to focus light onto the solar cell. The left and right halves of the chain are the positive and negative electrical sides. They are separated by the plastic insulator, making sure the current flows into the neck's back where your central nervous system starts. It produces 10% of the electric current of your body to make your nervous system healthier by exercising the nervous system.

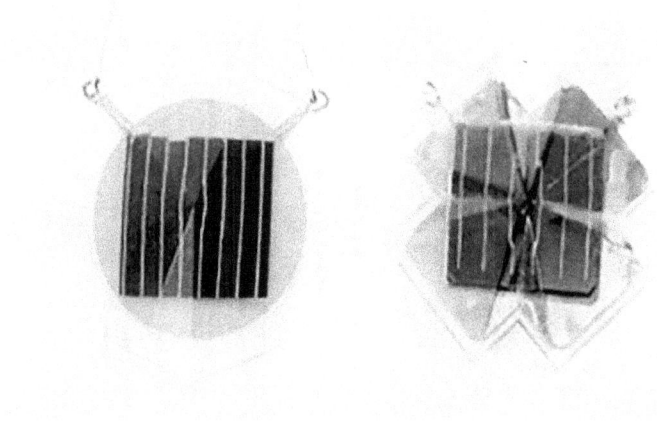

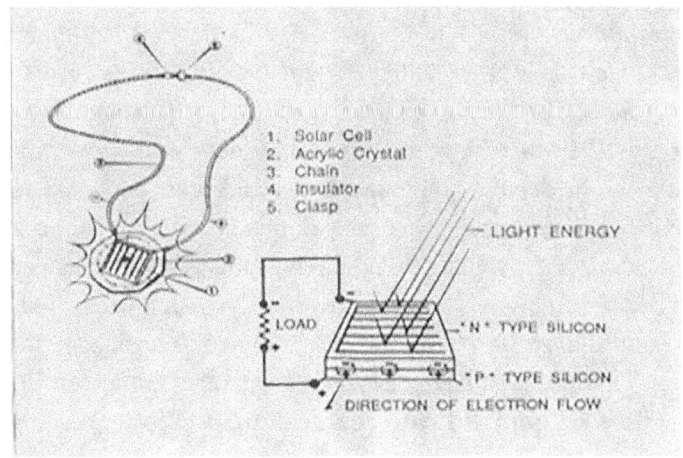

Leon D. Halfon

A HUMANE NON-FATAL MOUSETRAP

The little bit of food on the postcard should be very light, such as a smear of peanut butter or a small piece of cheese. The animal falls into the bucket and is not killed and lives to compete in Nature's Laws again. All inventors are free self-thinkers in wisdom. That gives humane-beings the confidence to be creative and make the world a better place. Please free self-think and use debating conversations for a more accurate understanding to find new wisdom that creates new knowledge!

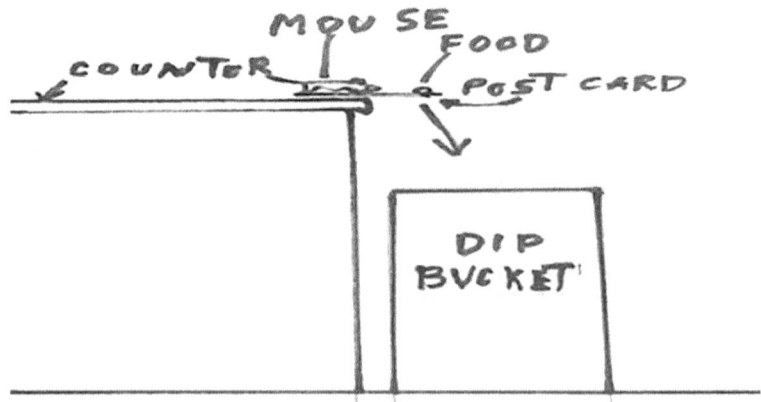

I lived through all of my exciting, sometimes scary life stories, from having confidence derived from free self-thinking by learning from my ancestors' inspiring stories, which taught me how to ask questions, the answers look like a puzzle board that seems impossible; however, by handling myself I was willing to learn from others, in the scientific method of thinking and by debating, I created a more accurate understanding of the spectrum of life magic reality because all the answers are in the questions. Even if you say: "I know that I do not know," this is a valid answer that will ultimately lead to new wisdom. However, if you don't question to know what you don't know, you will, believe leaders and preachers, that is why you mast ask questions and debate to learn from others in search of universal truth for wisdom, **and do not compete to create an ego, which is inhumane!**

The Enemy of Knowledge Is Not Ignorance

LIFEGUARD POEM

I liked to sit on the beach. In the evening,
After everyone was gone,
I would get a great feeling.
As it got darker,
Gazing at the glowing, pounding waves,
I would raise my eyes and stare at the horizon.
Then, as the universe meets the ocean, I understand.
**All these atoms
Created thinking Adams**

Leon D. Halfon

A FREE SELF-THINKING
PRAYER FOR LIFE TO CARE

This is my moral, humane prayer:
When I am looking at all this beauty out there,
I understand this Energy is in me and everywhere.
Give thanks that I was chosen for life to wear,
And realize it is my responsibility for all life to care.

THE REPRESENTATIVE OF THE CREATIVE COUNTRIES OF THE WORLD IS PLAYING A GAME OF CHEST FOR WORLD DOMINATION.

The game is simple? First, use your free self-thinkers realistic creative people that was created by the country of the people for the people, from the people, to create, the most powerful weapons, then that government is willing to sacrifice some of its peons, to create a reason for war, for world dominance, it is like taking candy from a baby, because the rest of the third world hierarchies created countries of sheep-people, by killing in the past, and are still killing today, their free self-thinkers as a norm, to protect their privileges. These wars hopefully are created to get rid of parasite hierarchy, that imposes their illusionary religion as reality on their people, and replaces them with a representative for the people, to protect the free self-thinkers, and gives them the freedom to debate in scientific God-reality to evolve into a creative humane being, **because it is ok to kill sheep that overgraze.** To create creative free self-thinkers for a safer world, it is working, as we are seeing, many people today are creative free self-thinking humane-being in the rest of the world countries, that we're obedient believers in blind faith because most free self-thinker are protected by internet understanding of word safety. However, illusionary religion hierarchy ran the world, today!

Leadership leads a flock of sheep, for their privileges.
A flock of sheep people create Leadership.
Free self-thinking people, create a democratic creative safe world, in God reality of science, to unite all!

Only by getting involved will you create a more accurate understanding of reality and become one of the greatest humane-beings of the future to make a better world for life!

Leon D. Halfon

I WAS BETRAYED BY MY BROTHER'S WIFE FOR AMERICAN MONEY, AND BY BRIBING MY BOAT PARTNER; IRONICLY, HIS NAME IS CRIES!

I am 77 years old, a general contractor with a, B license. I was hired in a verbal contract by my brother to renovate, is the second house, and I was requested to sell my home. And move with all my belongings, tools, and material to fix, and manage the place, and buy it , to be closer to my brother. to stay permanently, because we are getting older, however, after fixing for more than two years, the second house, and paying $3000 a month, plus I pay for the water & power& gas, wield wetting for my home to be sold,' and now that my home is sold, the value of my brother's house is up to because of my improvement, and the value of all homes are up. So, my brother wife said, she did not agree with her husband Verbal agreement, and she is selling the home and gave me 60 days' notice, without compensating for my work, my brother's wife after 60 days, the day I was in the hospital, she pouts 10% of my belonging in storage. Trash and sell the rest. When I came back from the hospital, I did not have a place to stay. My brother and his wife betrayed me for American money because they are not humane-beings. **As I realize now at 79 years old on 1-11-22 and have been told by my family and my religious friends is, that they want me to stop writing and stop lying, because I did not know and memorize a chapter in their religious and traditions book. However, any fool can memorize knowledge, the concept is to understand, God-reality of science that reveals the truth, and that will create pain, and all Pain is essential to let you know where the problem is**. All free self-thinking people in the God-reality of science have been tortured, and killed, to stopped revealing the God truth trout history. **Religious people believe that their religion, tradition, and money give them the right to destroy lives and the environment if not stopped by accurate reality understanding**. However, I will recover by free self-thinking understanding in God reality the magic of life that creates the confidence to overcome and the confidence to start the public coffee shop of wisdom necessary for a safer world, and a better life by reinventing myself from the love of life. This will happen, as the Energy of the Universe would not have it any other way. People have created all innovation of today's better world, only by scientific ways of thinking and debating throughout history, with no exceptions or excuses, because the voice of free self-thinking people in the search of universal truth, is the voice of God. The voice of beliefs, tradition or competition, or opinions in the search for comfort is the voice of leaders' greed, it made no creativity or universal understanding of today's world.

DEAR FRIEND

An accurate understanding of God-reality of science that is the essential to be a humane-being!

Not memorizing scholarly books to be computerized. Because the religious winners write all religious history books and hierarchy in illusion, write all illusory books, movies, media, and rewrite all books to prove that their prediction was right, as propaganda to increase their importance. For example, Abraham was a free self-thinker, not a Jew because the Word Jew came from the tribe of Juda and the tribe of Juda existed, only after Jacob had 12 children, that created the 12 tribes of the Israelites, and he named one of them Juda that created the name, Jew, and Judea, because al all-word will correlate. This is how leaders rewrite all books to create basket case stories for people that memorize books and become realleges schoolers believers in blind faith, so please be a free self-thinker in a scientific method of debating to increase your accurate understanding of **your significance**. Because all great civilization is created by free self-thinking people in a scientific way of debating for a more precise interpretation of the spectrum reality of life, and are destroyed by the greed of hierarchy, with the help of their ignorant obedient followers, religious schoolers believers in blind faith. This is the only way to have a scientific method of debating for a more accurate understanding of the magic reality of life, so you can have the wisdom to be creative for a better life, better government   better country, and a better world!

In search of universal-truth, by debating in God reality of science, for mor accurate understanding! Silence= to nothing, or 0, and opinion is a fort, everybody has one.

if you are having conversation, with dangers religious believers in blind fate. Silence= to gold.

If you are having an opinionated, or religious, or tradition, or atheist, in a debate conversation, you are wasting your time!

Freedom of religions, and traditions, will bring all the diseases and political problems, that exist in India, to America, it already started to happen, homeless people are dying on the street, the leprosy, now exist in America., and the caste system, that separate people in categories, that is created to increase, and protect leaders (the united nation) privileges, now exist in America., because., religion, tradition that kip people idol, and Creative democracy, cannot work together.

Is this what you want in the world? Challenge yourself, by free self-thinking and debating for the search of universal-truth, to create a majority of free self-thinkers. To be better today den yesterday. Not a majority of followers! of religions, and traditions in blind fate that destroy democracy!

The pen that writes God 'scientific reality for accurate understanding to create the new wisdom to unite all people and get rid of god players that create competing religion, tradition, and wars, that kip people idol. Is the God realistic mightiest weapon of all. If it is not a democracy, it will not unite all the people, and it is not, God reality!

All general saying is wrong including the general saying in this book because Wisdom is in the understanding of meaning not in memorizing words! However, by free self-think and debating for a more accurate understanding you will find the meaning of the saying from understanding the magic of life!

The end of this book has empty pages, so the readers can comment on what aspects they disagree with for other readers to create a more accurate understanding of what is the meaning? .

CONTACT INFORMATION
323-449-2325
Leonhalfon777@ gmail.com

HALFONBOOKS.COM & HALFONBOATS.COM

As a humane-being, I freely self-think to debate this book in wisdom, to be better today than yesterday. It is not to create competition or new religions, dogmas, cognitive dissonances, prejudices, or hatred!

The end of this book has empty pages, so the readers can comment on what aspects they disagree with for other readers to create a more accurate understanding of God magic of life.

Always in friendship.

www.ingramcontent.com/pod-product-compliance
Lightning Source LLC
Chambersburg PA
CBHW070730020526
44118CB00035B/1150